IMAGES
of America

KINGSTON

IMAGES
of America

KINGSTON

Betty J. Cotter

ARCADIA
PUBLISHING

ISBN 978-0-7385-6364-0

Published by Arcadia Publishing
Charleston, South Carolina

Printed in the United States of America

Library of Congress Catalog Card Number: 2008937075

For all general information contact Arcadia Publishing at:
Telephone 843-853-2070
Fax 843-853-0044
E-mail sales@arcadiapublishing.com
For customer service and orders:
Toll-Free 1-888-313-2665

Visit us on the Internet at www.arcadiapublishing.com

CONTENTS

Acknowledgments		6
Introduction		7
1.	A Village Tour	9
2.	Taverns	23
3.	Old Houses	33
4.	School and Church Life	47
5.	Clubs and Organizations	57
6.	Famous Families	65
7.	Town and Gown	99
8.	West Kingston	117
Bibliography		127

Acknowledgments

The majority of the photographs in this book are the property of the Pettaquamscutt Historical Society, which maintains an archive at the Old Jail in Kingston. The author expresses her gratitude for the Society's continued support of her work.

The following people also supplied photographs for this book: Diane Smith, Elaine Pereira, Everett J. Hopkins, Betty Faella, the Kingston Fire District, Pat Wyatt, Joy Utter, and Virginia Arnold. Many of these people also supplied caption information, for which the author is grateful.

The author is indebted to Dr. William D. Metz, professor emeritus at the University of Rhode Island, for his assistance in proofreading this manuscript. Any errors that remain are the sole responsibility of the author.

INTRODUCTION

The history of Kingston stretches back to the Pettaquamscutt Purchase of 1657–58, which marked the beginning of European settlement in South Kingstown. Both the educational and religious legacy of Kingston village are tied directly to the purchase, through the setting aside of ministerial lands for a church pastor and the Sewall educational fund that was created by the sale of some of the Pettaquamscutt property. The Kingston Congregational Church had its origins in the ministerial lands, as the Kingston Academy benefited from the Sewall Fund. But perhaps the most important key to the development of the village was its selection for a county courthouse in 1752 and then for one of Rhode Island's five statehouses, built in 1775–76. This ensured Kingston's place as a cultural, political, and intellectual center. By the time the courthouse had been moved to West Kingston and the general assembly had stopped rotating its meetings among five sites, Kingston had a new anchor for its prominence in South County—the Rhode Island College of Agricultural and Mechanic Arts, to become Rhode Island State College and eventually the University of Rhode Island.

Much of Kingston's familiar history is tied to the Colonial period, when the village was called Little Rest. Several stories have been told as to how the village got that name, one being that the Colonial soldiers halted there for a little rest on their way to the Great Swamp Fight of King Philip's War. Other stories are that the mischievous, joke-playing residents gave little rest to their victims, or simply that the taverns of the village gave weary travelers a little rest on their way between Newport and points west. The name was officially changed to Kingston in 1825.

Kingston's history is full of personalities, from evangelist Jemima Wilkinson, who was the "Publick Universal Friend" claiming to be able to raise the dead, to counterfeiter and silversmith Samuel Casey, who escaped his death sentence when villagers freed him from jail. Villagers here have always been of the intellectual bent and perhaps more tolerant than other New Englanders of people's differences. George Fayerweather, whose bride, Sarah Harris, was one of the black students in teacher Prudence Crandall's fated Connecticut school, found a welcoming home in Kingston, where he and his brothers were respected members of the community.

Kingston's strong sense of community also may relate to its size. The village proper encompasses only a few square miles. No river bisects Kingston, and even the railroad was built on the outskirts. Behind picket fences, the Colonial- and Federal-style houses that line the main street appear today much as they did when built—tidy and close together, a metaphor for village life. It is easy to imagine merchant Nathaniel Helme, who kept an exhaustive record of his activities in diaries written from the 1880s to the 1950s, walking through the village and saying hello to everyone he passed. His diaries tell of a tightly woven community of simple pleasures. On the Fourth of July, village streets were lit with Chinese lanterns, and on a summer evening every August, the village turned out to be entertained on the Kingston Free Library lawn. Missionary and Sunday school groups picnicked beside the aptly named Boiling Spring, and excursions to Larkin's Pond were popular. Villagers organized themselves into clubs to concern themselves with temperance and abolition and a host of other issues.

Kingston's lively intellectual tradition has not abated. Many of its clubs, including the Tavern Hall Club, the Kingston Improvement Association, and the Kingston Hill Gardeners, are still active. Villagers remain committed to preserving their rich architectural history. Kingston also continues to be home to all sorts of people from all sorts of places, who are united in one thing: their love for the village once called Little Rest.

Betty J. Cotter

One

A Village Tour

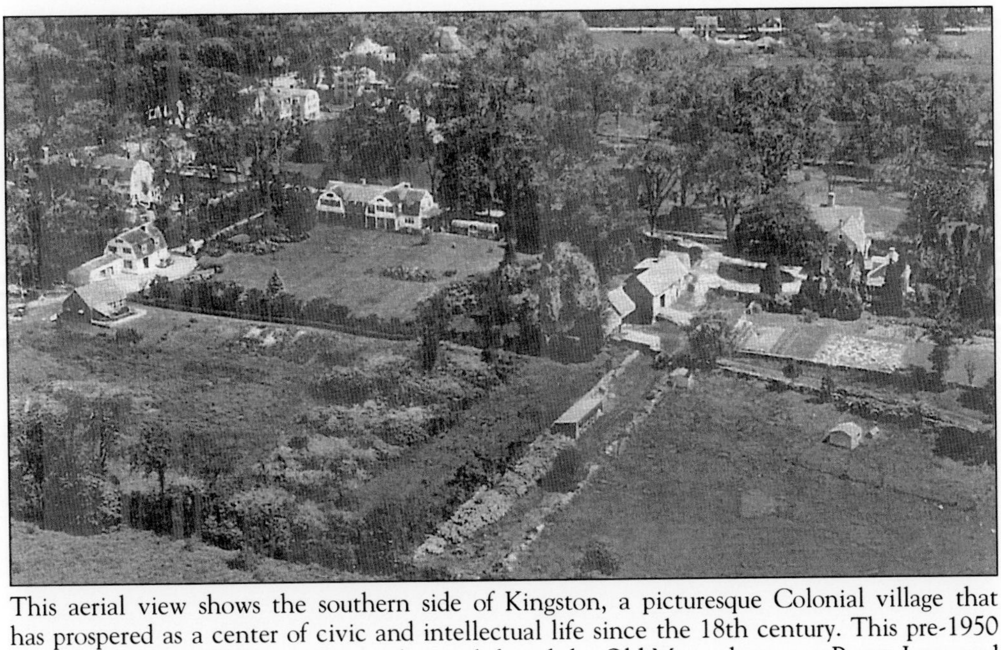

This aerial view shows the southern side of Kingston, a picturesque Colonial village that has prospered as a center of civic and intellectual life since the 18th century. This pre-1950 postcard shows the Kingston Inn at the top left and the Old Manor house on Potter Lane and the Homestead, or Elisha Reynolds Potter house, on the right. (Courtesy of Pettaquamscutt Historical Society.)

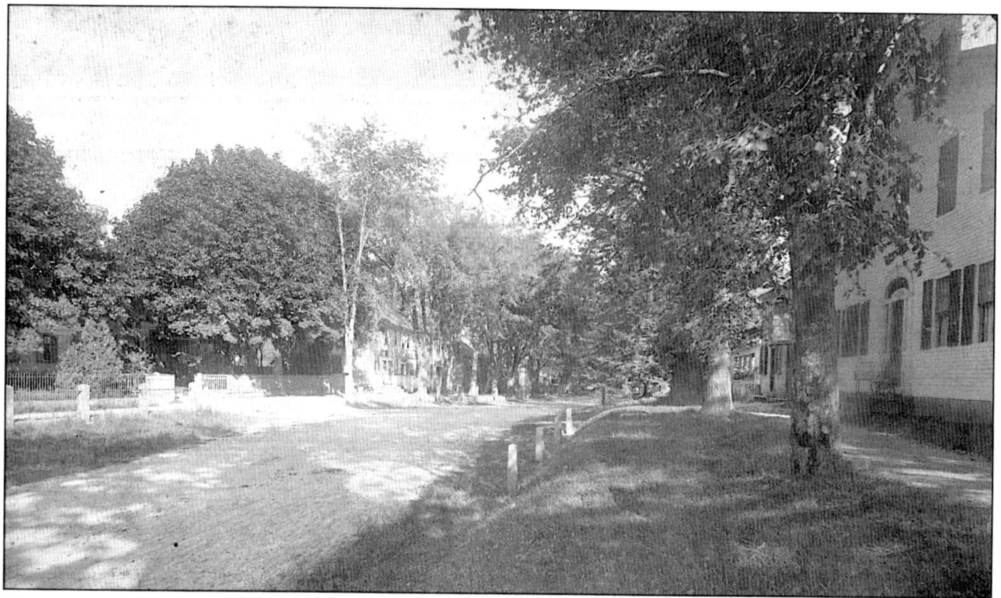

This view of Kingston's peaceful village thoroughfare is looking east along Kingstown Road, or what is now Route 138. But at the time this photograph was made, the road was known as Main Street. (Courtesy of Pettaquamscutt Historical Society.)

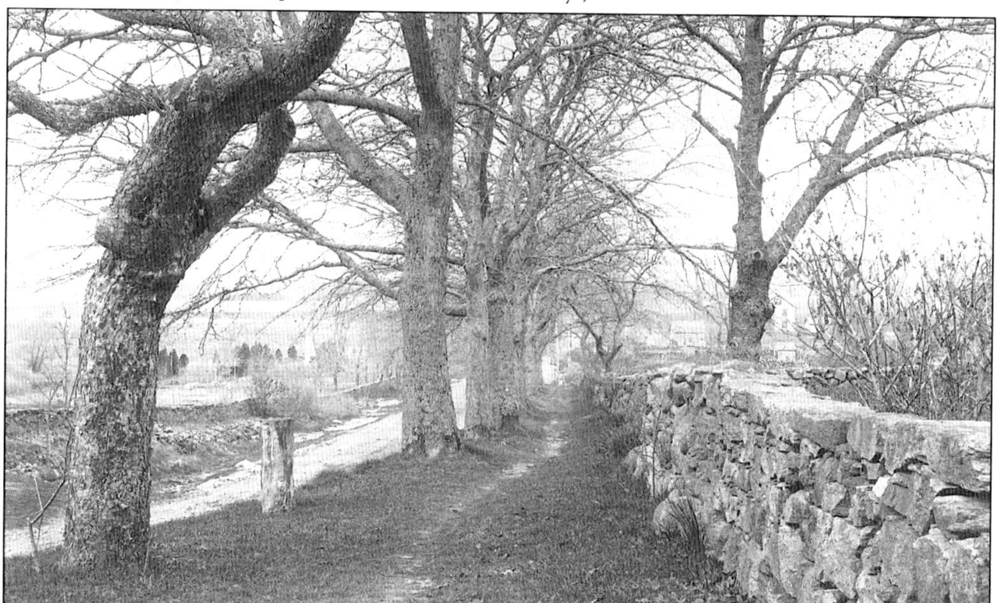

This bucolic view shows Lover's Lane, a byway that crossed through what is now the University of Rhode Island campus. Writing in 1922, an anonymous man who called himself "G" described the lane as beginning about where the French house stood (where the URI sign is today at Upper College Road) and running the length of the French property. In his epistle published in the *Narragansett Times* in 1947, "G" wrote, "The lane has always been shaded by fine large trees, and there used to be a number of rest benches towards the lower part of the lane, [which] were freely occupied both day and night by young and old." (Courtesy of Pettaquamscutt Historical Society.)

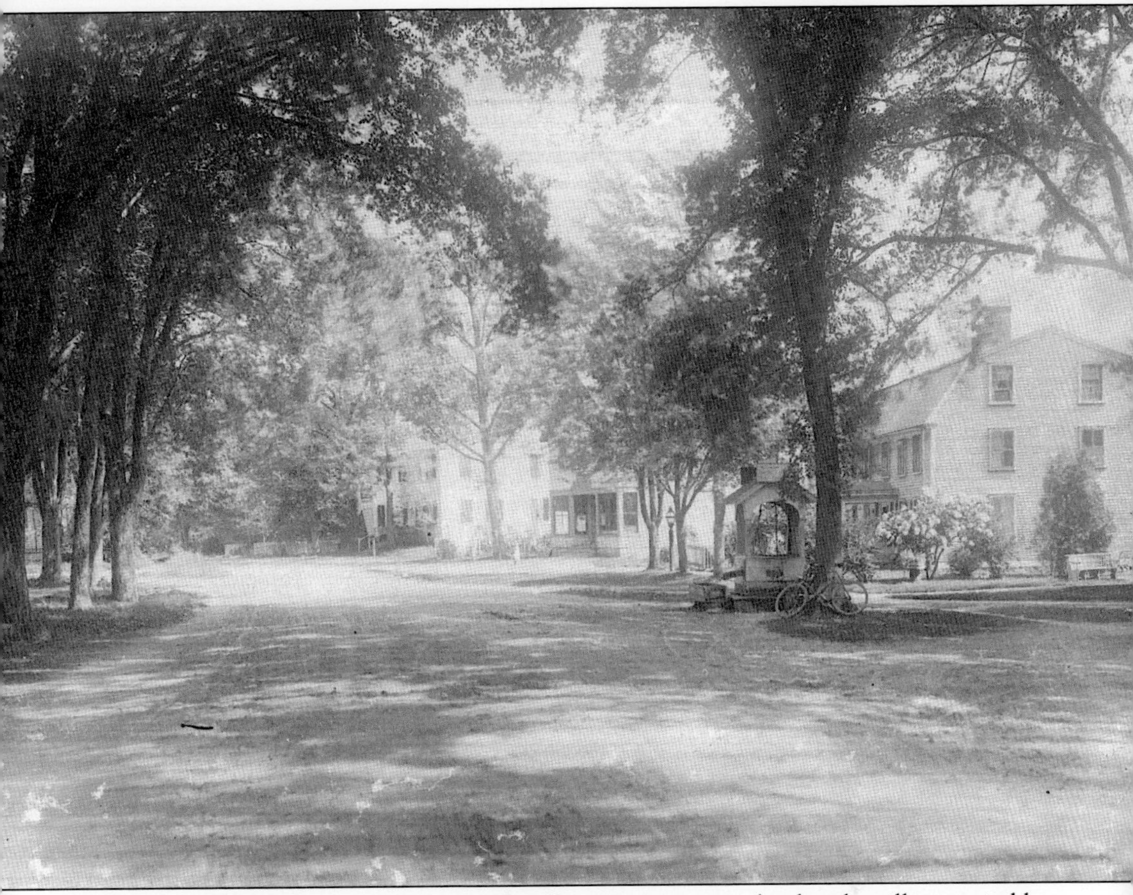

Looking east on Main Street, or Kingstown Road, one can see many landmarks still recognizable today. They include the well house at the intersection with South Road, the Moore house in the immediate foreground, the Kingston Hill Store following, and finally, in the background, the Wilkins Updike house. Part of the Moore house is believed to be the oldest house in Kingston, dating to 1710, and the Wilkins Updike house dates to 1819. Note the bench next to the Moore house. (Courtesy of Pettaquamscutt Historical Society.)

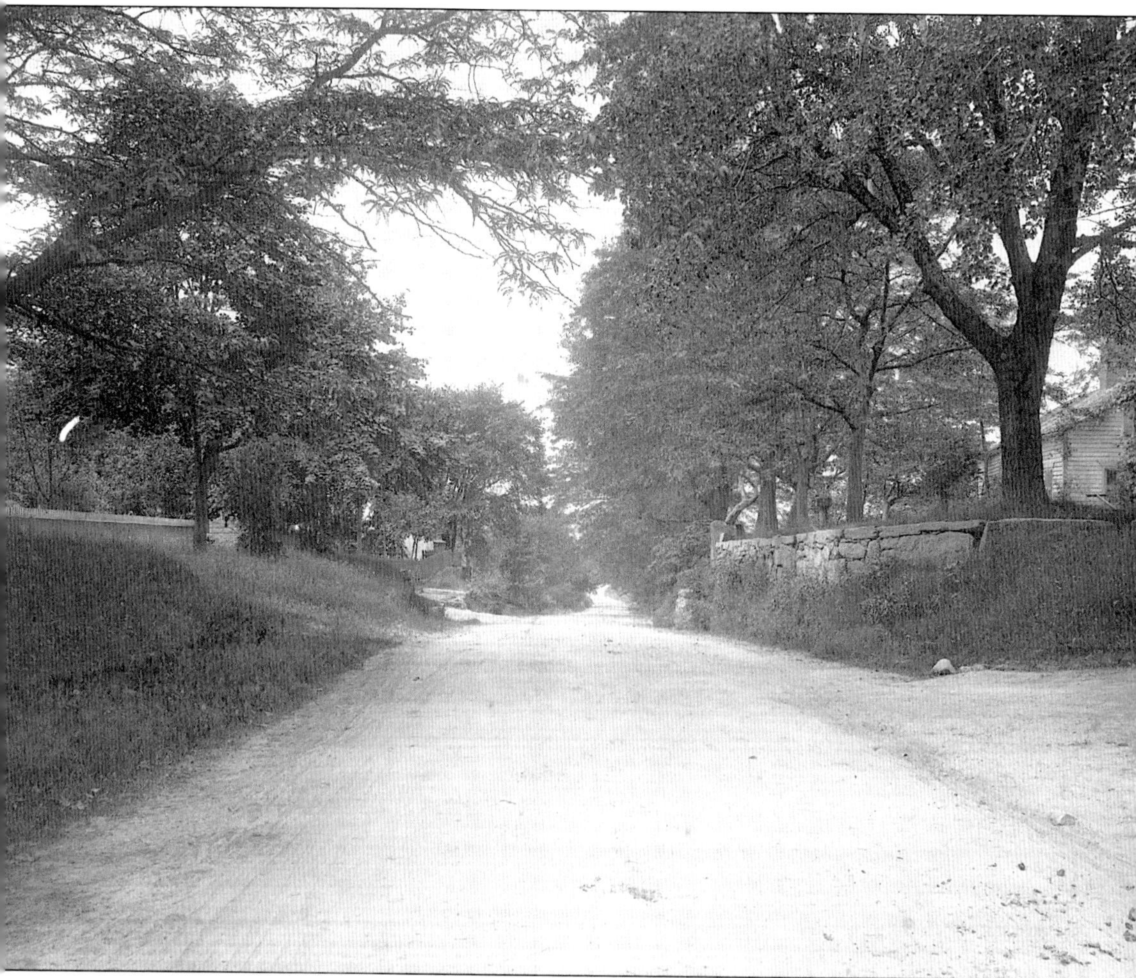

Kingston, previously called Little Rest, was a village of tree-lined streets, where walking was a popular pastime. In his diaries, Kingston merchant Nathaniel Helme often described taking long walks as a form of amusement. The lack of sidewalks was no impediment, although the roads must have been dusty at certain times of the year. (Courtesy Pettaquamscutt Historical Society.)

This view is looking west, with the Kingston Congregational Church spire in the background. The Kingston Inn is in the foreground. (Courtesy Pettaquamscutt Historical Society.)

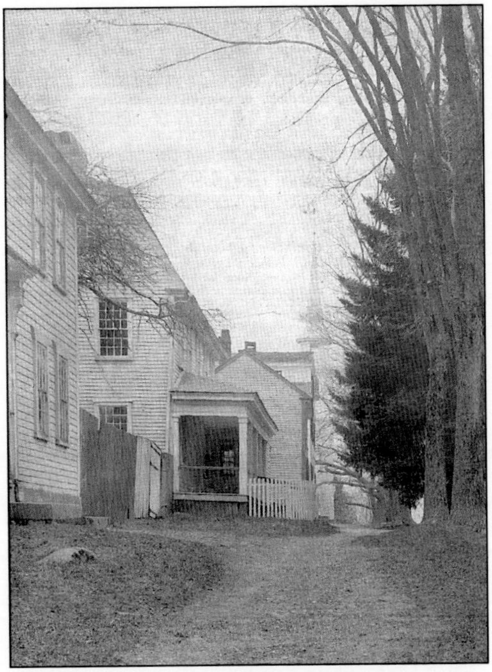

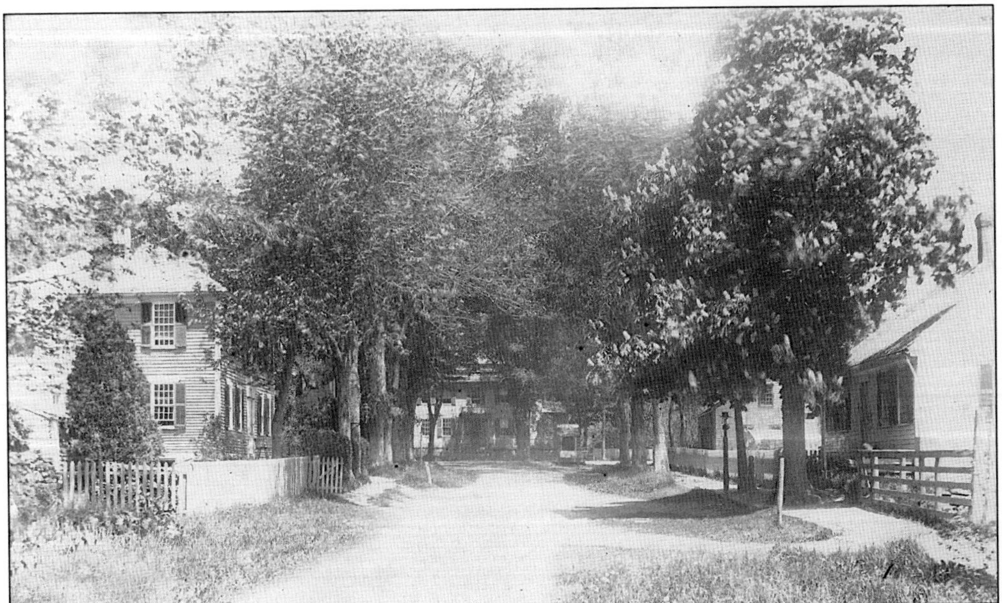

This view of South Road is looking north toward the village, with the well at the head of the street. South Road opened on May 30, 1850, and according to the Reverend J. Hagadorn Wells's "Kingston Annals, Reminiscences of Little Rest," the road "greatly relieved travel between Kingston and the rapidly growing section of the town in the southeast," which previously had been carried out in a "long circuitous route into the old south or east roads, much longer and more difficult." The development of South Road demonstrates the shifting of the town's business toward Wakefield and Peace Dale. (Courtesy Pettaquamscutt Historical Society.)

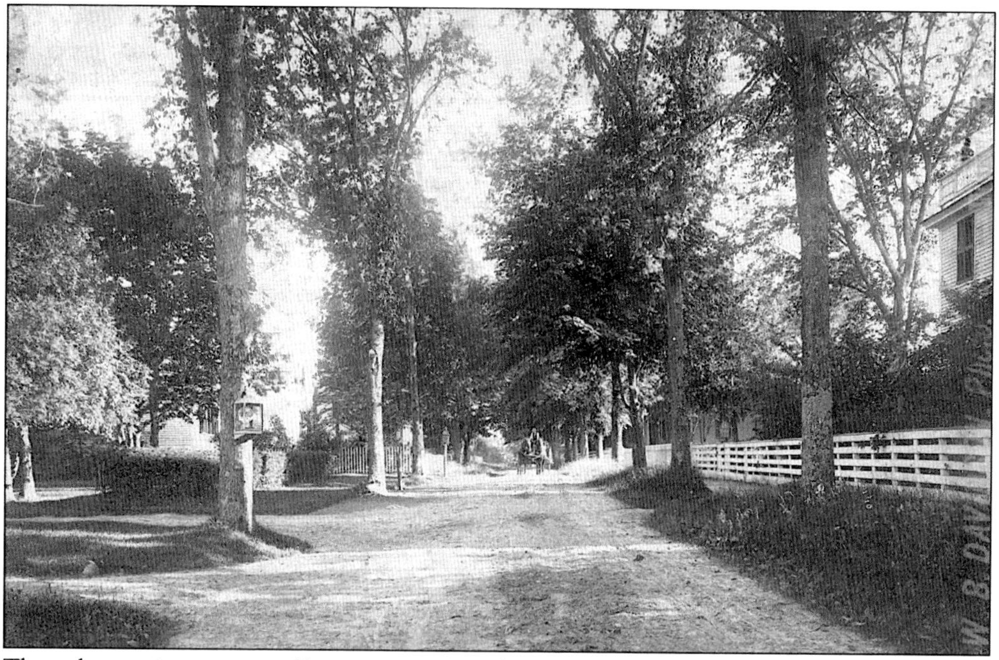

The other major street in Kingston was North Road, now Old North Road, home to the Kingston Seminary and several residences of Federal, Victorian, and Greek Revival design. (Courtesy of Pettaquamscutt Historical Society.)

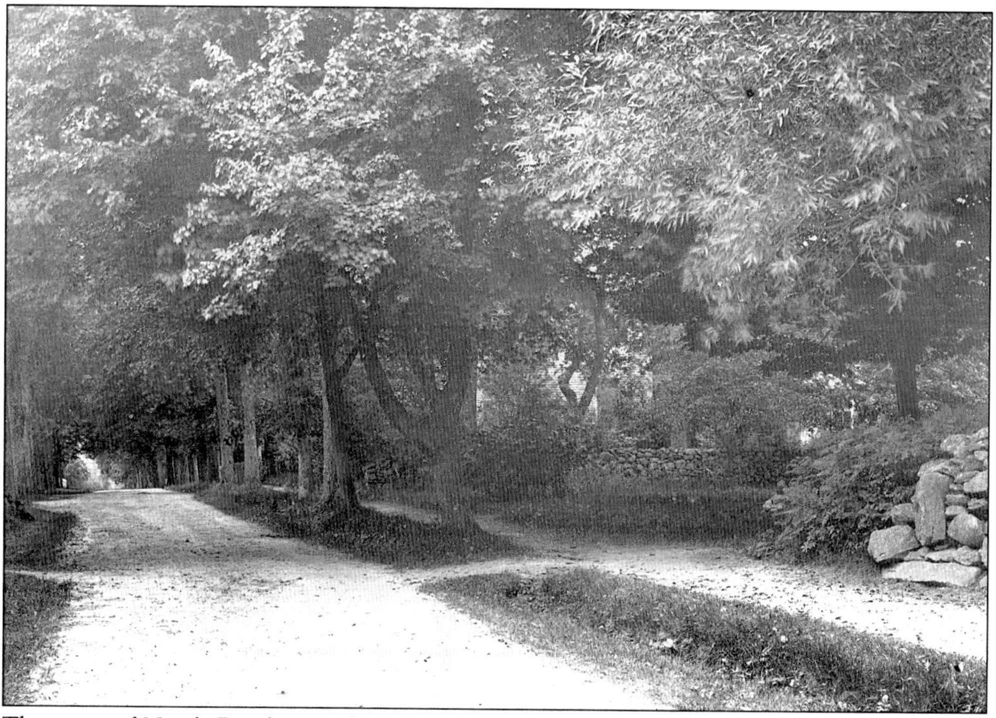

This view of North Road was taken *c.* 1898 and is part of a collection of photographs that belonged to Bernon Helme, a prominent member of the village. In the center is the Job Watson house. (Courtesy of Pettaquamscutt Historical Society.)

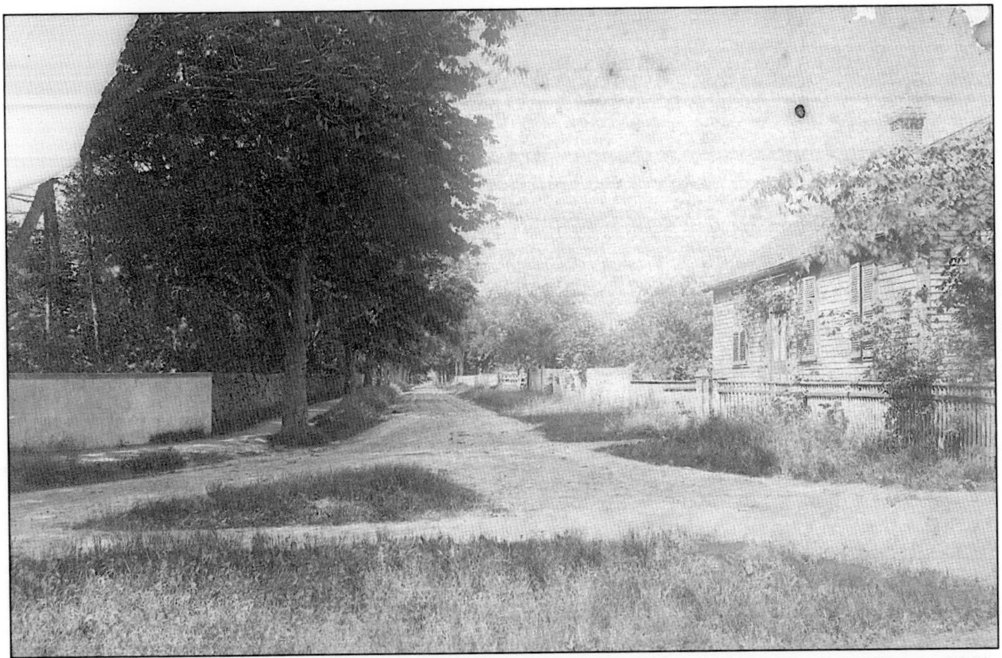

This grassy triangle is the intersection of Old North Road and Main Street (Route 138). (Courtesy of Pettaquamscutt Historical Society.)

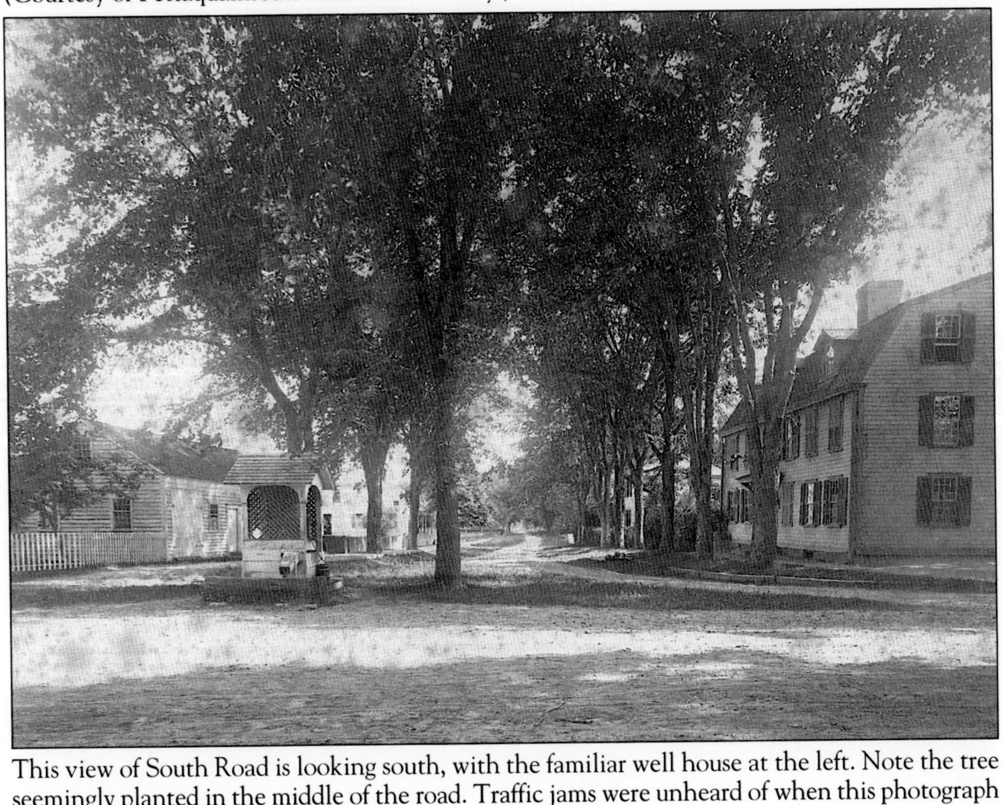

This view of South Road is looking south, with the familiar well house at the left. Note the tree seemingly planted in the middle of the road. Traffic jams were unheard of when this photograph was taken. (Courtesy of Pettaquamscutt Historical Society.)

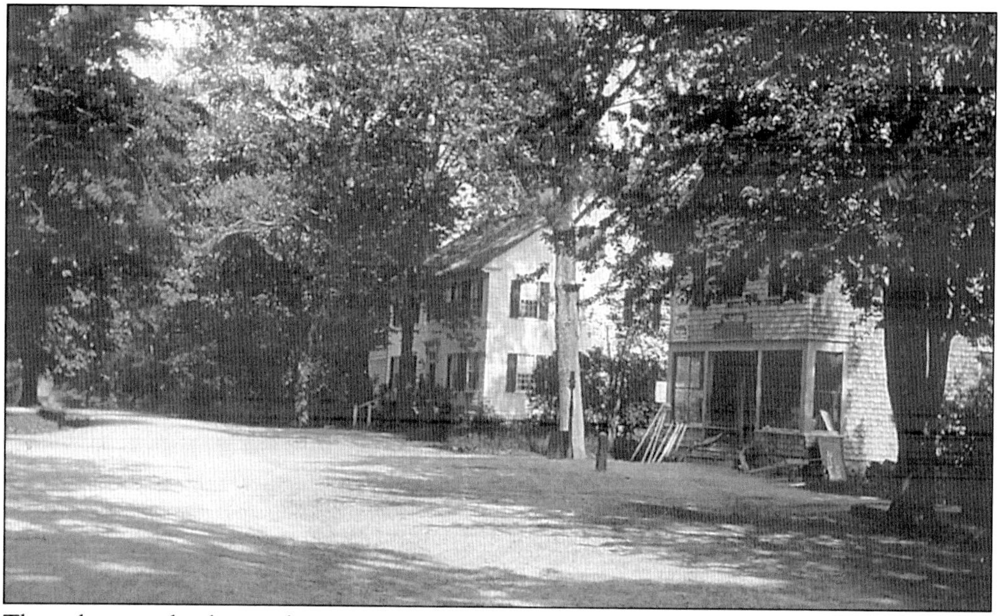

This photograph shows the Kingston Hill Store in the foreground, with the Wilkins Updike house just beyond. Originally the site of a marble shop where cemetery stones were carved, the store also was home to a grocery and liquor store. (Courtesy of Pettaquamscutt Historical Society.)

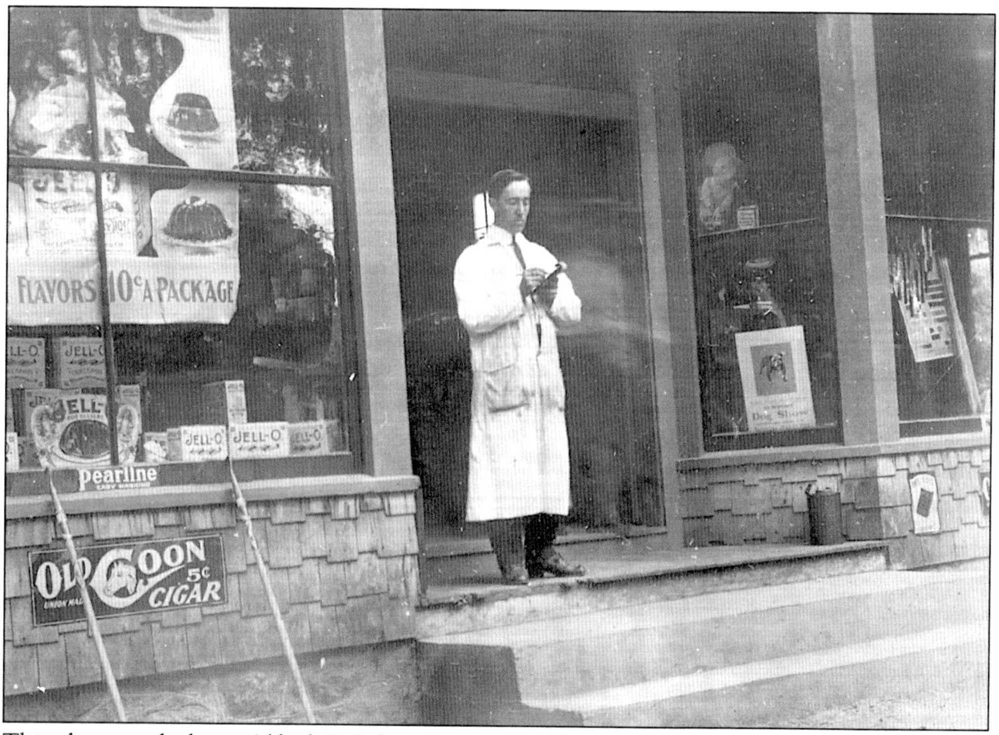

This photograph shows Alfred C. Schmidt when he was proprietor of what is now the Kingston Hill Store. Note the Jell-O mold advertisements in the window. (Courtesy of Pettaquamscutt Historical Society.)

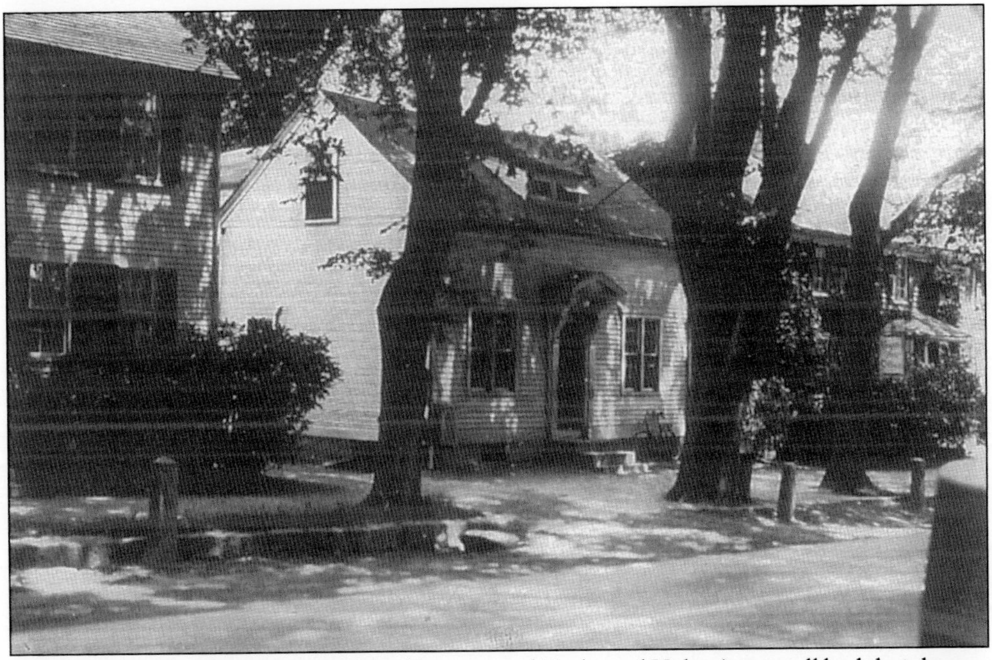

The Kingston Post Office, a school, and Bernon and Nathaniel Helme's store all had their homes in this building at one time or another. (Courtesy of Pettaquamscutt Historical Society.)

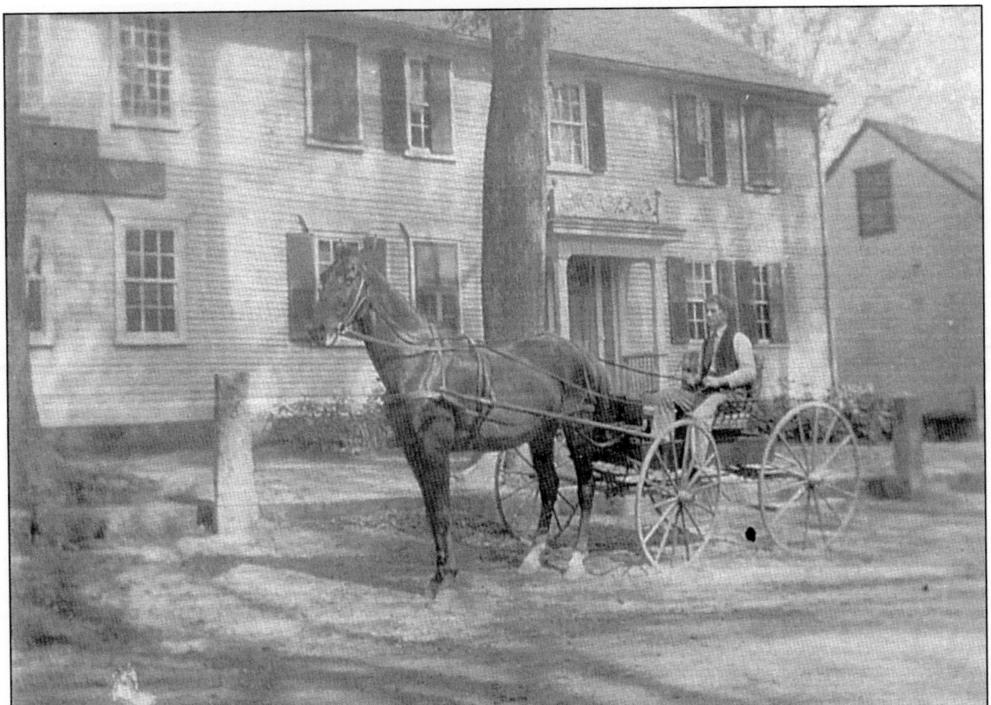

Part of the sign for the Landholders Bank is visible on this building at 2587 Kingstown Road, which is now owned by the South County Art Association. Bernon Helme and his brother Nathaniel left the society a bequest that was used to buy the house. (Courtesy of Betty Faella.)

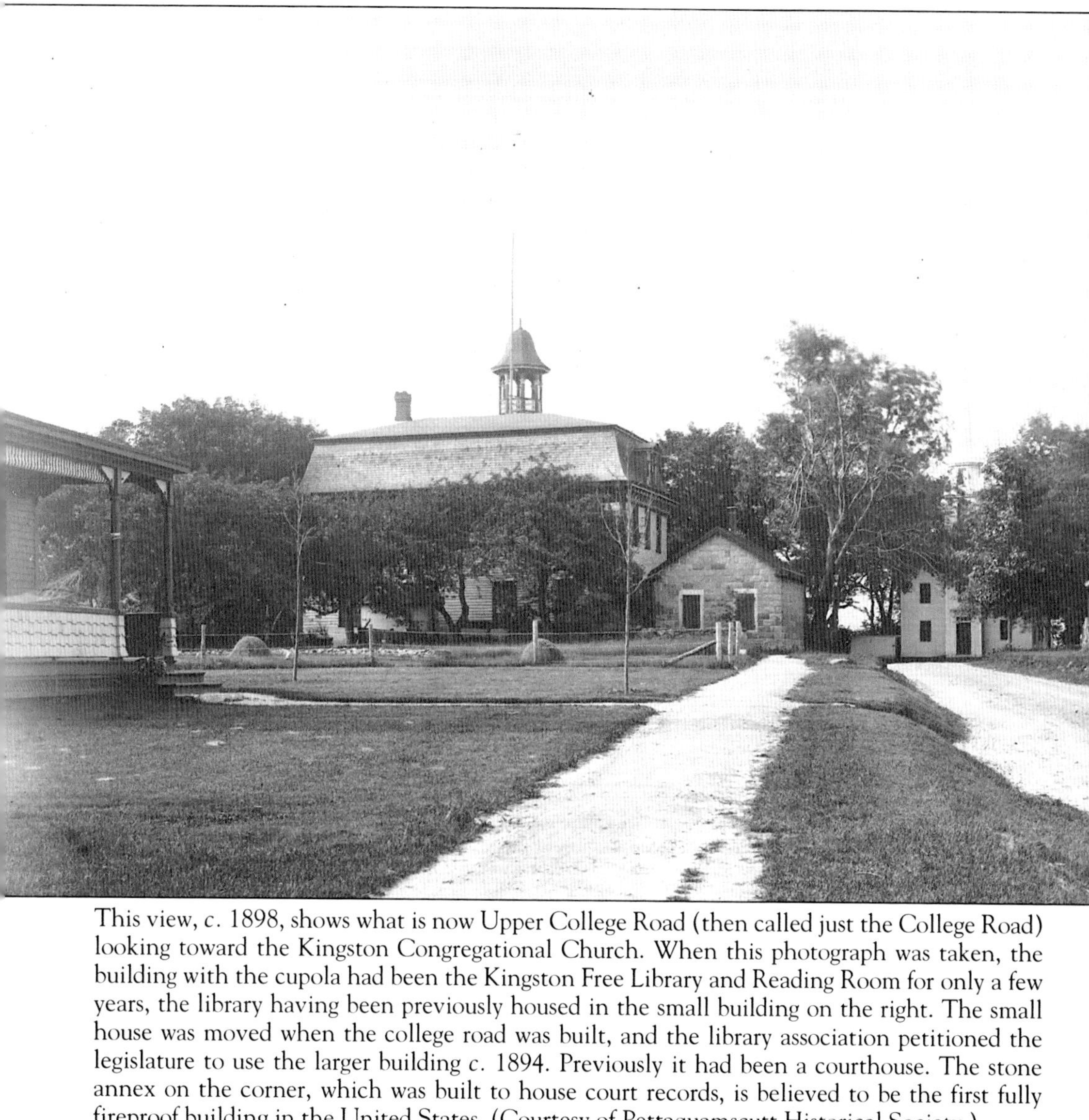

This view, *c.* 1898, shows what is now Upper College Road (then called just the College Road) looking toward the Kingston Congregational Church. When this photograph was taken, the building with the cupola had been the Kingston Free Library and Reading Room for only a few years, the library having been previously housed in the small building on the right. The small house was moved when the college road was built, and the library association petitioned the legislature to use the larger building *c.* 1894. Previously it had been a courthouse. The stone annex on the corner, which was built to house court records, is believed to be the first fully fireproof building in the United States. (Courtesy of Pettaquamscutt Historical Society.)

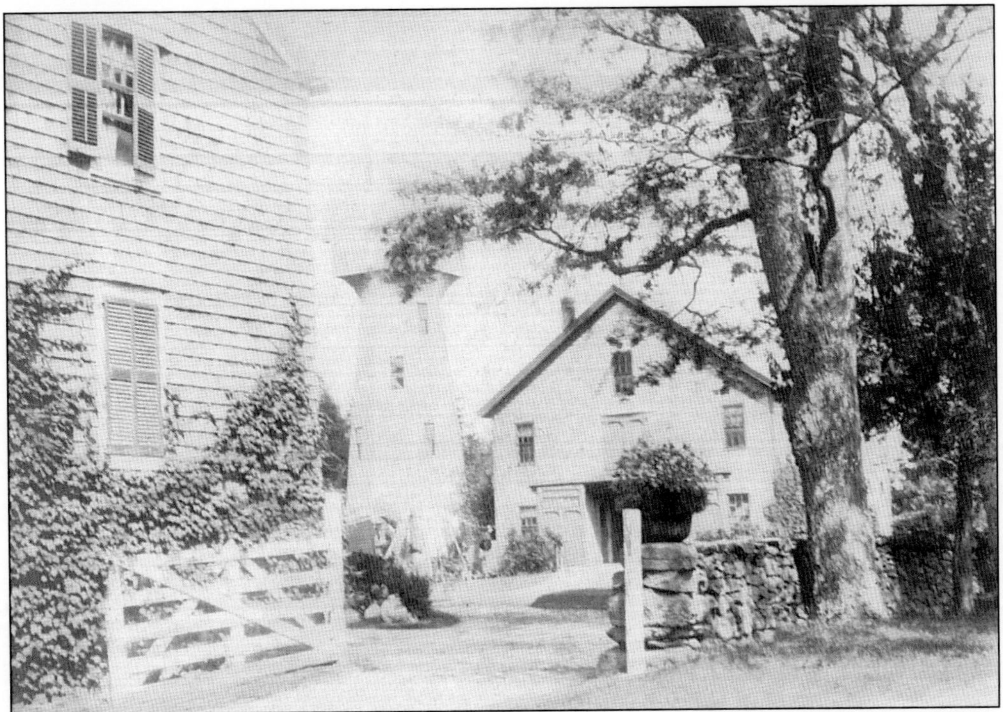

This view off Kingstown Road shows the village water tower in the distance. The tower has since been dismantled. (Courtesy of Pettaquamscutt Historical Society.)

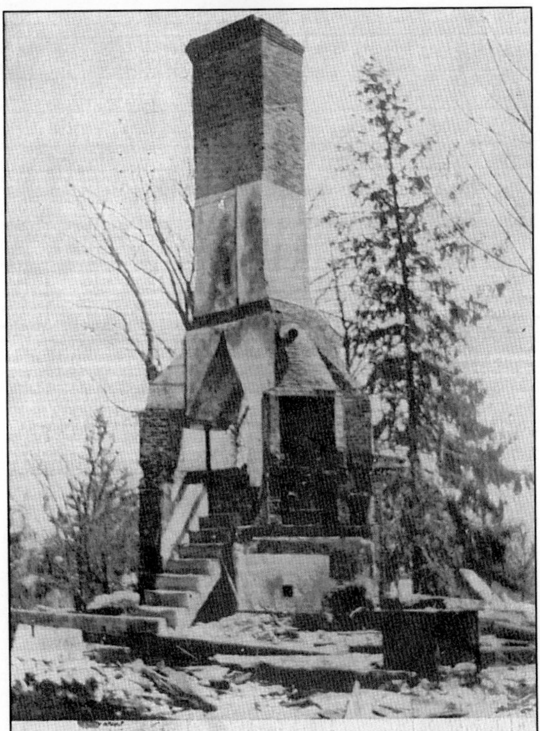

This wishbone chimney, a sign of good luck, was located behind the Helme house, northeast of the four corners. (Courtesy of Pettaquamscutt Historical Society.)

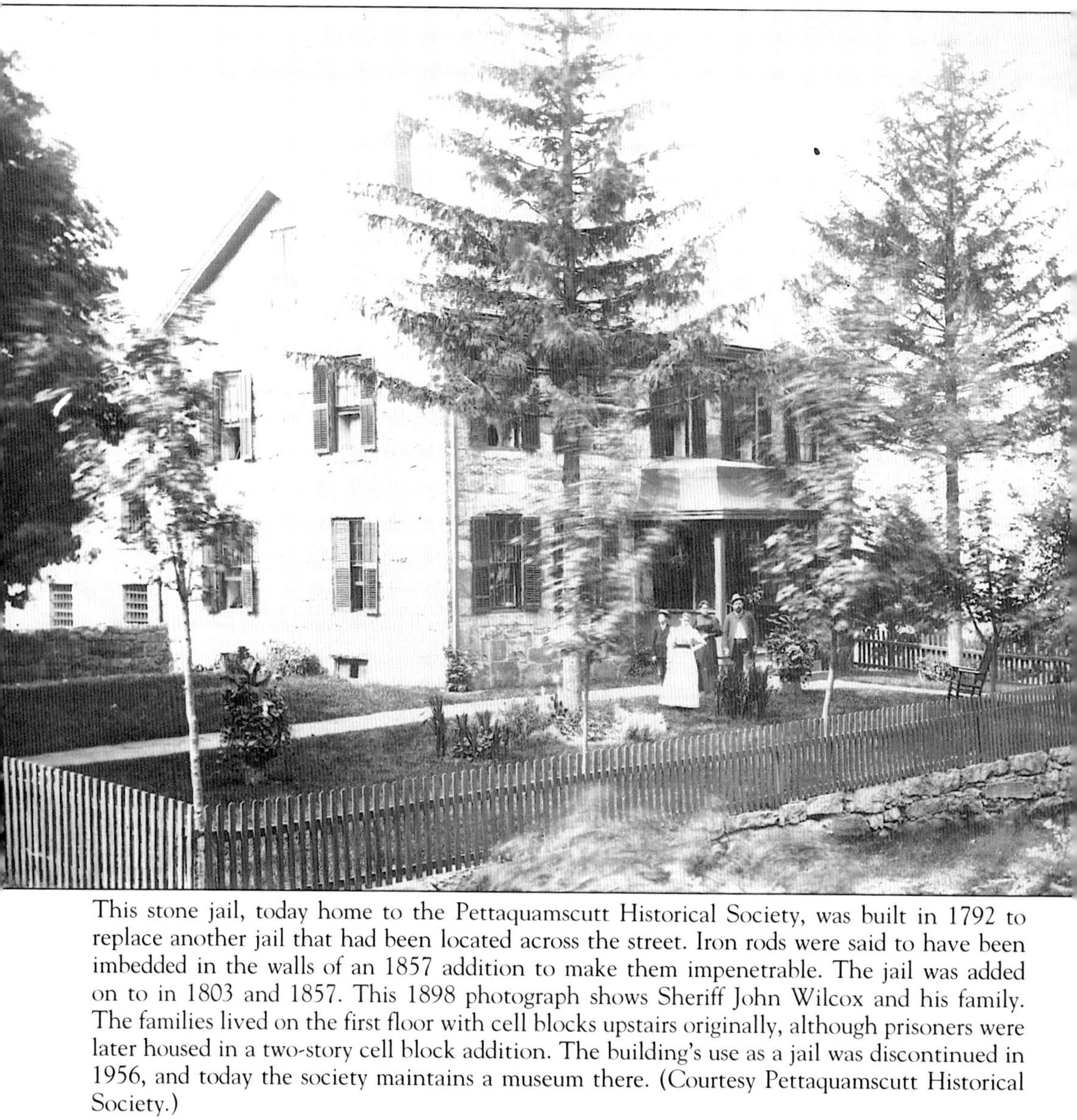

This stone jail, today home to the Pettaquamscutt Historical Society, was built in 1792 to replace another jail that had been located across the street. Iron rods were said to have been imbedded in the walls of an 1857 addition to make them impenetrable. The jail was added on to in 1803 and 1857. This 1898 photograph shows Sheriff John Wilcox and his family. The families lived on the first floor with cell blocks upstairs originally, although prisoners were later housed in a two-story cell block addition. The building's use as a jail was discontinued in 1956, and today the society maintains a museum there. (Courtesy Pettaquamscutt Historical Society.)

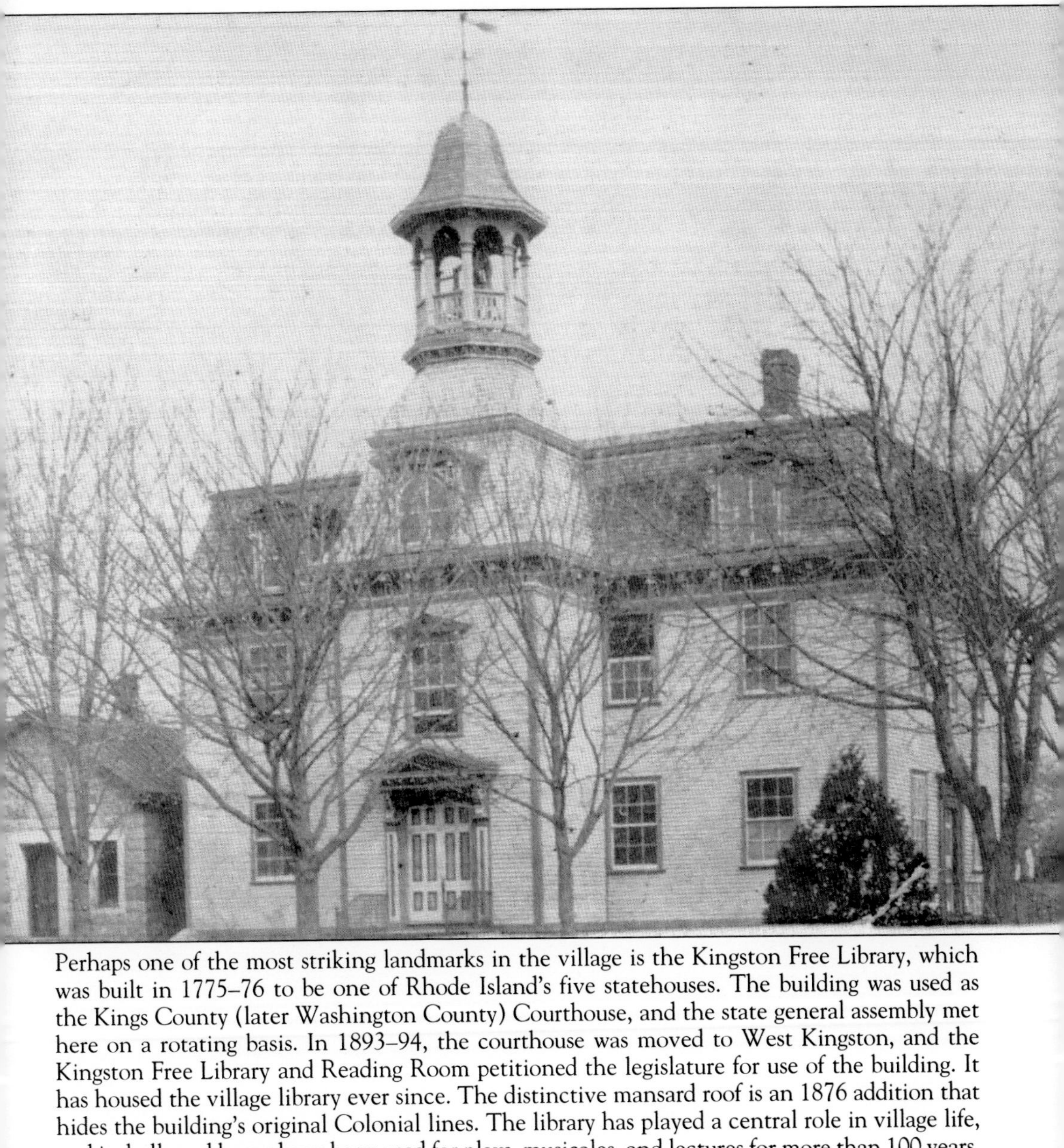

Perhaps one of the most striking landmarks in the village is the Kingston Free Library, which was built in 1775–76 to be one of Rhode Island's five statehouses. The building was used as the Kings County (later Washington County) Courthouse, and the state general assembly met here on a rotating basis. In 1893–94, the courthouse was moved to West Kingston, and the Kingston Free Library and Reading Room petitioned the legislature for use of the building. It has housed the village library ever since. The distinctive mansard roof is an 1876 addition that hides the building's original Colonial lines. The library has played a central role in village life, and its halls and lawns have been used for plays, musicales, and lectures for more than 100 years. (Courtesy of Pettaquamscutt Historical Society.)

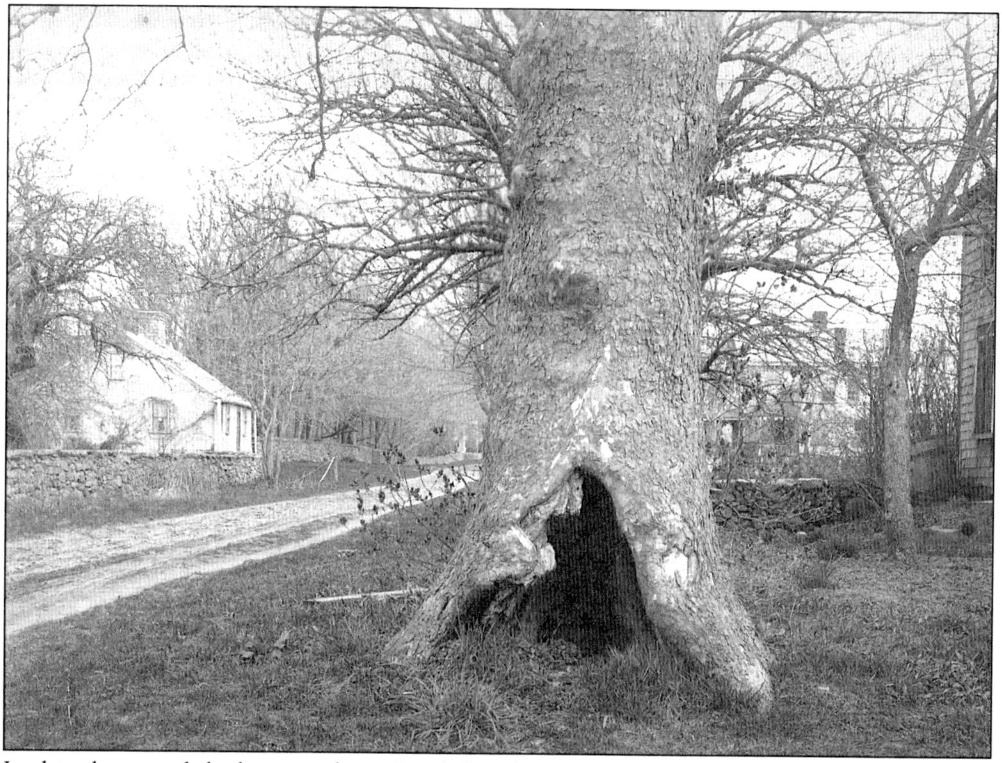

In this photograph looking north on South Road, one can see a large tree, the trunk of which still stands, and the Judge William Case Clarke house on the right, which is no longer standing. (Courtesy of Pettaquamscutt Historical Society.)

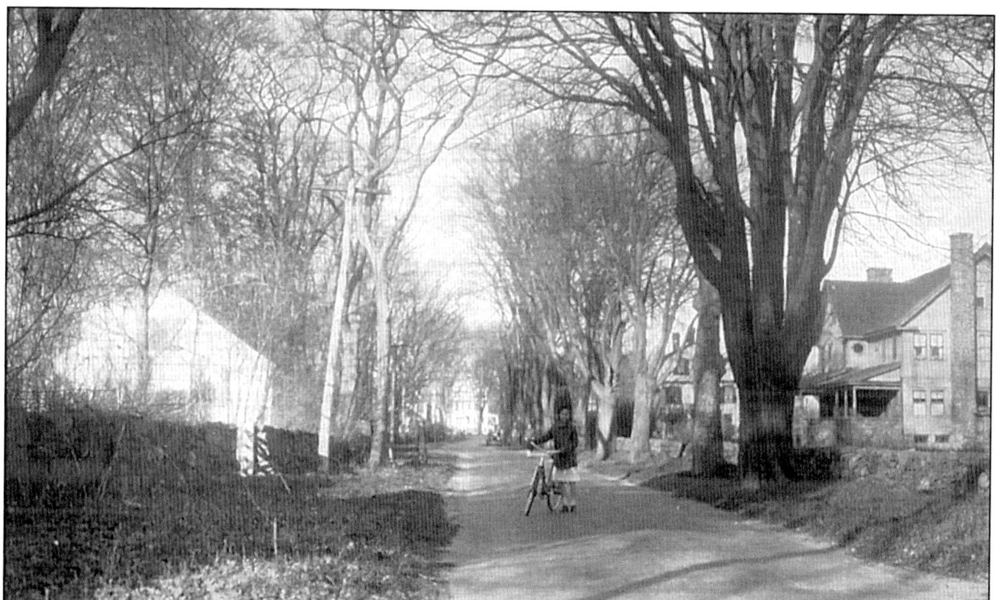

A girl on a bicycle looks wistfully behind her, down South Road, in this undated photograph. (Courtesy of Pettaquamscutt Historical Society.)

Two

TAVERNS

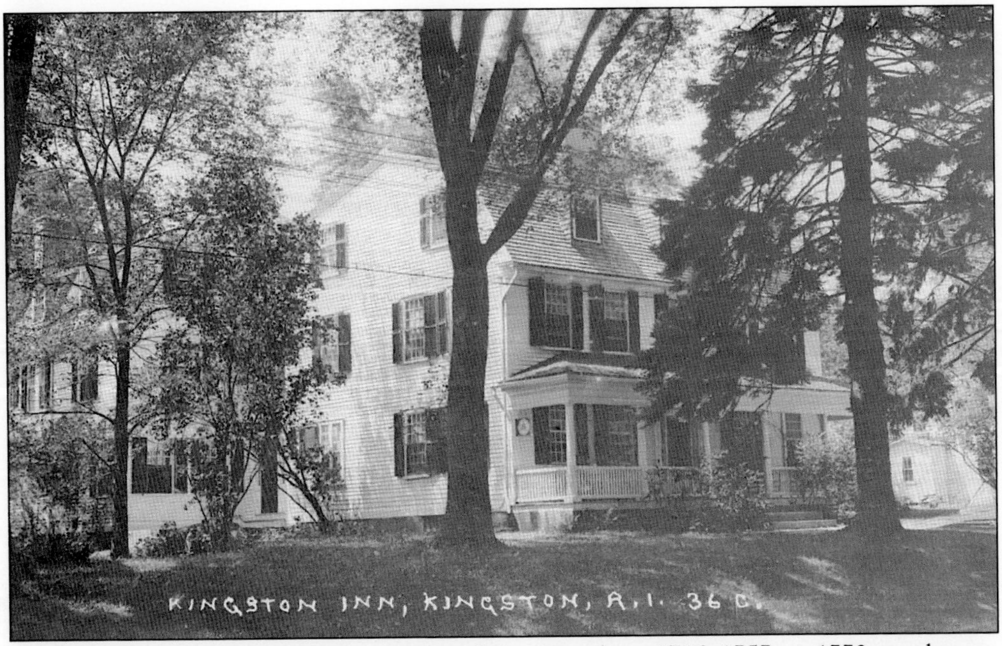

The Kingston Inn, which written accounts date variously to 1746, 1757, or 1770, was kept as a tavern by John Potter and later as Barker's Tavern and Babcock House. The inn played an important role in the village's development as a stagecoach stop between Newport and points west. A mail stop and headquarters for militia groups, the tavern was restored in 1912 by a group of villagers who reopened it as an inn. (Courtesy of Pettaquamscutt Historical Society.)

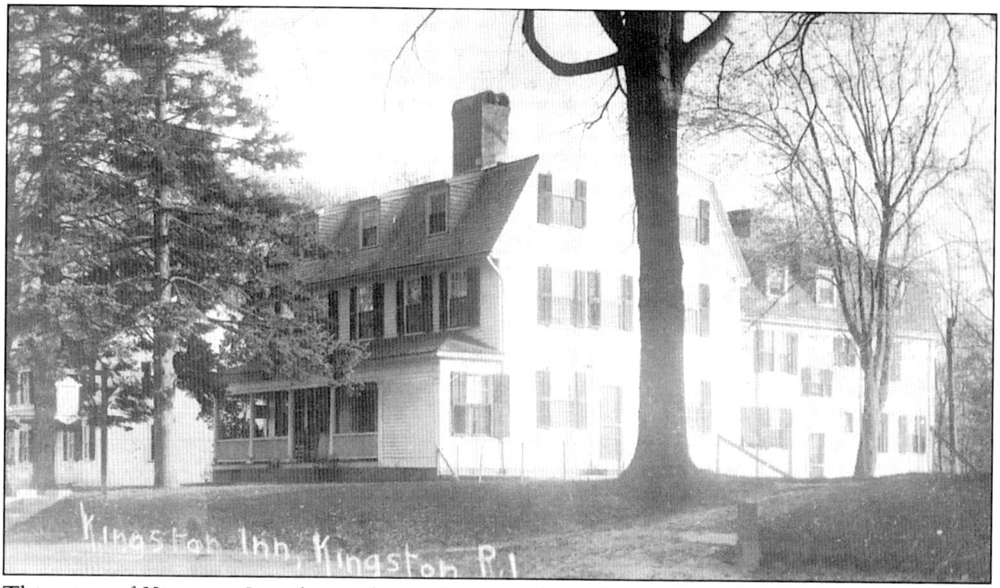

This view of Kingston Inn shows the inn's west side and the 1912 addition in the rear. This imposing structure, located at 2590 Kingstown Road, is still used as a roominghouse. (Courtesy of Pettaquamscutt Historical Society.)

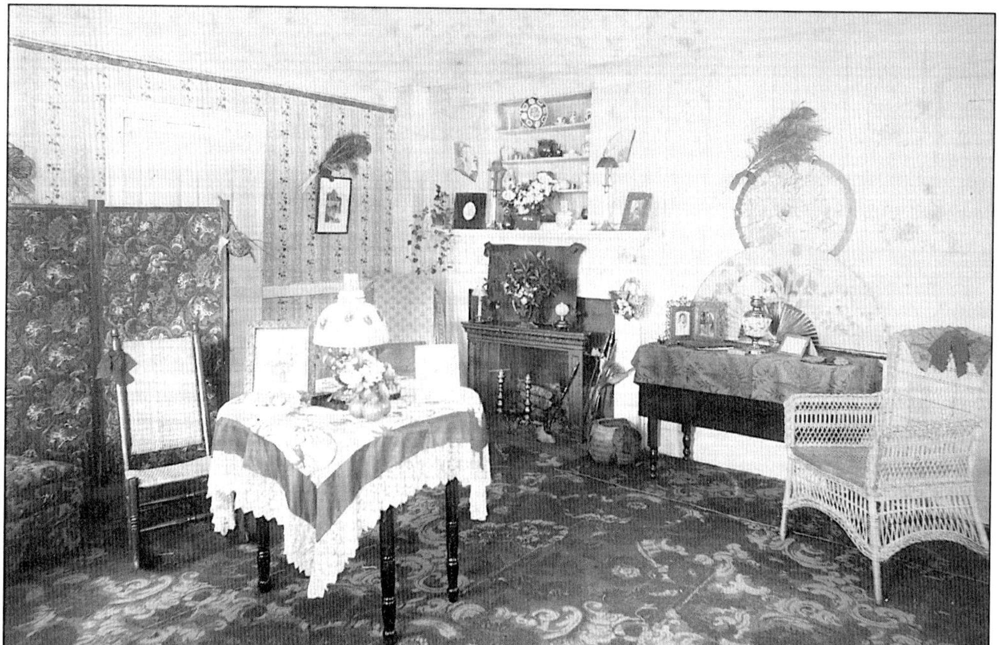

This interior shows the Northeast Room of the Kingston Inn, probably at the time of its renovation in 1911–12. Architects Angell and Swift of Providence were hired by a landholders' corporation to design a 60-by-30-foot addition three stories tall that would include 20 sleeping rooms. "The wall decorations and the paper and the rugs are in keeping with the quiet elegance and the century-old air which the architects and decorators have aimed to give the inn," the *Narragansett Times* wrote in its account of the inn's dedication in October 1912. (Courtesy of the Pettaquamscutt Historical Society.)

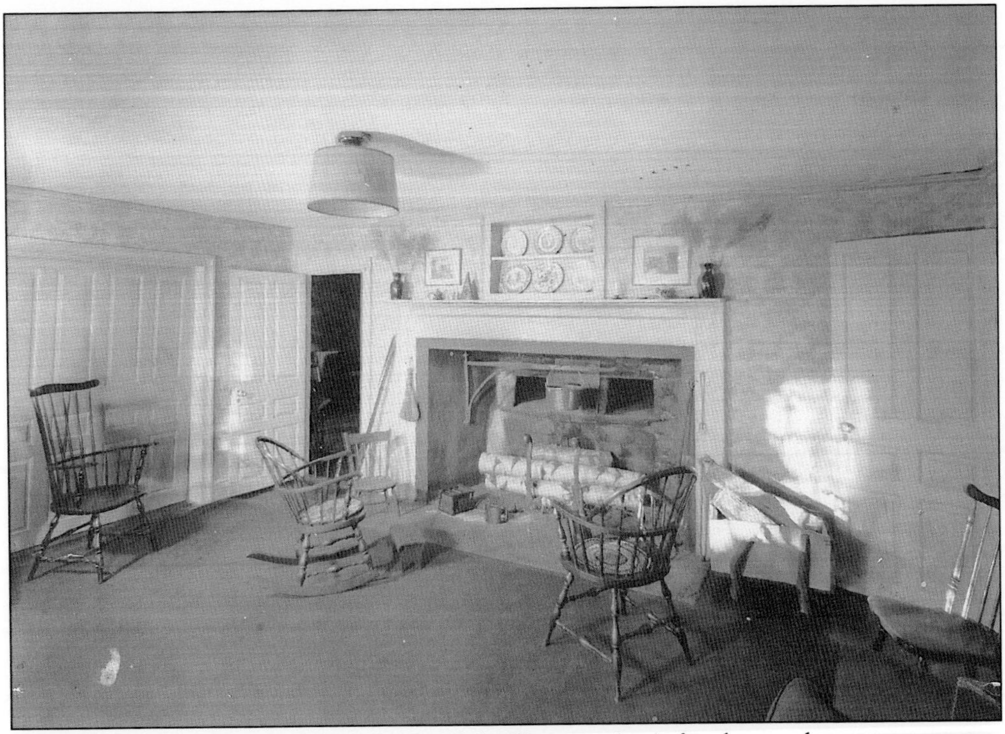

Another interior photograph shows one of the Kingston Inn's fireplaces, where many a weary traveler settled to warm his bones after a long stagecoach ride. Note the hardware from which cooking pots were hung. (Courtesy of Pettaquamscutt Historical Society.)

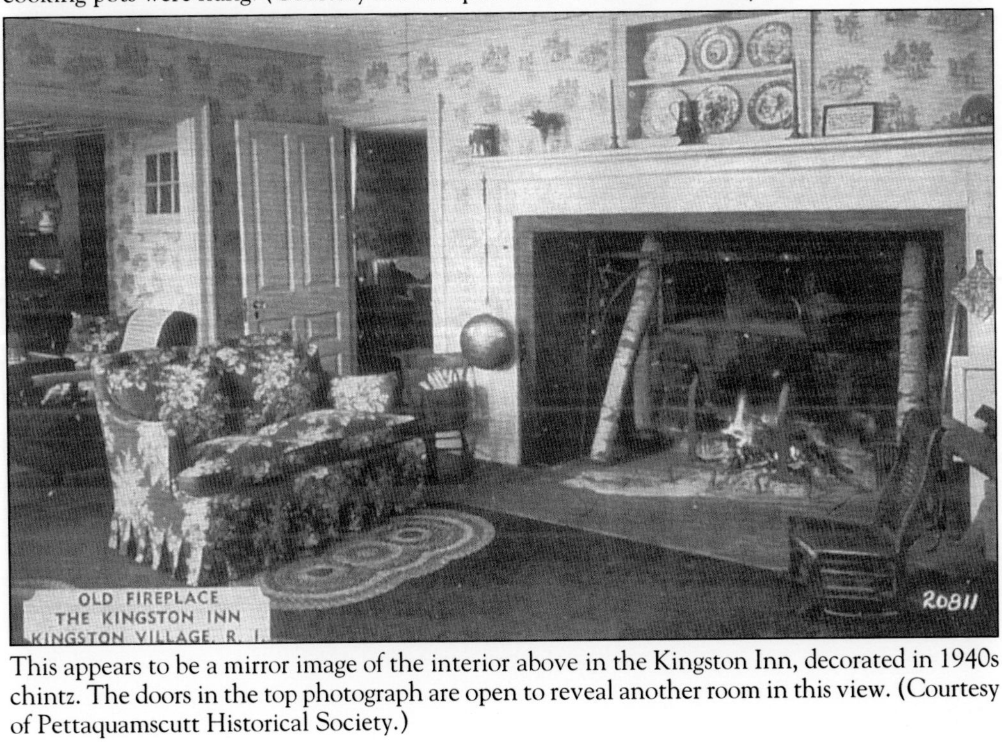

This appears to be a mirror image of the interior above in the Kingston Inn, decorated in 1940s chintz. The doors in the top photograph are open to reveal another room in this view. (Courtesy of Pettaquamscutt Historical Society.)

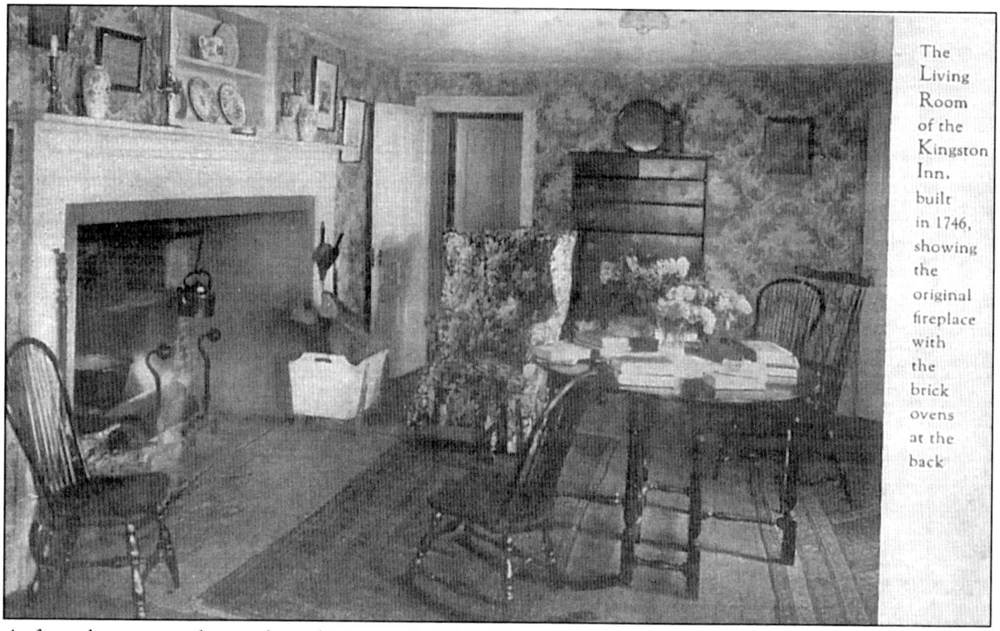

A fire glows merrily in this photograph of a fireplace at the Kingston Inn, with its original brick ovens. Note the teakettle warming over the blaze. (Courtesy of Pettaquamscutt Historical Society.)

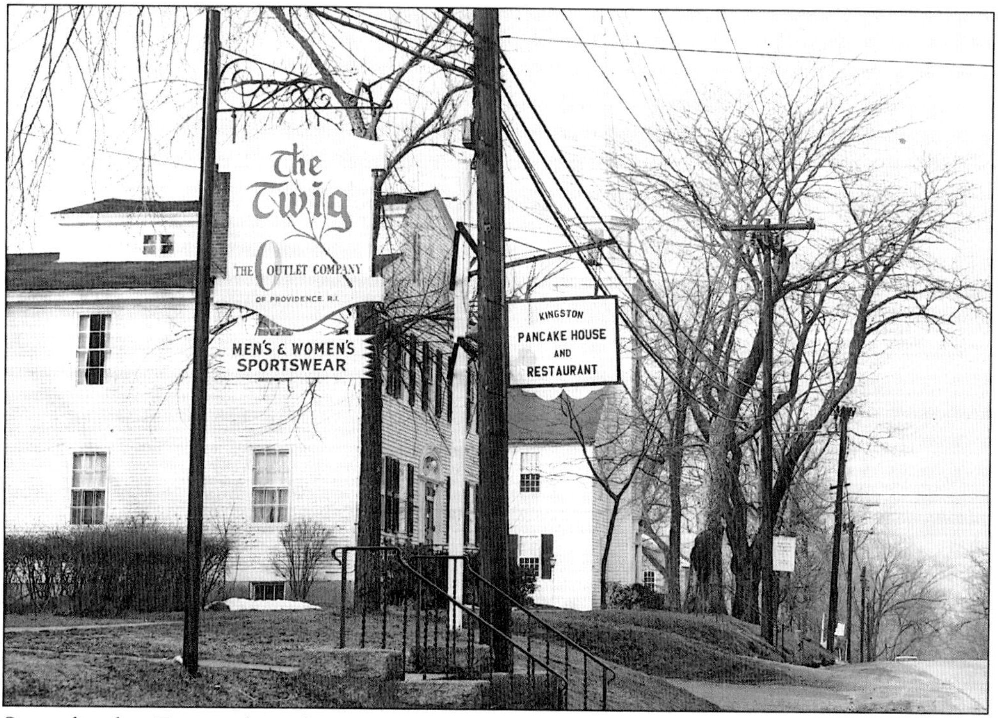

Signs for the Twig, a branch of the Outlet Company department store, and the Kingston Pancake House and Restaurant are located in front of the Kingston Inn in this mid-20th-century photograph. The view is looking west on Kingstown Road. (Courtesy of Pettaquamscutt Historical Society.)

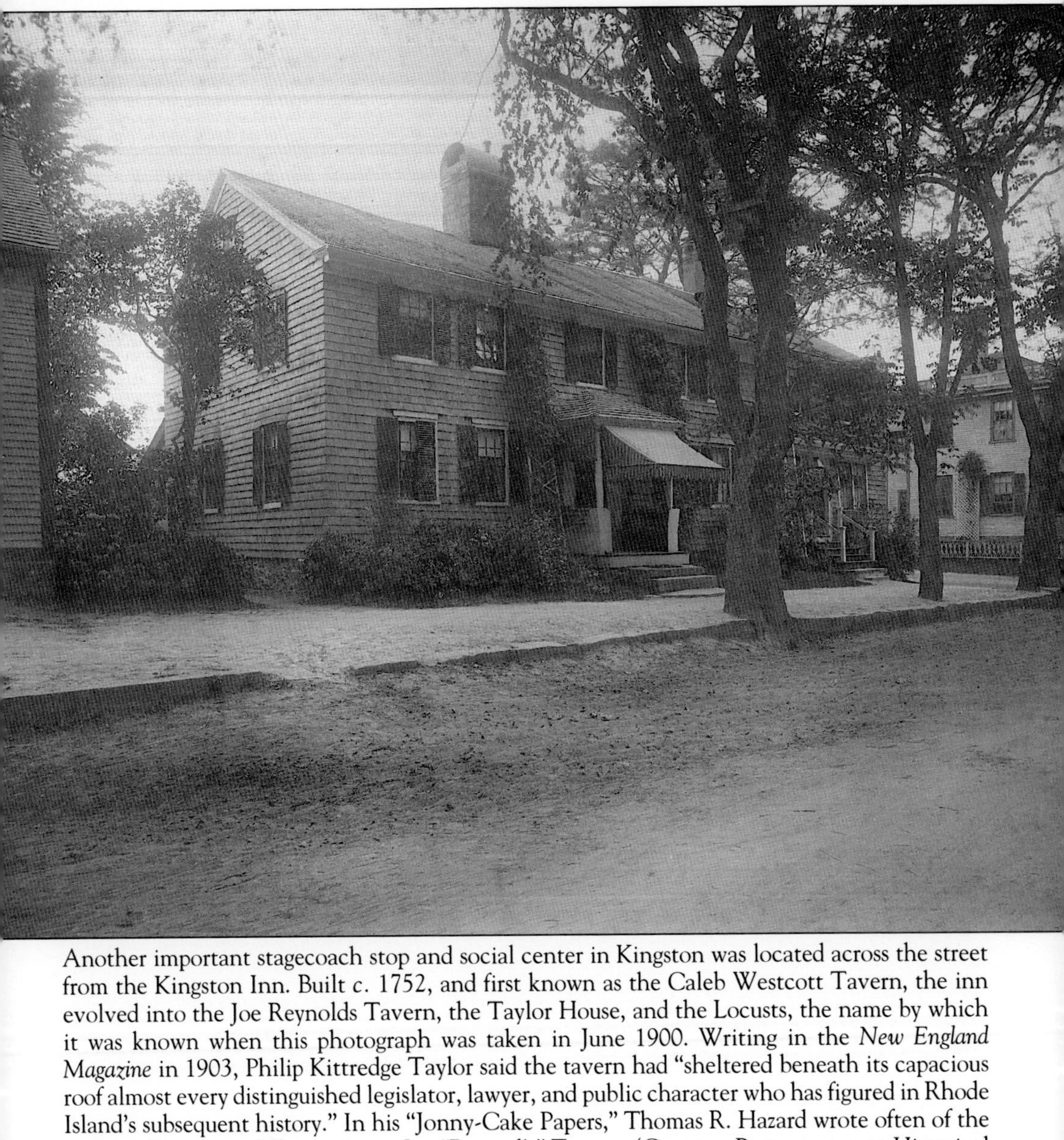

Another important stagecoach stop and social center in Kingston was located across the street from the Kingston Inn. Built c. 1752, and first known as the Caleb Westcott Tavern, the inn evolved into the Joe Reynolds Tavern, the Taylor House, and the Locusts, the name by which it was known when this photograph was taken in June 1900. Writing in the *New England Magazine* in 1903, Philip Kittredge Taylor said the tavern had "sheltered beneath its capacious roof almost every distinguished legislator, lawyer, and public character who has figured in Rhode Island's subsequent history." In his "Jonny-Cake Papers," Thomas R. Hazard wrote often of the conviviality of menfolk meeting at Joe "Runnel's" Tavern. (Courtesy Pettaquamscutt Historical Society.)

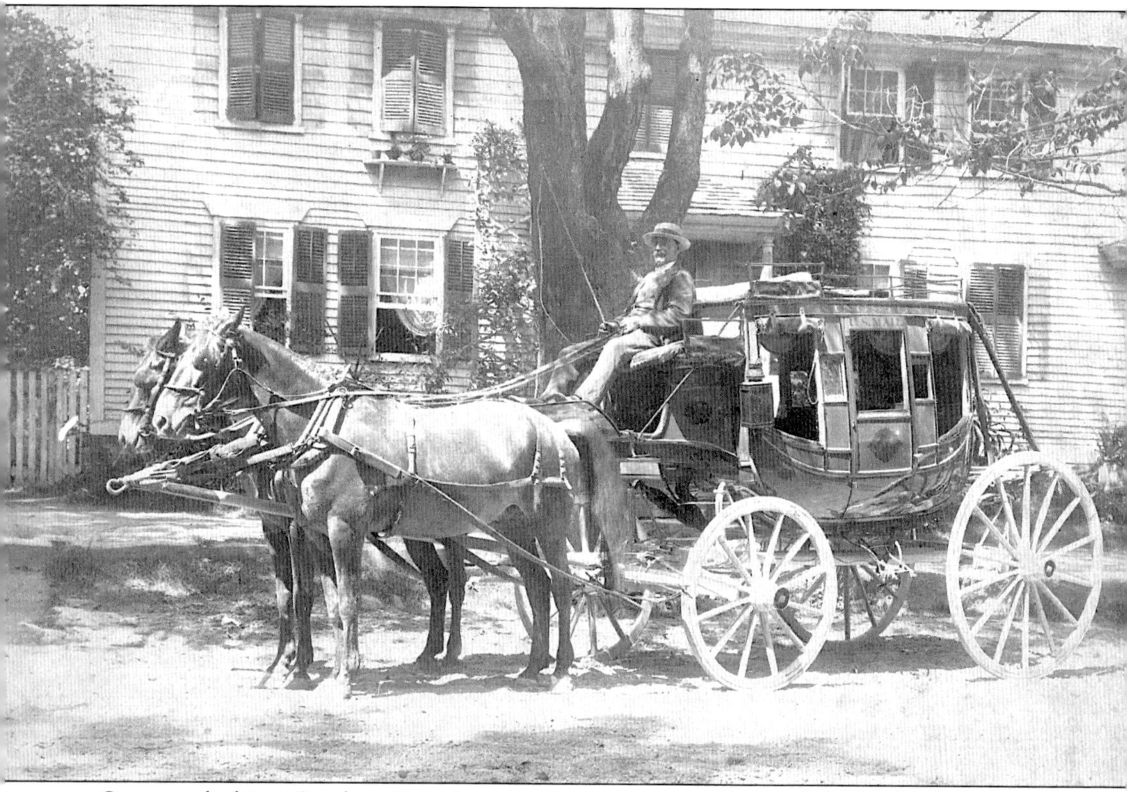

Stagecoach driver Stephen Knowles waits for passengers in front of the Joe Reynolds Tavern, probably during the time it was operated by John N. Taylor. Knowles met all trains at the Kingston Station with his coach. The railroad bypassed the village when it was constructed in 1837. When the Narragansett Pier Railroad was launched in 1876, creating a direct rail link between the Kingston Station and the resort at Narragansett Pier, the real decline of the stage routes began. The stage ceased to run a year after the Narragansett Pier Railroad began. (Courtesy Pettaquamscutt Historical Society.)

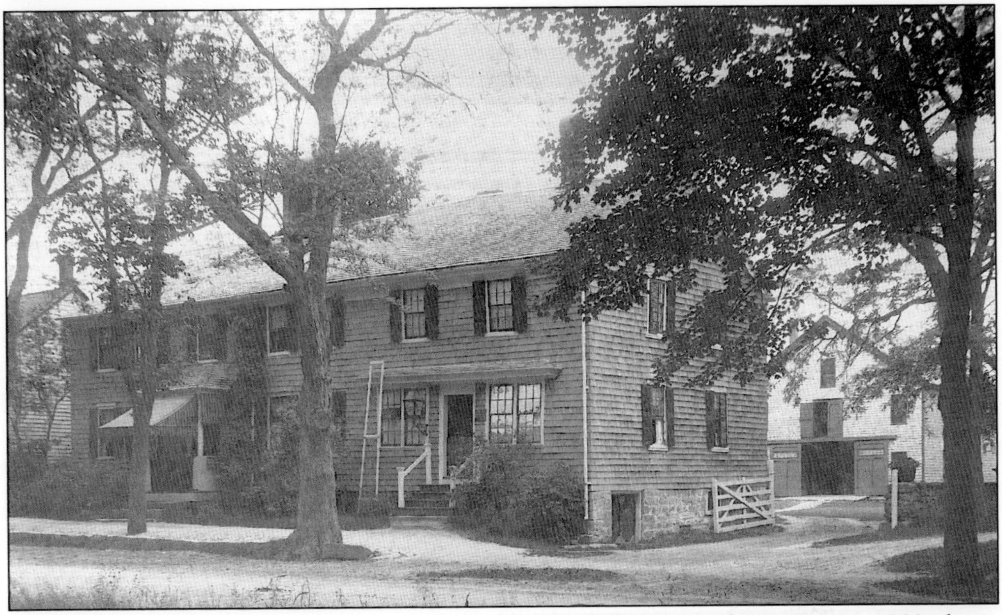

This view of the Joe Reynolds Tavern, taken when it was known as the Locusts in 1900, shows the barn in the back. Over the years, the tavern's proprietors included Caleb Westcott, a carpenter; Joe Reynolds, who died in 1823; John Reynolds, his son; Philip Taylor, who acquired the building in 1836 and died in 1856; and his son John N. Taylor. (Courtesy Pettaquamscutt Historical Society.)

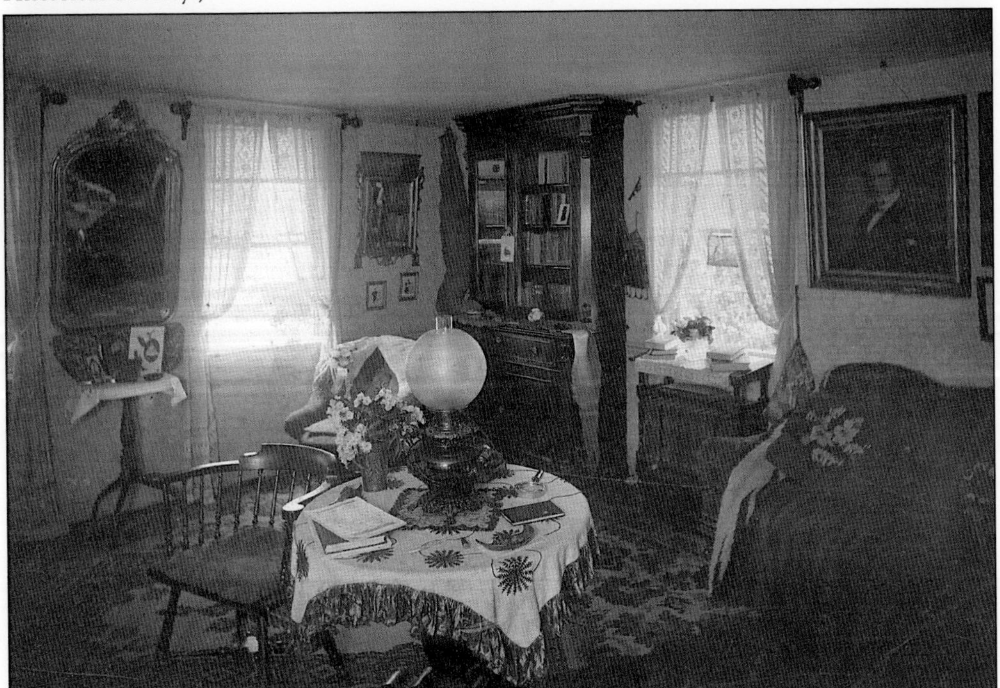

This view shows the interior of the tavern when it was known as the Locusts. The lamps, furnishings, and curtains are typical of the Victorian period and bear little relationship to the tavern's beginnings. (Courtesy Pettaquamscutt Historical Society.)

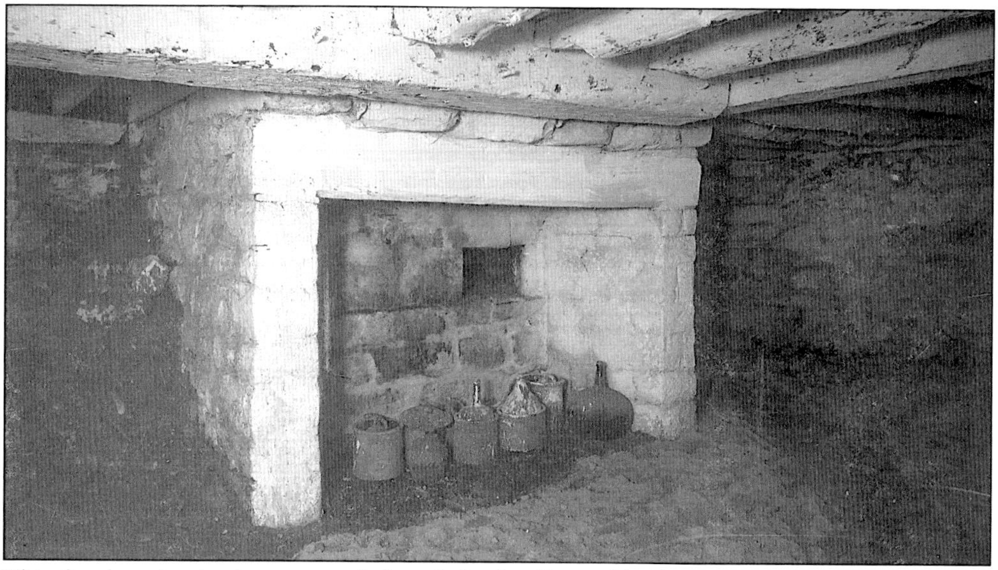

This fireplace in the basement of the of the Joe Reynolds Tavern was described by Philip Kittredge Taylor in 1903 as having "a massive lintel of oak" and in its rear "an oven large enough to hold a suckling pig." Taylor went on to write that it was believed the slaves cooked in the cellar fireplace, hanging pots not from a crane but on "chains or withes from an oaken beam built into the throat of a flue." (Courtesy of Pettaquamscutt Historical Society.)

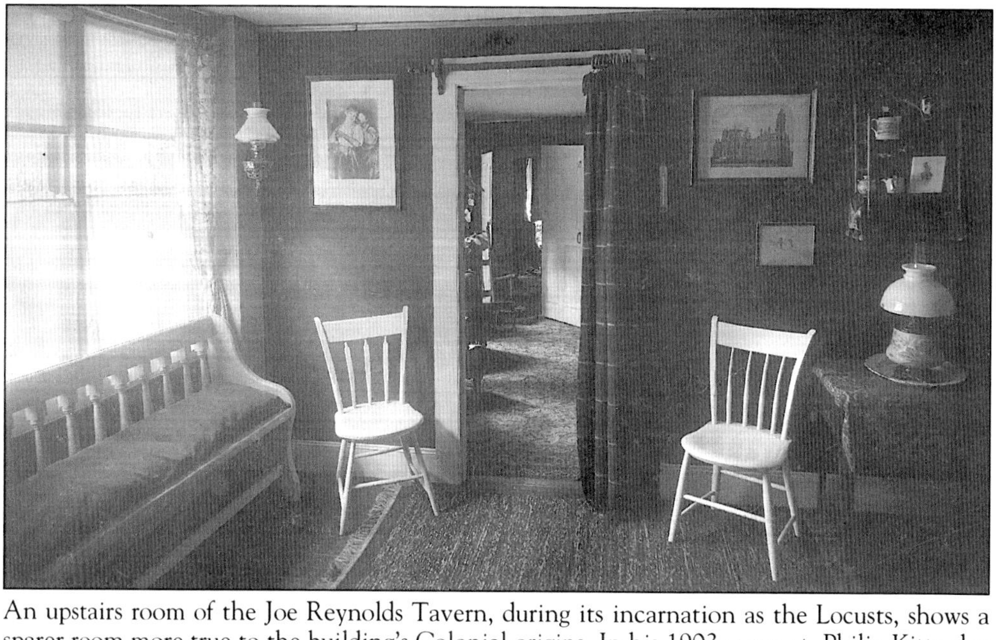

An upstairs room of the Joe Reynolds Tavern, during its incarnation as the Locusts, shows a sparer room more true to the building's Colonial origins. In his 1903 account, Philip Kittredge Taylor notes that the second floor of the building once contained a large hall where legislators and other officials in town on business at the Kings County Courthouse were entertained. (Courtesy Pettaquamscutt Historical Society.)

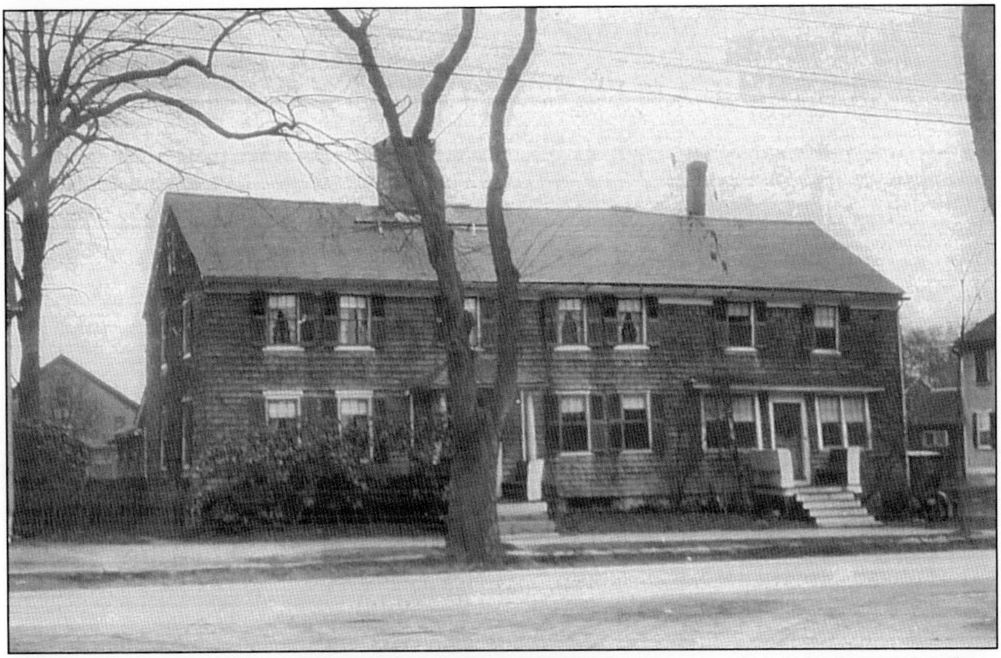

This view, *c*. 1920s, shows the exterior of the Joe Reynolds Tavern after it had ceased to be a public inn. (Courtesy Pettaquamscutt Historical Society.)

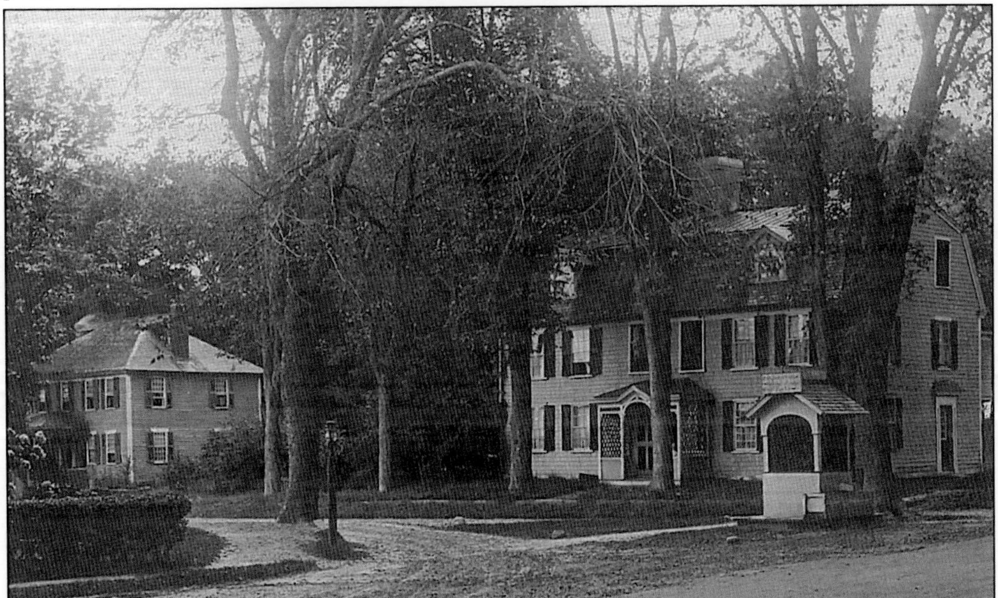

The Tavern Hall Club, the building in the foreground, is a familiar landmark in Kingston, and its history touches on many facets of village life. Built *c*. 1738 by Elisha Reynolds, the tavern was the site of the county's first newspaper, *the Rhode Island Advocate*. After Reynolds, the building was for many years in the Potter family, one of whom added a story on to an ell and made the attic into lodging rooms. Kingston Academy students boarded here for a time, and the tavern also served as a grocery store, tavern, library, lecture hall, and boot and shoe factory. (Courtesy Pettaquamscutt Historical Society.)

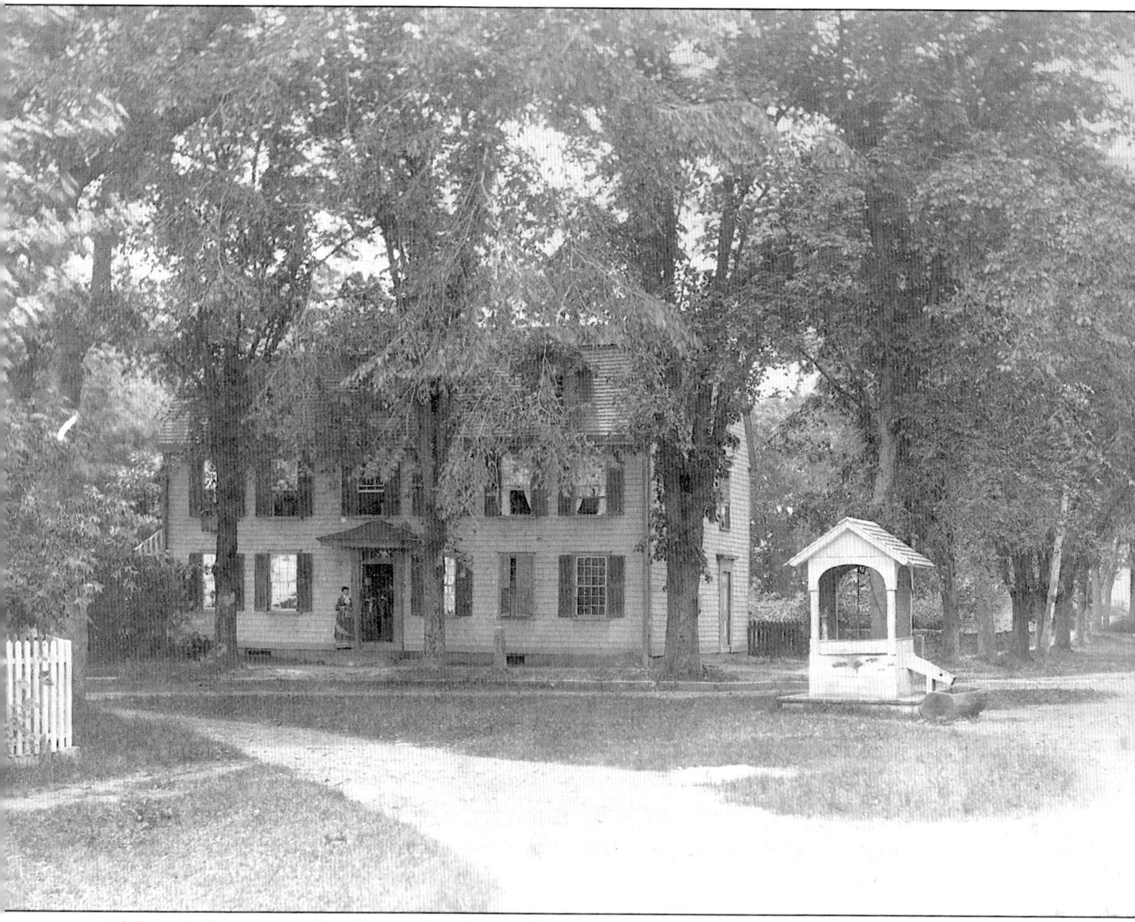

Although known today for its familiar yellow paint and familiar name, the Tavern Hall Club was red for many years and sported a number of different names, including the Lucca House, after the Viennese opera singer who stayed there and demanded that her portrait be displayed while she was in residence. In his *Kingston Annals*, the Reverend J. Hagadorn Wells describes the stacks of slaughtered hogs that were stored at the Tavern Hall Club when its bottom floor was a grocery. (Courtesy Pettaquamscutt Historical Society.)

Three

Old Houses

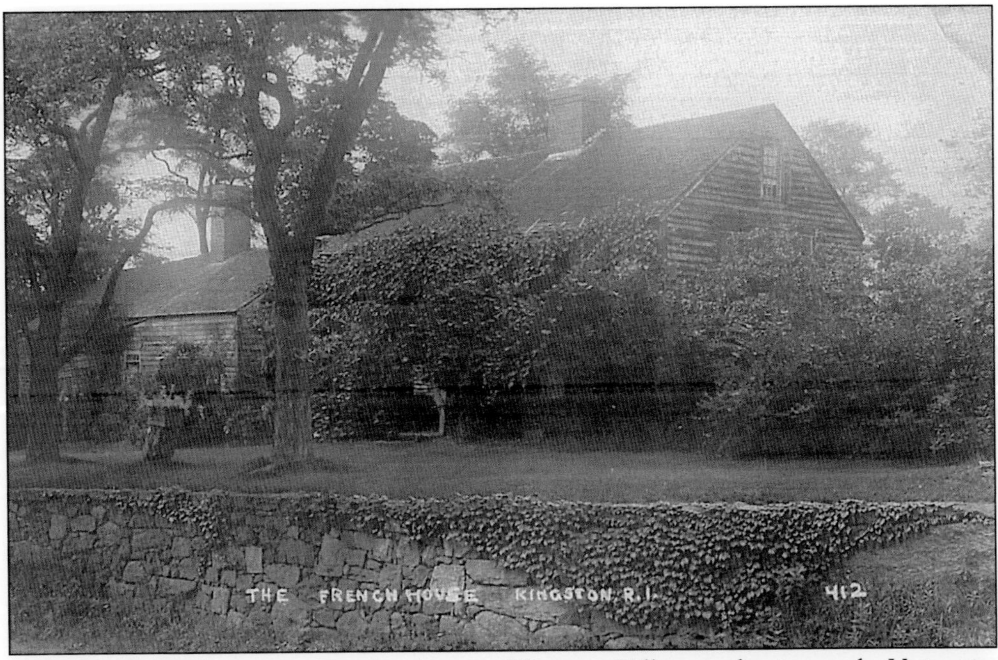

The Cyrus French house once stood at the top of Kingston Hill, near what is now the University of Rhode Island sign at the intersection of Upper College Road. French, who was a hatmaker from Grafton, Massachusetts, bought the property from Robert Potter in 1792 and fashioned the house from three buildings on the lot, including parts of the original Kingston Jail. (Courtesy Pettaquamscutt Historical Society.)

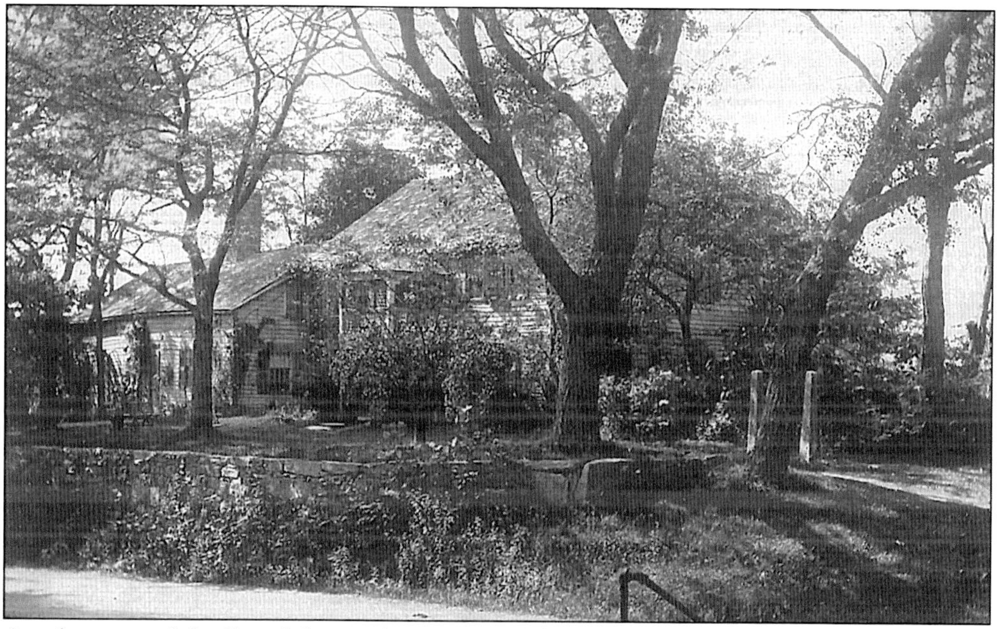

Another view of the French house shows more of the corner and French's wall. Cyrus French made beaver hats in this house and was succeeded in the trade by his son William. Historical accounts describe both father and son as tall, bulky men who loved to regale listeners with stories at the Joe Reynolds Tavern. (Courtesy Pettaquamscutt Historical Society.)

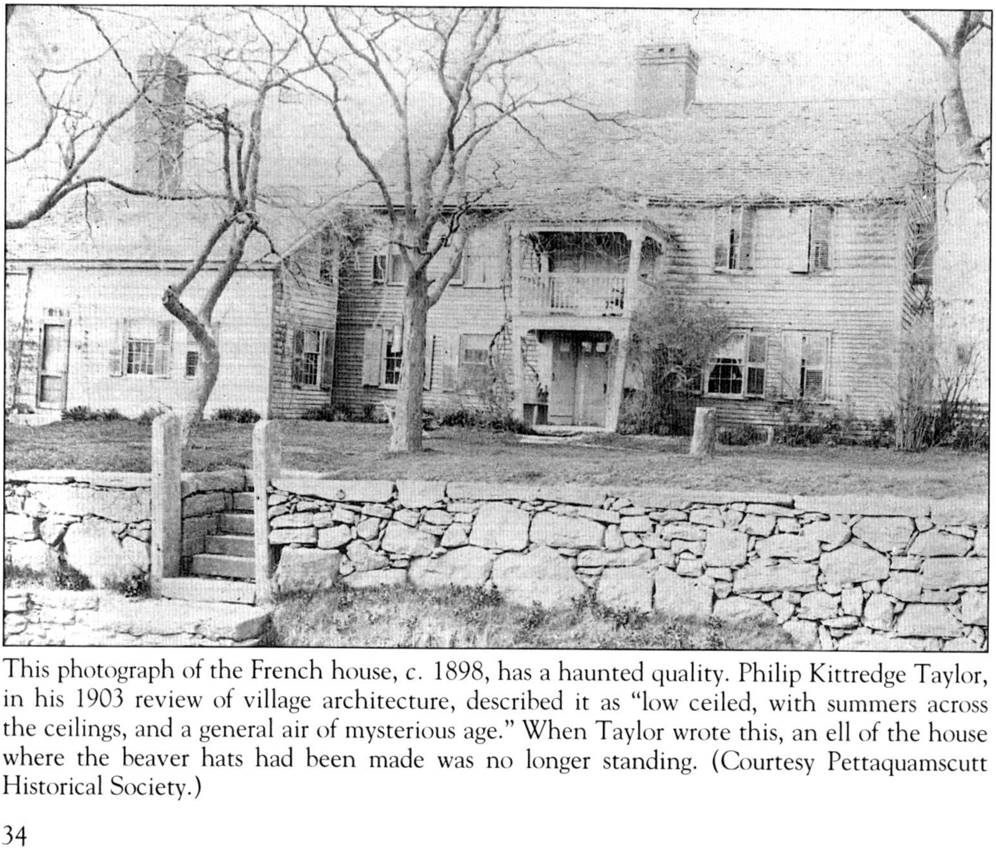

This photograph of the French house, *c.* 1898, has a haunted quality. Philip Kittredge Taylor, in his 1903 review of village architecture, described it as "low ceiled, with summers across the ceilings, and a general air of mysterious age." When Taylor wrote this, an ell of the house where the beaver hats had been made was no longer standing. (Courtesy Pettaquamscutt Historical Society.)

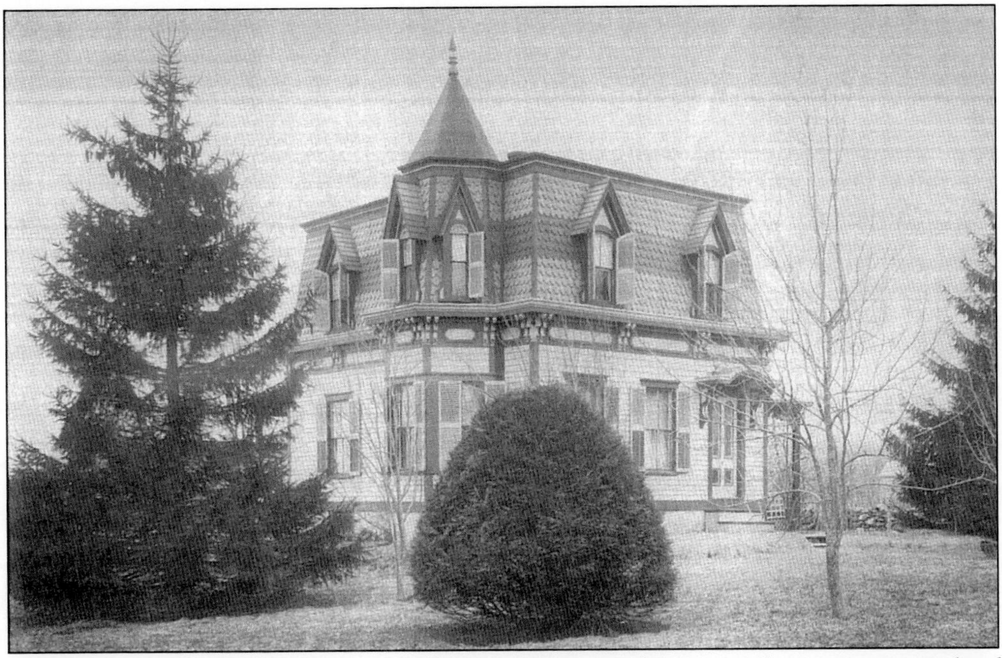

The B.F. Brown house, an elaborate residence of the Second Empire style, is a rare example of Victorian architecture to survive in Kingston. Although several houses were built in similar styles in the late 19th century, some fell to the wrecking ball while their older Colonial cousins survived. (Courtesy Pat Wyatt.)

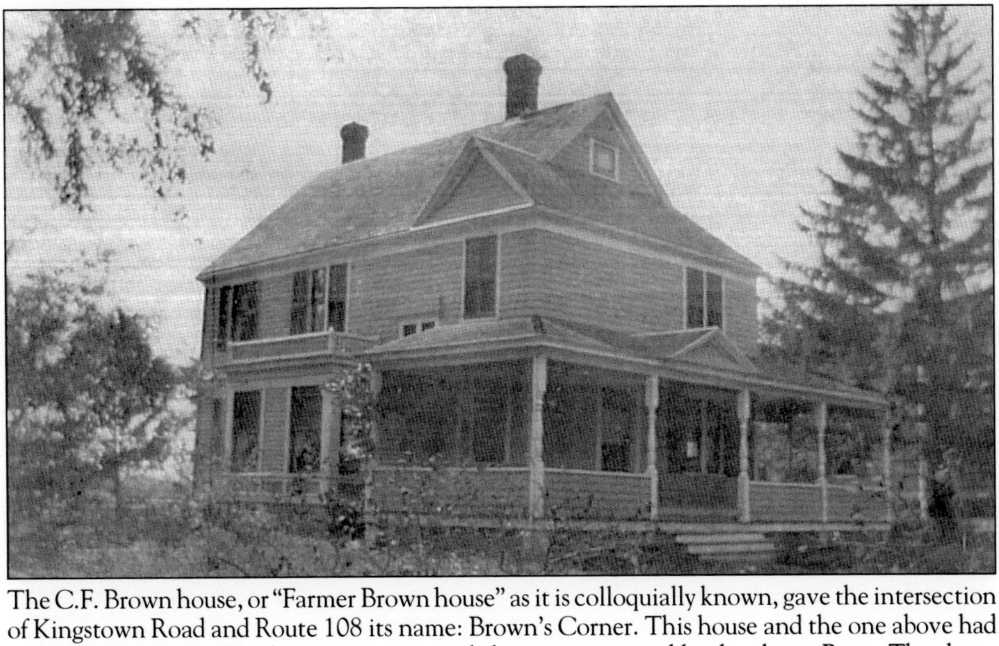

The C.F. Brown house, or "Farmer Brown house" as it is colloquially known, gave the intersection of Kingstown Road and Route 108 its name: Brown's Corner. This house and the one above had a haunted-house quality for many years until they were restored by developer Bruce Thunberg. (Courtesy Pat Wyatt.)

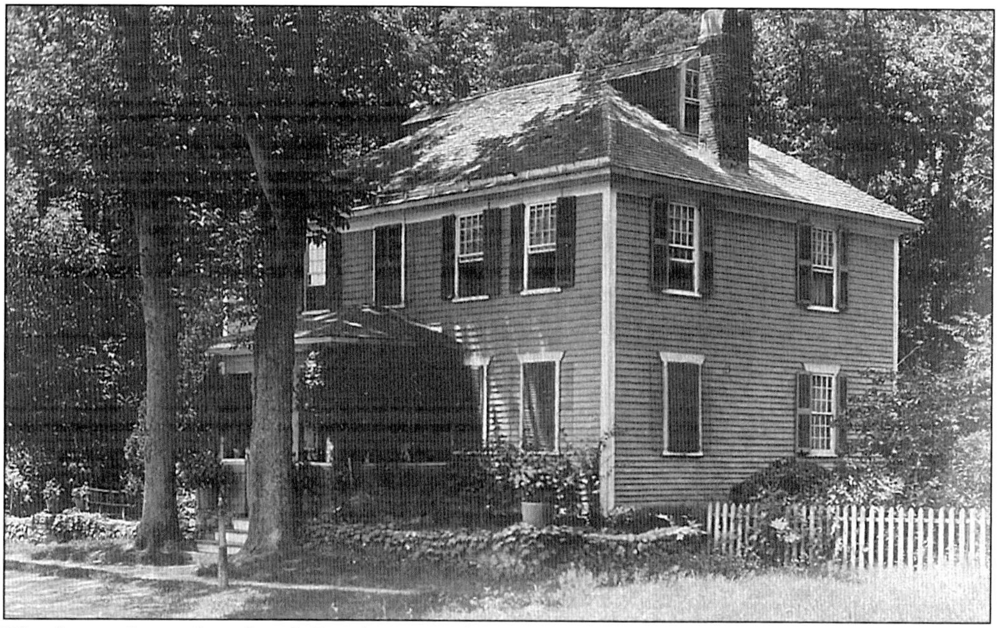

This house, located on South Road next to the Tavern Hall Club, is known as the Christopher Gardner house, after its builder. It dates from 1862 and replaced a gambrel-roofed house built in 1820 by Sarah Fellows. (Courtesy Pettaquamscutt Historical Society.)

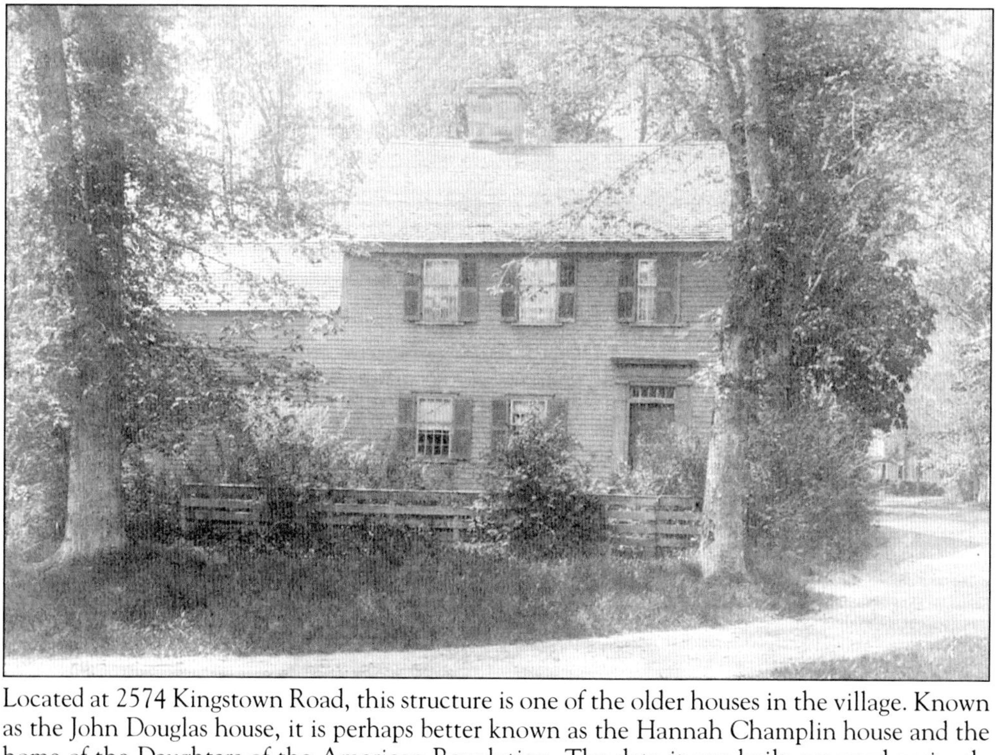

Located at 2574 Kingstown Road, this structure is one of the older houses in the village. Known as the John Douglas house, it is perhaps better known as the Hannah Champlin house and the home of the Daughters of the American Revolution. The date it was built, reported variously as 1756 or 1765, is carved in the chimney. Another view of this house appears on page 40. (Courtesy Pettaquamscutt Historical Society.)

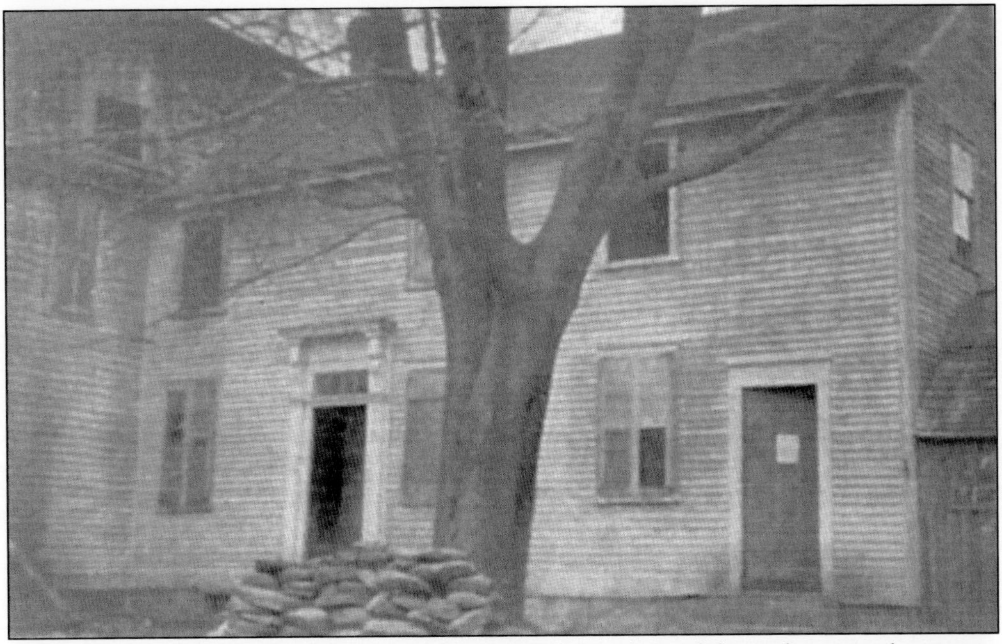

This side view of the Wells-Comstock house at 59 Old North Road shows the original structure, which faced toward what is now Route 138 or Kingstown Road. The original house of post-and-beam construction dates from 1750. In 1820, Thomas R. Wells added a two-story addition in the Federal style to front on Old North Road. Fifteen years later he sold the rambling house to Christopher Comstock, an instructor at the Kingston Academy, next door. Students at the academy boarded upstairs, and the house became a social center for academy students. It served as a bookstore, a faculty study, a dormitory, and a laundry. (Courtesy Joy Utter.)

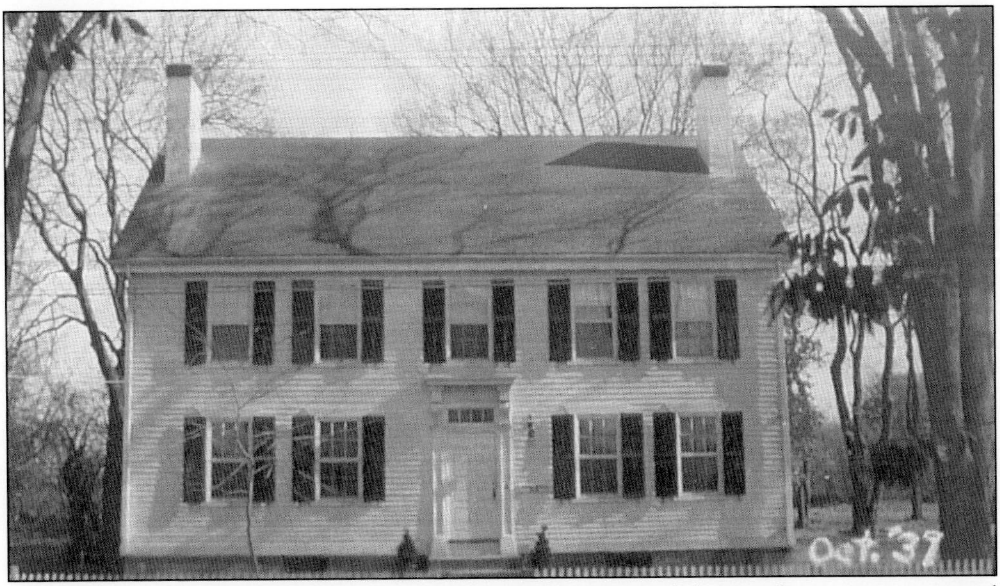

This photograph shows the front view of the Wells-Comstock house after it was renovated in 1937. The house has six fireplaces, and a large keeping room in the original 1750 portion features a beehive oven. (Courtesy of Joy Utter.)

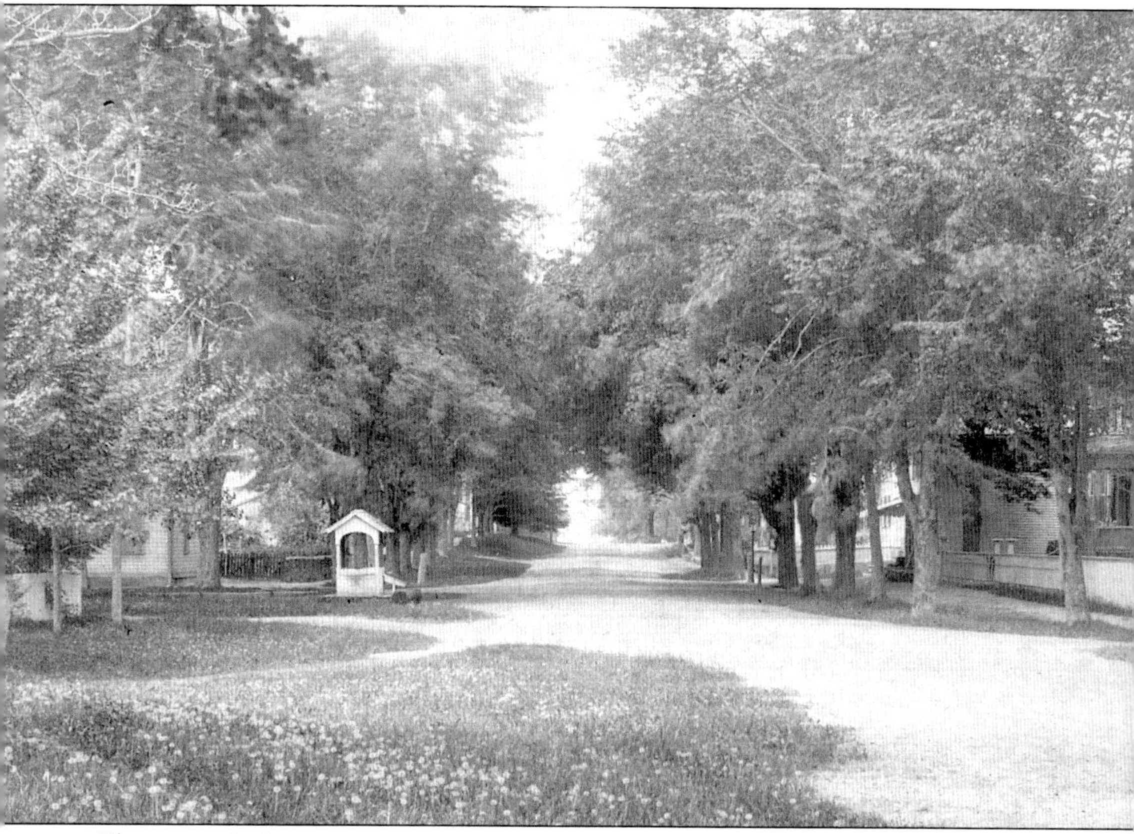

This view of what was Main Street shows the setting of many of Kingston's old houses: a tree-lined street with white picket fences and posts for tying up horses. The road was narrow enough and so little-used that a flower-strewn lawn could spring up alongside it. (Courtesy Pettaquamscutt Historical Society.)

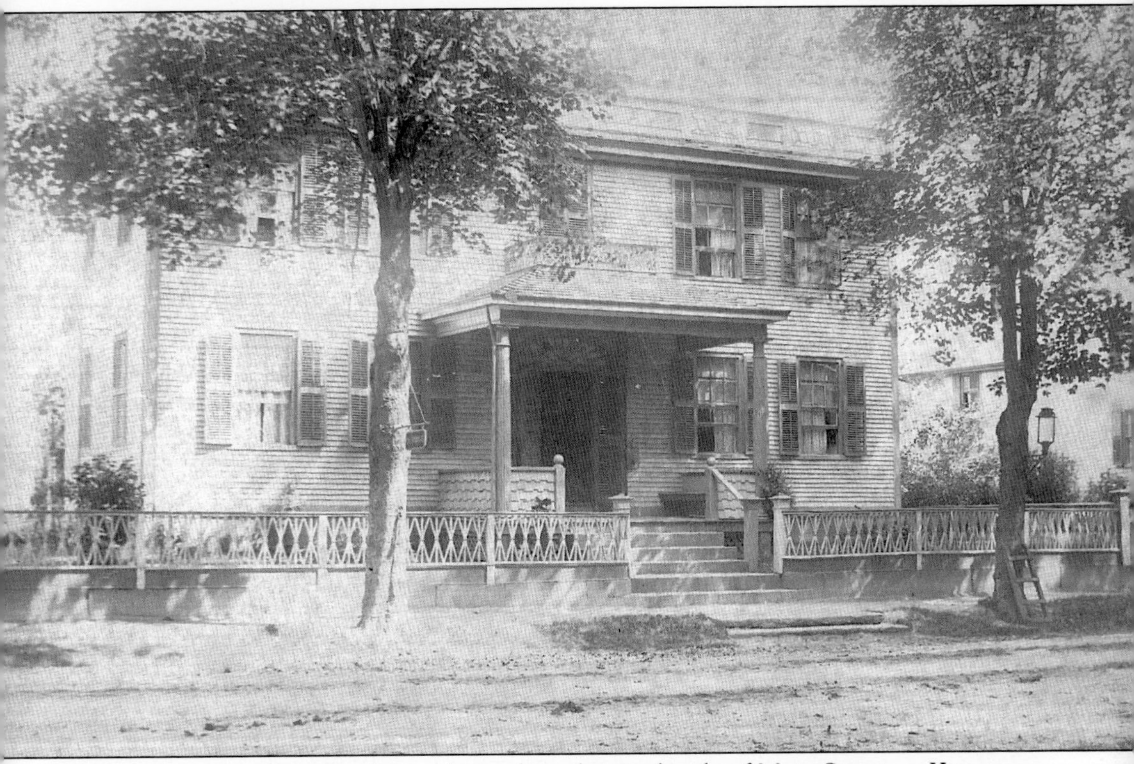

The Hawthorne or Hagadorn house, located on the north side of Main Street, or Kingstown Road, was named after its one-time owner John Hagadorn, whose German surname translated to "hawthorne." The original part of the house was built in 1775 by silversmith Joseph Perkins and later turned to face west to accommodate an addition. In 1827, merchant Thomas Stoddard Taylor, who had married Hagadorn's niece, built the addition facing Kingstown Road, and two parts of the original structure were moved off the site. (Courtesy Pettaquamscutt Historical Society.)

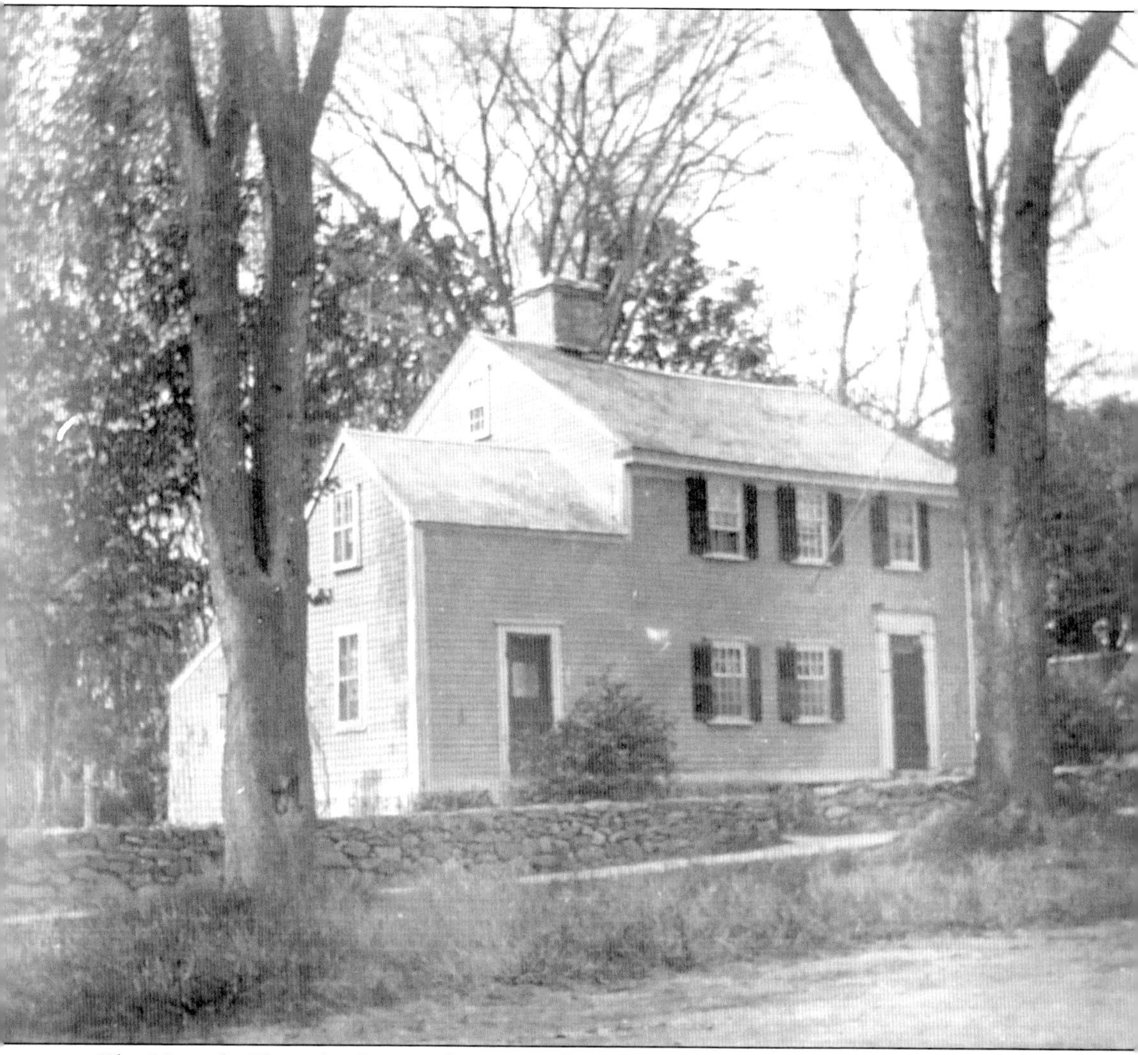

The Hannah Champlin house, also pictured on page 36, was built in the mid-18th century. In 1912, the Narragansett Chapter of the Daughters of the American Revolution converted the first floor into a museum, evidence of the growing recognition in the 20th century of the village's historic importance. The DAR held its first meeting in the house in June of that year. The *Narragansett Times* reported that the DAR museum contained "interesting relics of the older times" and would be open every Thursday afternoon. (Courtesy Pettaquamscutt Historical Society.)

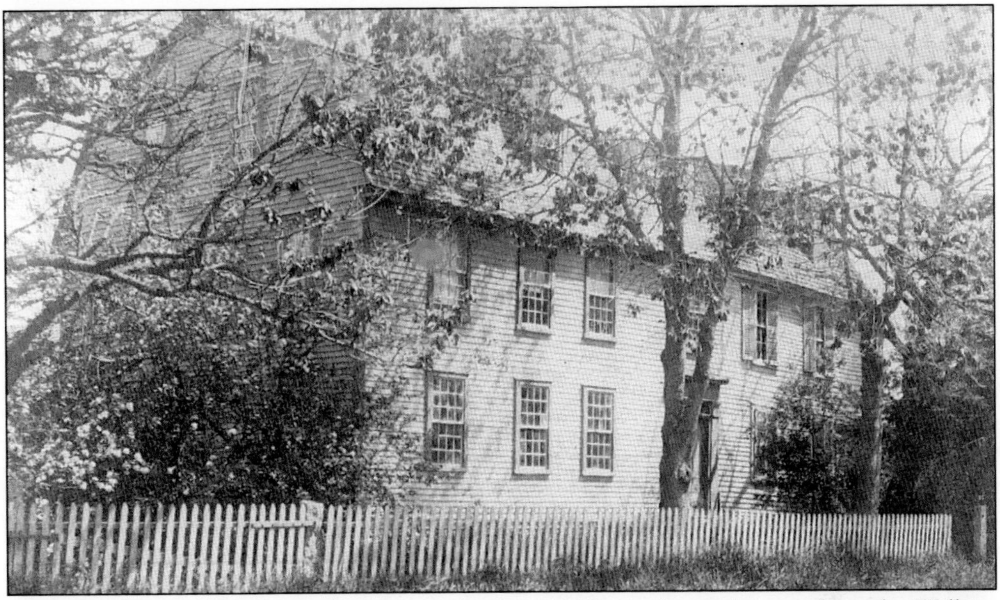

The James Helme house, which was torn down in 1910, was located across from the Wilkins Updike house on Kingstown Road. The Reverend J. Hagadorn Wells reported in his reminiscences that the house was moved "a few rods east" and used as a tenement. The east end was home to Sarah Fayerweather from 1855 until her death in 1878. Wells recalled that Helme was "a man of affairs holding responsible positions" in the community and that his father, James Helme Sr., was also prominent. (Courtesy Pettaquamscutt Historical Society.)

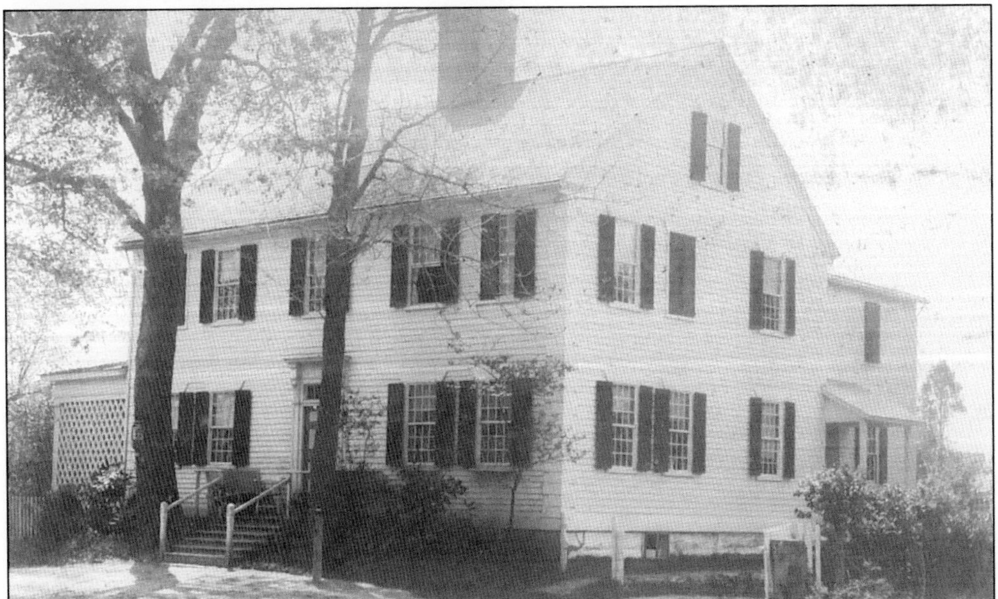

The Wilkins Updike house at 2520 Kingstown Road was named for Mr. Updike, who moved from Smith's Castle in the Cocumcussoc section of North Kingstown in the early 19th century to build this house in Kingston. The Reverend J. Hagadorn Wells reports that the house was built in 1812 and was occupied by a Mr. Hunt later in that century. (Courtesy Pettaquamscutt Historical Society.)

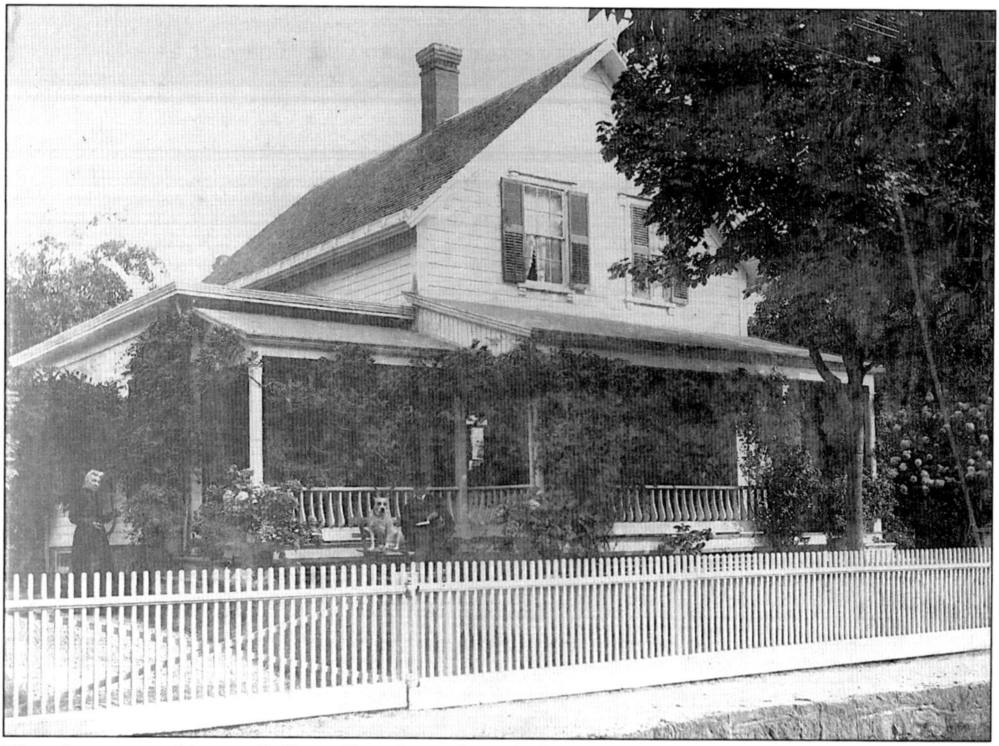

This house on Upper College Road is identified as Dr. Hartwell's house. The reference is probably to Burt L. Hartwell, who was hired by the Rhode Island College of Agricultural and Mechanic Arts in 1891 as an assistant director of the Experiment Station. Hartwell later became the director and also served as a music instructor. (Courtesy Pettaquamscutt Historical Society.)

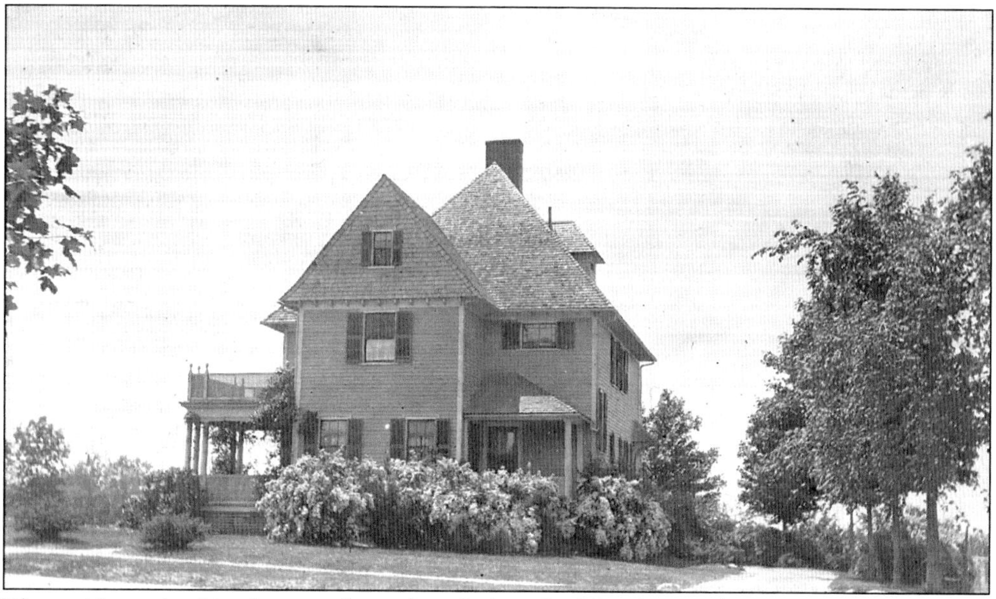

The residence in this photograph is identified as the Hart house. (Courtesy Pettaquamscutt Historical Society.)

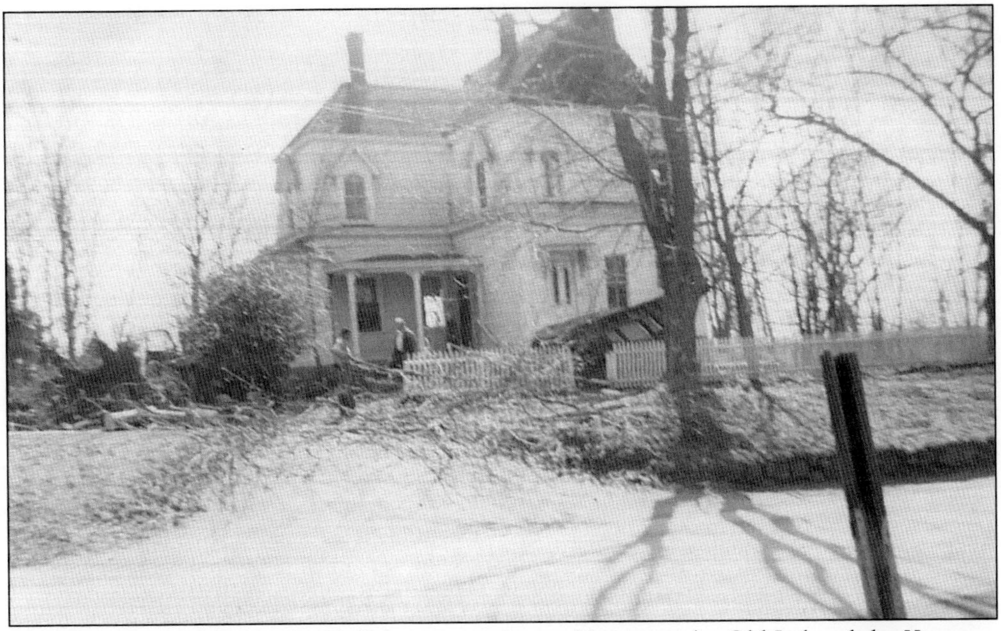

This Victorian residence, the Tefft house, was located between the Old Jail and the Kingston Congregational Church on Kingstown Road. It was torn down in 1962 to make room for a church parking lot. (Courtesy Pettaquamscutt Historical Society.)

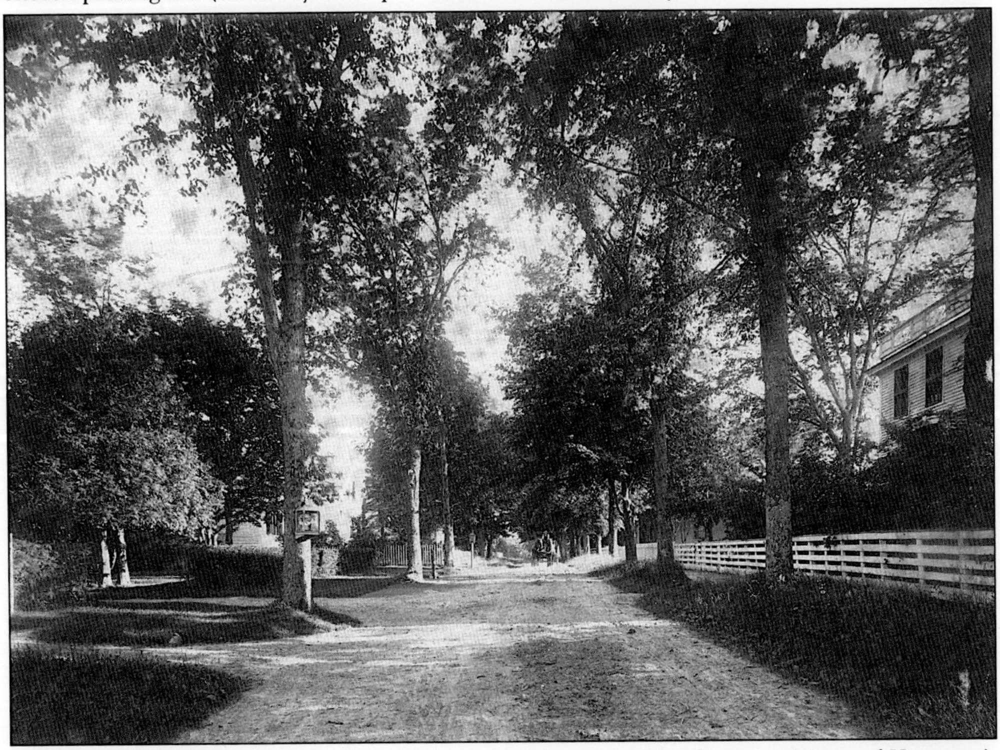

This view of Old North Road shows a horse and buggy in the distance. Many of Kingston's homes were built close to the road, with a barn or stable in the back. (Courtesy Pettaquamscutt Historical Society.)

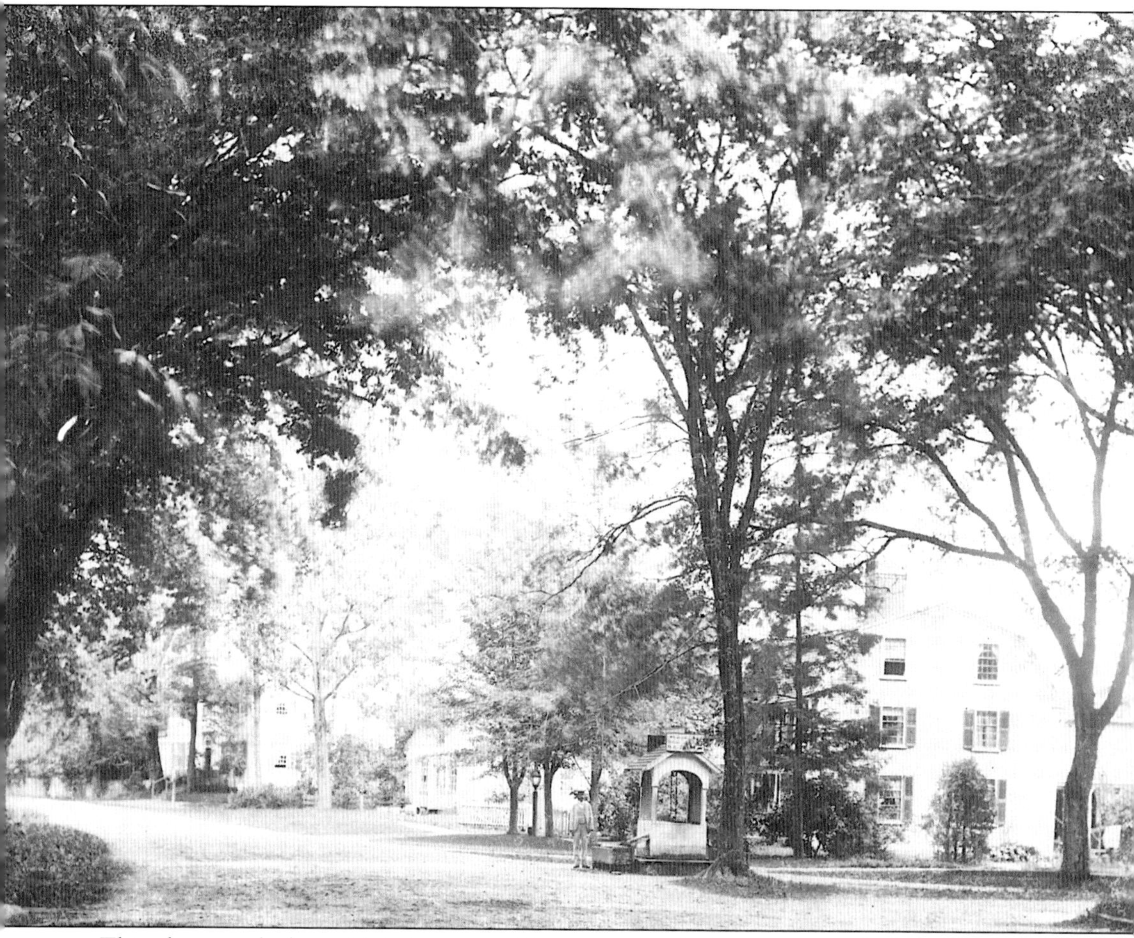

This photograph shows Main Street, or Kingstown Road, facing east, with the Aldrich Marble Shop where the Kingston Hill Store is now at the center and a kerosene lantern hanging from a tree at the extreme left. At one time, kerosene lanterns were the only form of illumination on village streets. (Courtesy Pettaquamscutt Historical Society.)

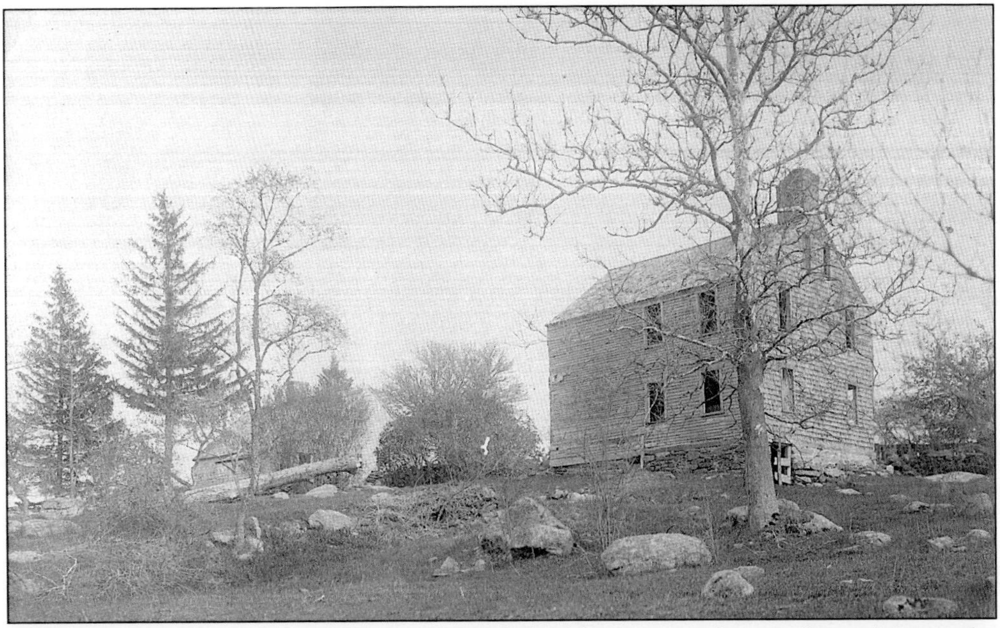

This part of Kingston was called Biscuit City, legend has it, after the traveling salesman who was rebuffed at the door by housewives busy baking biscuits. This view was taken *c.* 1895, when the area was in decline. (Courtesy Pettaquamscutt Historical Society.)

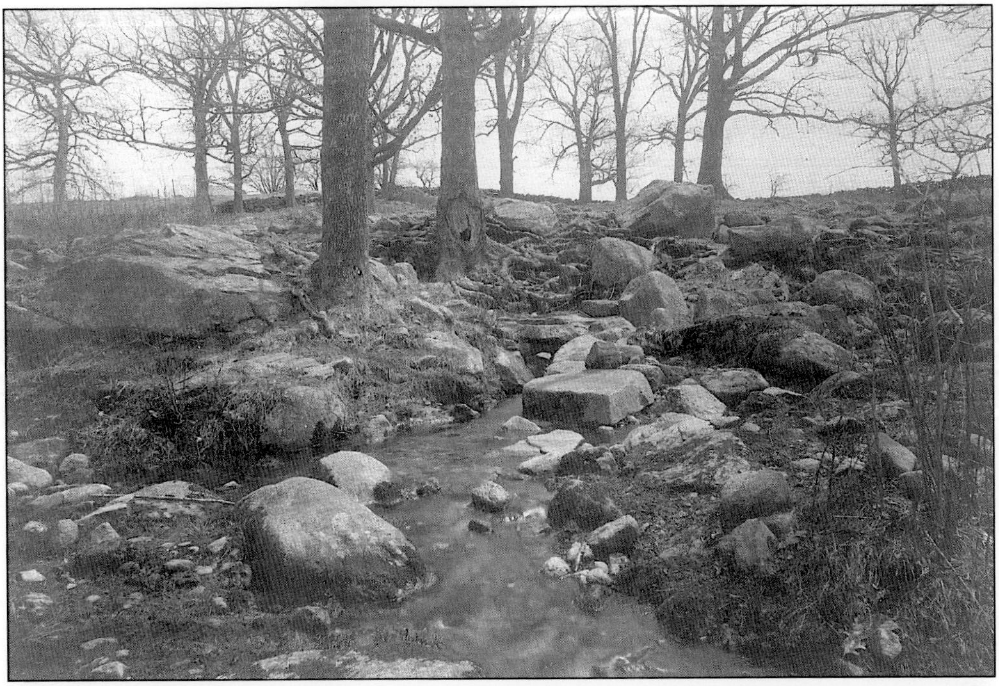

This is Boiling Spring, a favorite site of picnics and the former source of Kingston's water supply. The spring, named for its bubbly nature, flowed into a pond that powered a gristmill, which may have been the town's first textile mill. Philip Kittredge Taylor, in his 1903 account of the village, noted that a second spring joined the waterway to make "a chattering little rivulet which runs to a quiet mill pond." (Courtesy Pettaquamscutt Historical Society.)

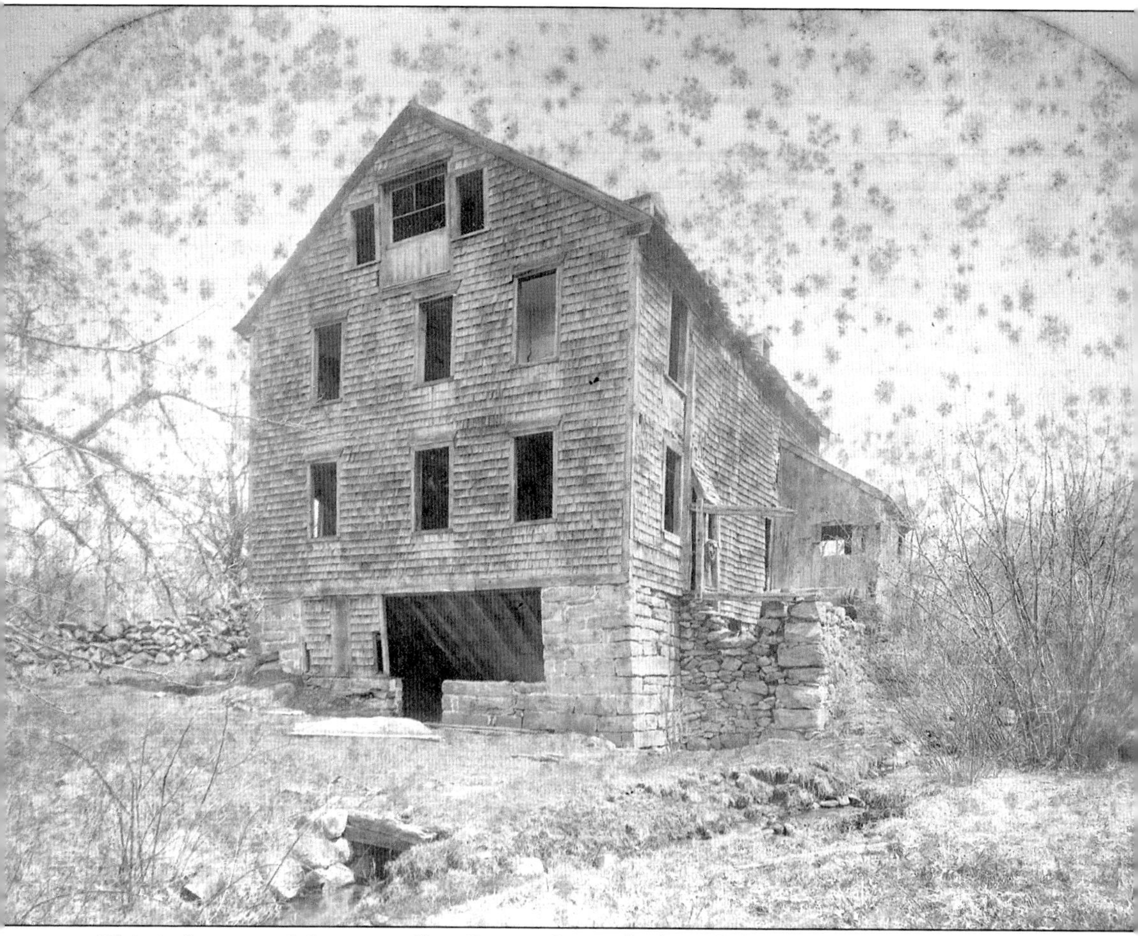

This is the ruin of the gristmill at Biscuit City, which probably began as a cotton or woolen mill. An anonymous writer called "G," giving his account of village memories in 1922, said that when he was a young man, the mill had been known as Holley's gristmill after miller Solomon Holley, who lived nearby. "G" also reported that the second floor of the mill was occupied by Aunt Nobby Potter, who had been a servant and nurse for Judge Elisha R. Potter Jr. Others operating the mill were James W. Mowry and J. Henry Wells, who made hay rakes. At one time a portion of the mill was used to paint and repair wagons. Still, in the mind of "G," the mill "ground the best johnnycake meal that was ever eaten." Philip Kittredge Taylor, writing in 1903, also spoke sadly of the mill's decline when a modern turbine replaced the wooden waterwheel, the flume was lowered, "and one of the chief fascinations of the place was gone." (Courtesy Pettaquamscutt Historical Society.)

Four

School and Church Life

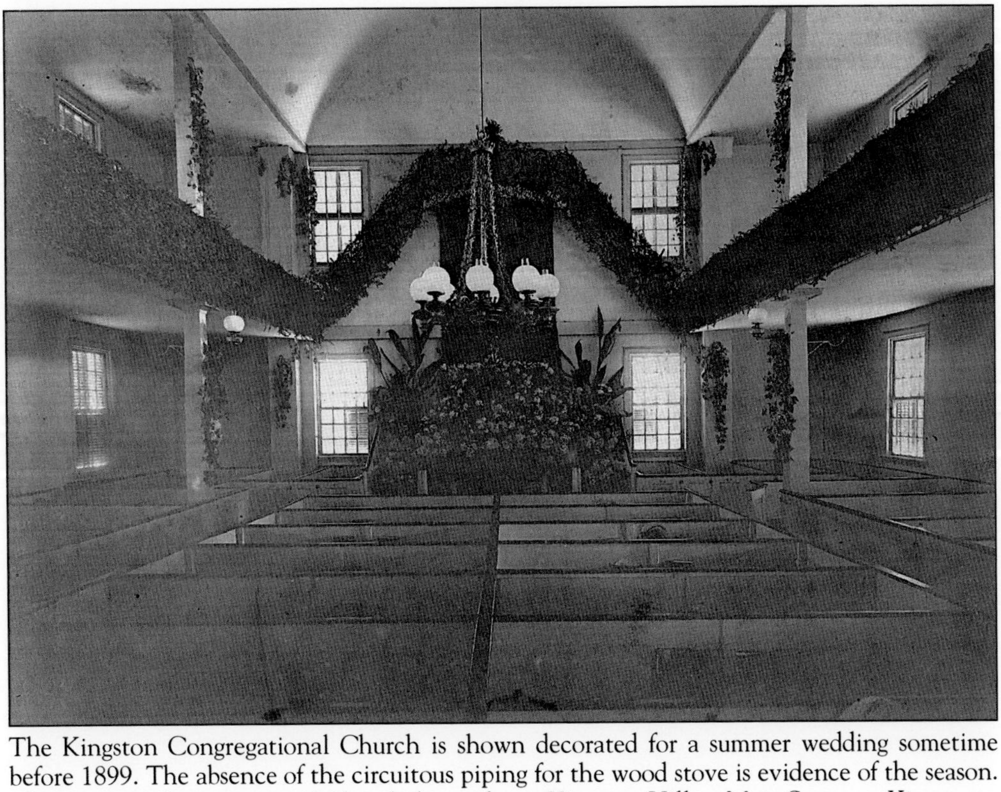

The Kingston Congregational Church is shown decorated for a summer wedding sometime before 1899. The absence of the circuitous piping for the wood stove is evidence of the season. The Kingston Congregational Church, located atop Kingston Hill on Main Street, or Kingstown Road, was built in 1820 but has roots dating from the Pettaquamscutt Purchase. (Courtesy Pettaquamscutt Historical Society.)

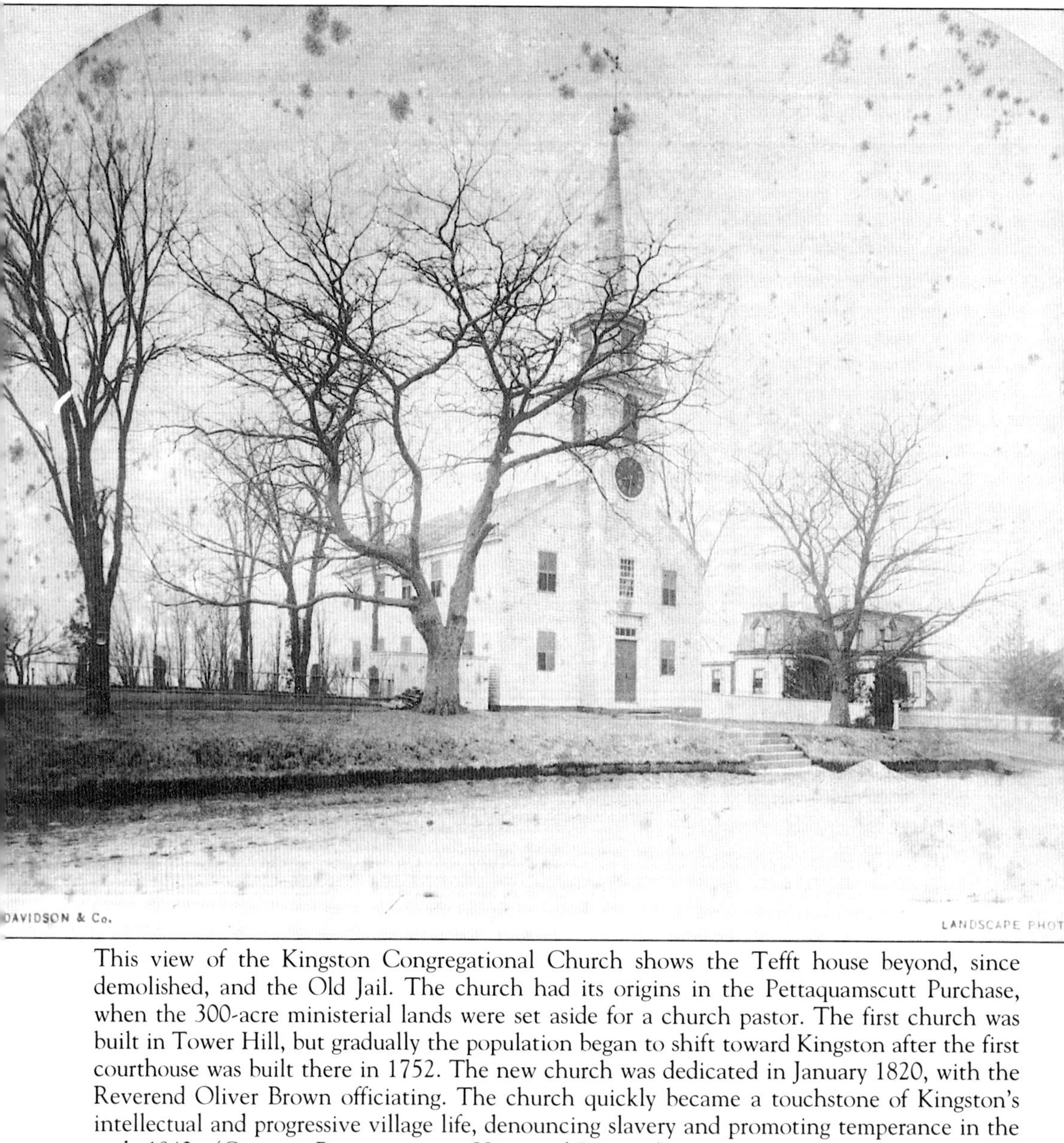

This view of the Kingston Congregational Church shows the Tefft house beyond, since demolished, and the Old Jail. The church had its origins in the Pettaquamscutt Purchase, when the 300-acre ministerial lands were set aside for a church pastor. The first church was built in Tower Hill, but gradually the population began to shift toward Kingston after the first courthouse was built there in 1752. The new church was dedicated in January 1820, with the Reverend Oliver Brown officiating. The church quickly became a touchstone of Kingston's intellectual and progressive village life, denouncing slavery and promoting temperance in the early 1840s. (Courtesy Pettaquamscutt Historical Society.)

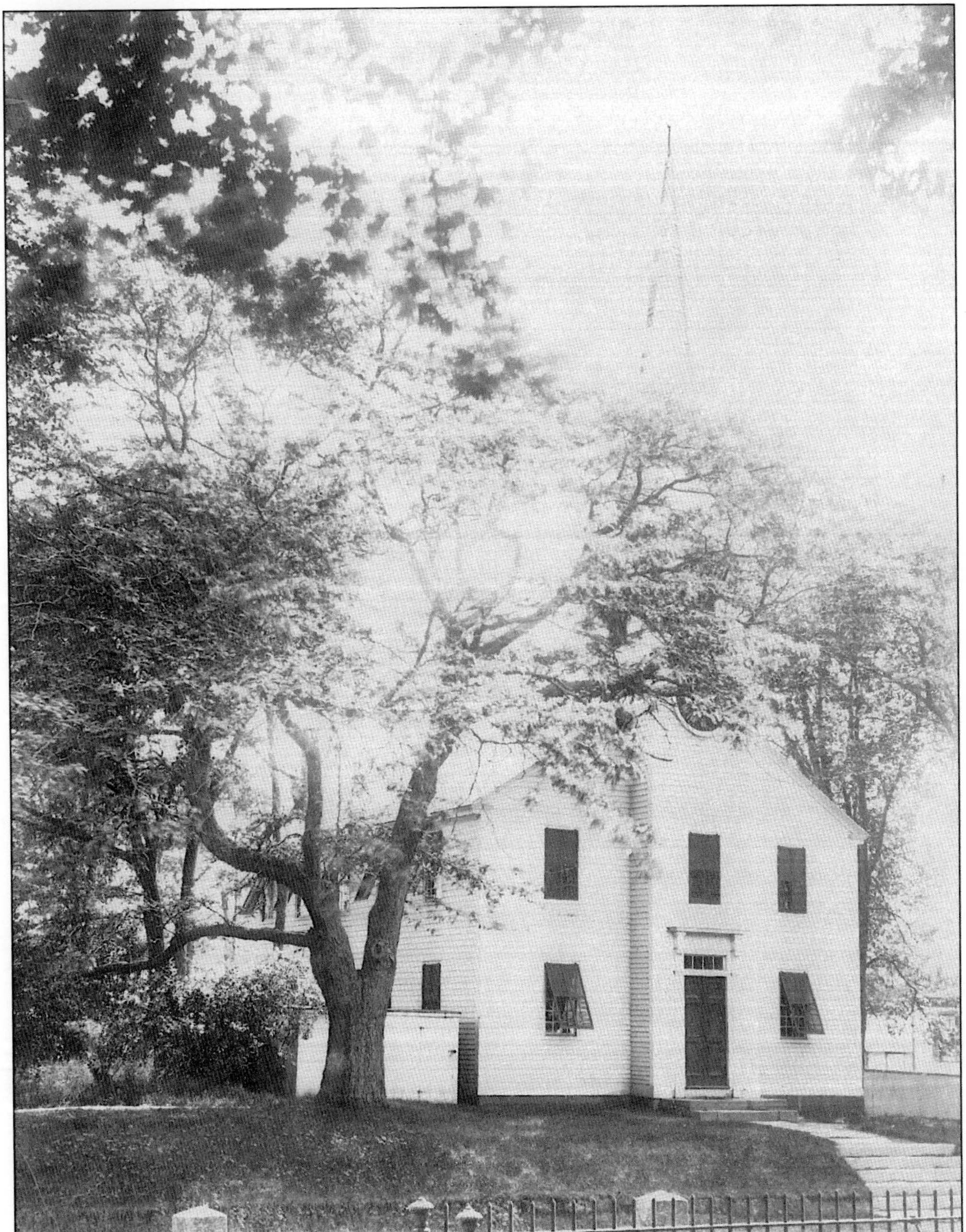

In January 1857, the steeple of the Kingston Congregational Church blew over in a gale. When it was repaired, the front was modified to have four windows instead of eight. Among the church's pastors was the Reverend J. Hagadorn Wells, who at age 80 penned memoirs that are still relied on by historians. In his account he takes an acerbic view of some modern-day alterations, such as the "great, unseemly wooden coal hod," located on the church's front and visible in this photograph. Wells was the church's pastor from 1862 to 1877. (Courtesy Pettaquamscutt Historical Society.)

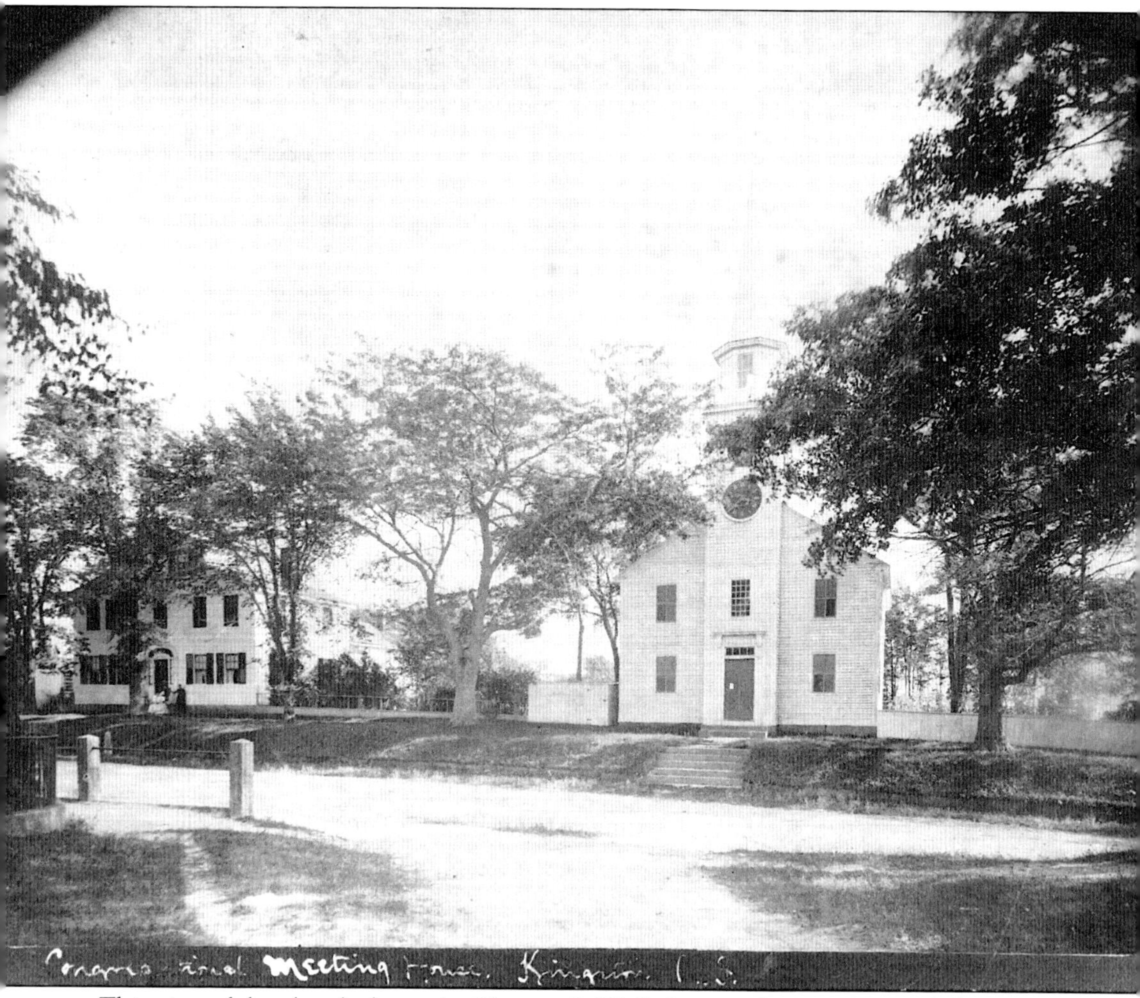

This view of the church shows the Thomas P. Wells house, which is the parish house of the Kingston Congregational Church. The first Kingston courthouse was built here in 1752 and was replaced by the house built by Thomas P. Wells in 1832. The residence became the church's parish house in 1933 and today is connected to the sanctuary by an auditorium built in 1962. (Courtesy Pettaquamscutt Historical Society.)

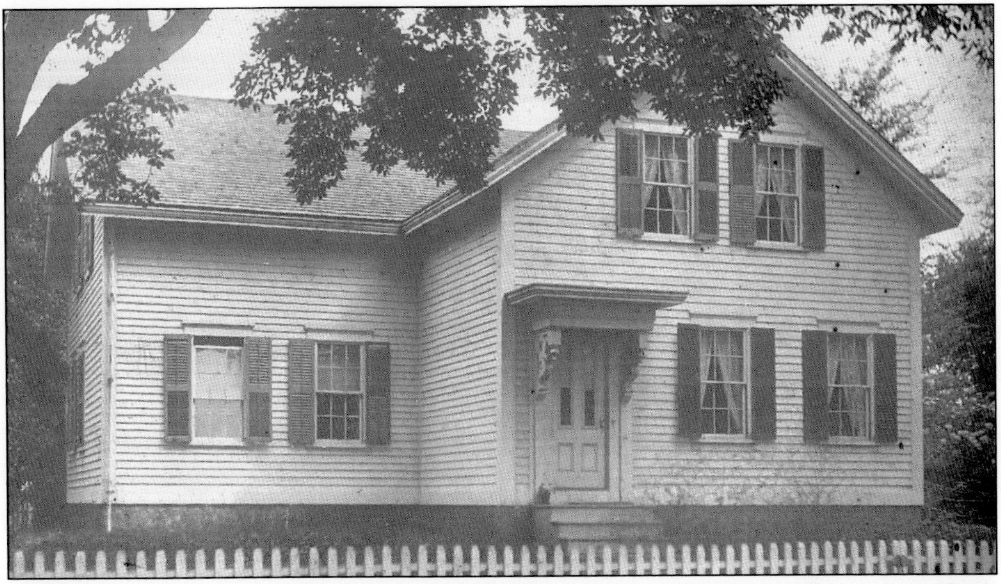

This house was at one time the parsonage of the Kingston Congregational Church. It was built in 1871 by village carpenter John Risley Eldred for his sisters Susan and Maria. Susan Eldred bequeathed it to the church. John Risley Eldred worked on a number of village buildings, including the Old Jail, and was killed at age 60 in an accident during construction of the Kingston Grammar School on Old North Road. (Courtesy Pettaquamscutt Historical Society.)

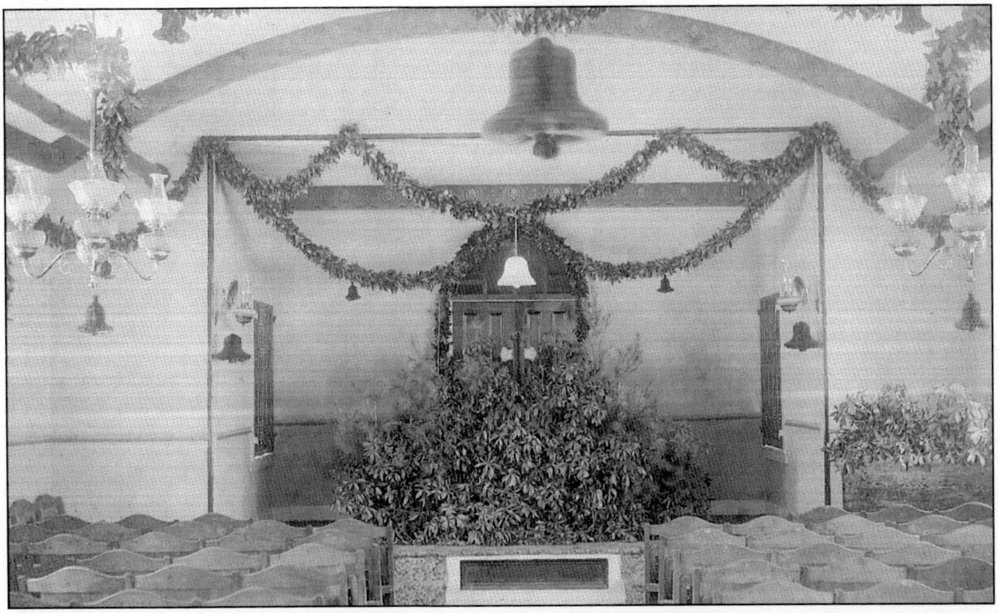

This was the scene inside the Waites Corner Church in West Kingston on Christmas Day of 1912, when Lulu Emma Burton became the bride of Millard Fillmore Perry of Kingston. The *Narragansett Times* reported that the church "was gay with Christmas green and flowers" for the 5:00 ceremony. Ushers included Oliver Watson and merchant Bernon E. Helme. Perry at one time had been a bank cashier, although his occupation at the time of the wedding is unknown. The couple left on the 9:20 train for a Providence honeymoon before settling in Kingston. (Courtesy Pettaquamscutt Historical Society.)

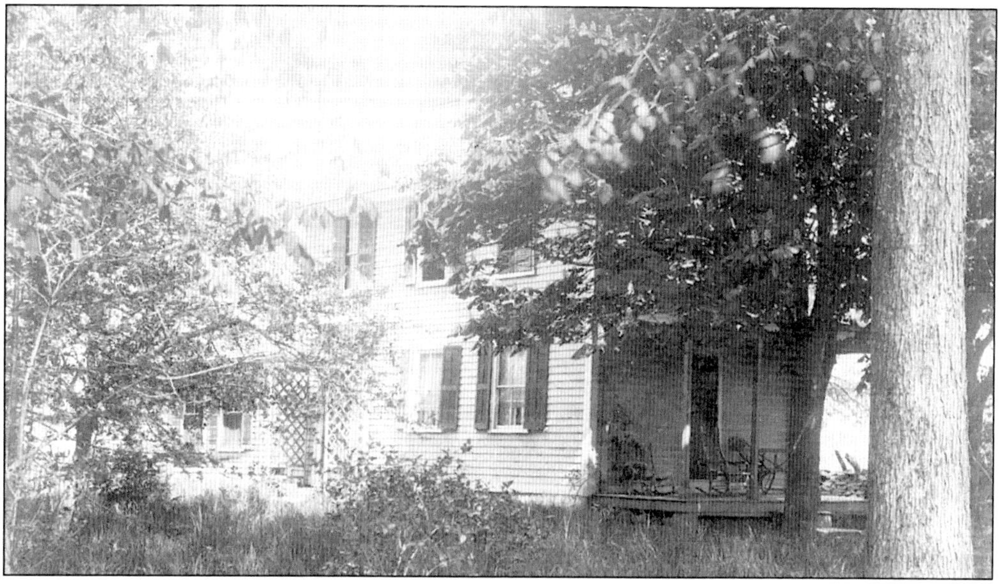

Kingston's first district school was held in this house. Later the District No. 3 schoolhouse, or Kingston Grammar School, was built on Old North Road. That building stands vacant today. (Courtesy Pettaquamscutt Historical Society.)

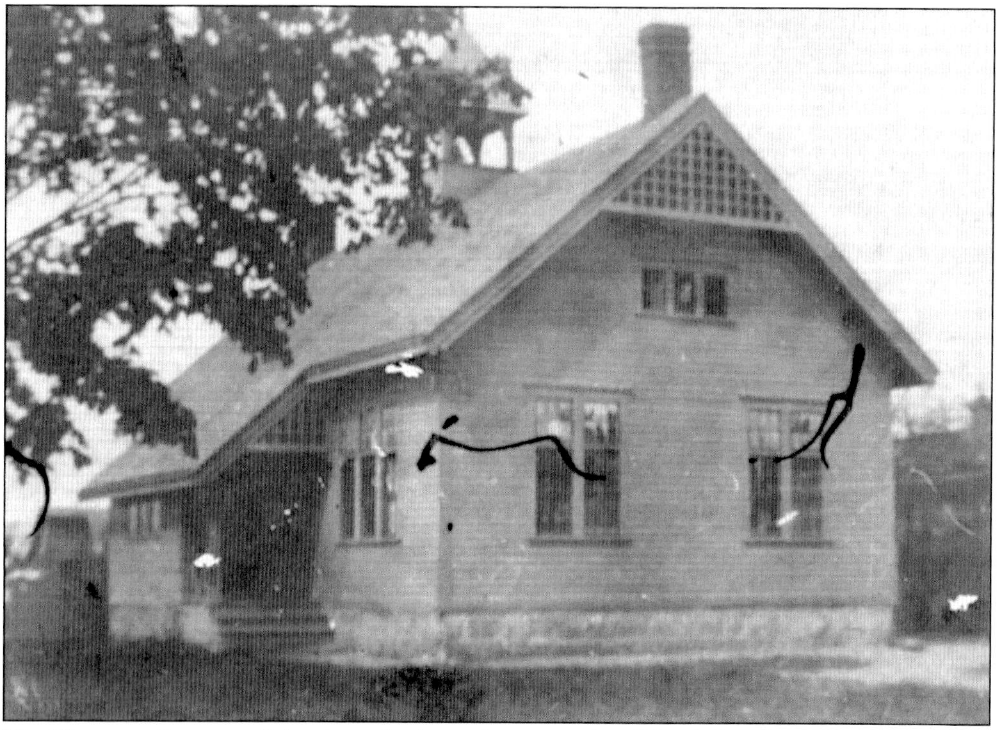

The Kingston Grammar School was built on the west side of North Road in 1882–83 at a cost of $3,000. John Risley Eldred, who designed and worked on the building's construction, was killed November 9, 1882, when a derrick gave way and fell on him. In 1913–14, a second story was added, and the school served the district until 1964 when the South Road School opened. (Courtesy Pettaquamscutt Historical Society.)

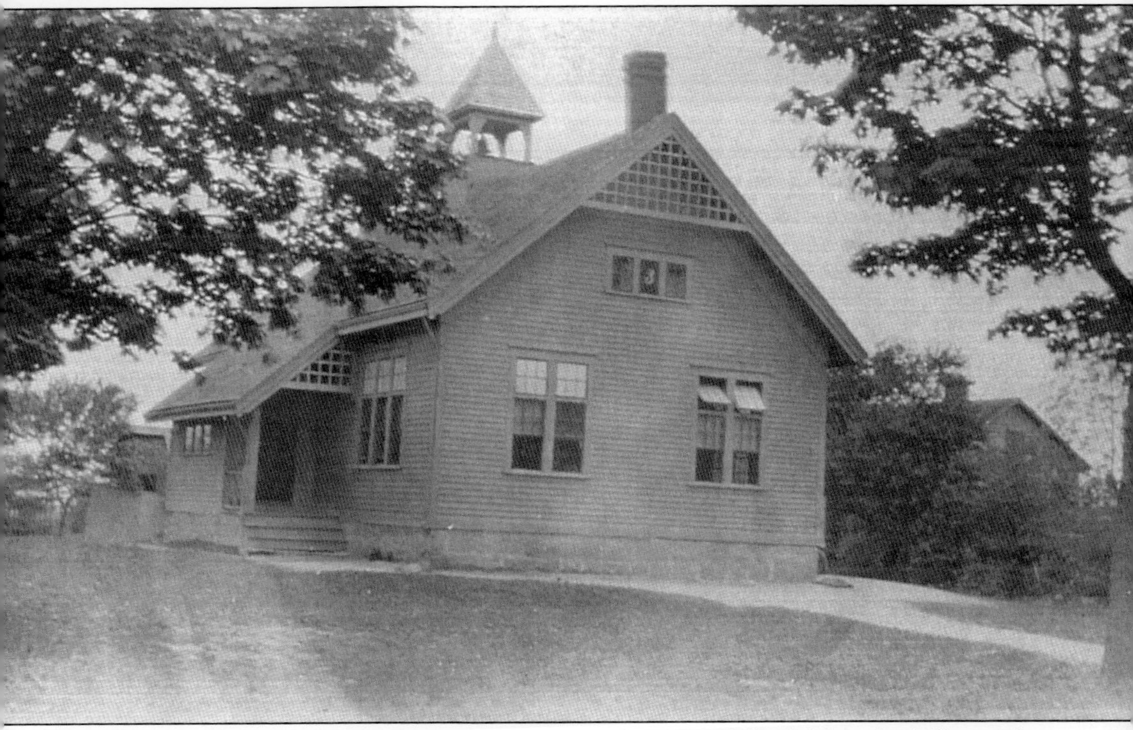

This photograph shows another view of the Kingston Grammar School. Note the bell atop the school and the top windows that opened out. The school is directly linked to an educational legacy in Kingston that, like the church's beginnings, can be traced to the Pettaquamscutt Purchase. Land set aside for educational purposes by the purchasers eventually was sold, and that money created the Sewall Fund, which funded the Kingston Academy and later the Kingston Seminary and the Kingston Female Seminary. The fund was eventually used to support the public schools and still exists. (Courtesy Pettaquamscutt Historical Society.)

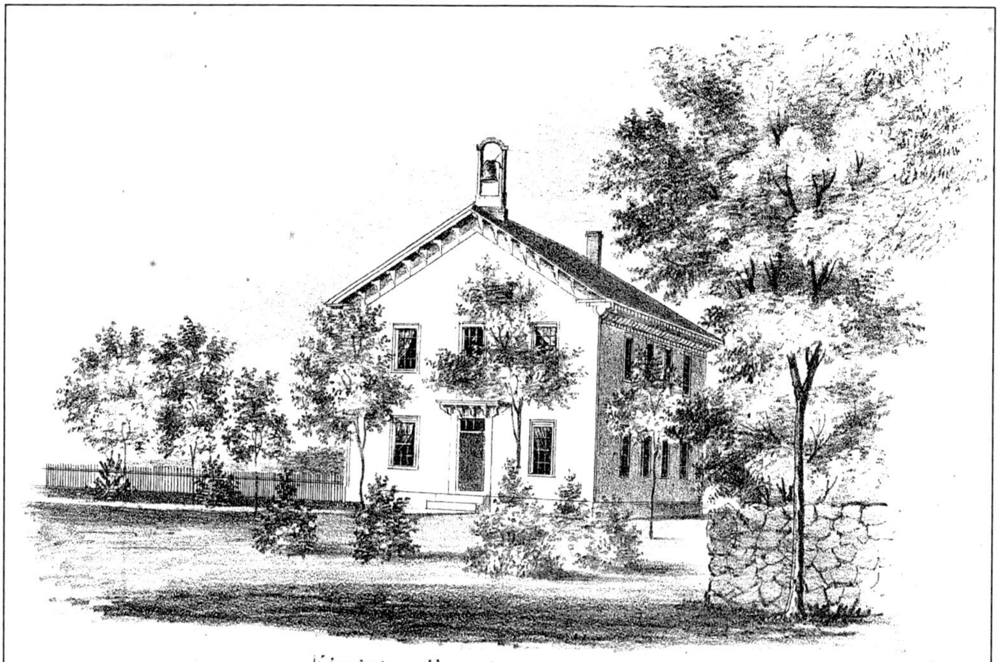

This sketch shows the Kingston Female Seminary on Old North Road, which operated from 1855 to 1863, and for two years prior to that as a coeducational institution. The building still stands at 81 Old North Road. (Courtesy Pettaquamscutt Historical Society.)

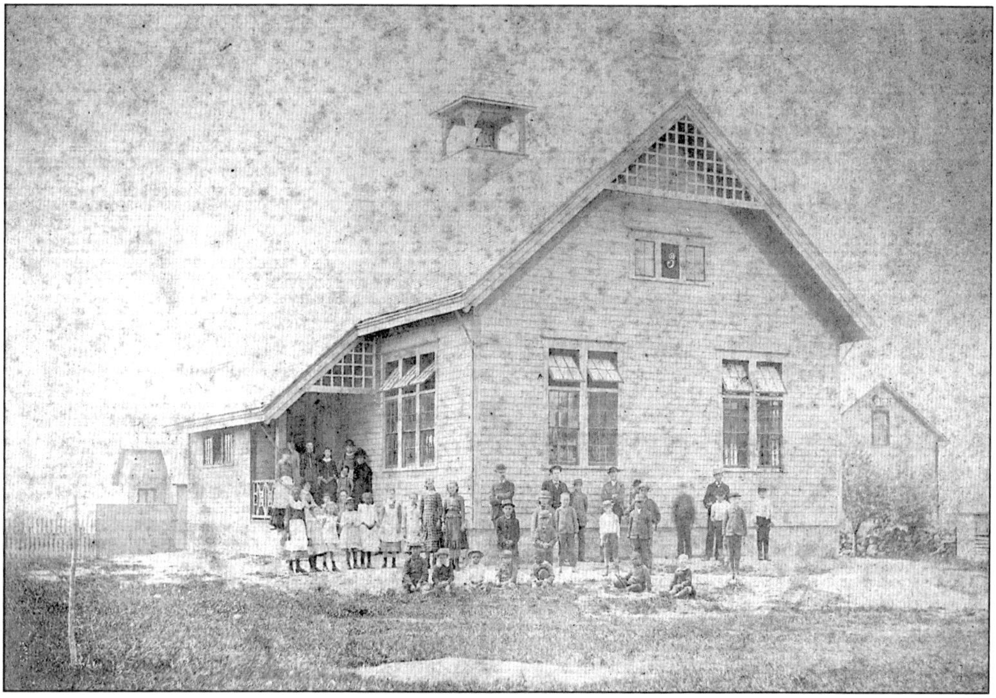

This photograph, *c.* 1884, shows students standing in front of the Kingston Grammar School. (Courtesy Pettaquamscutt Historical Society.)

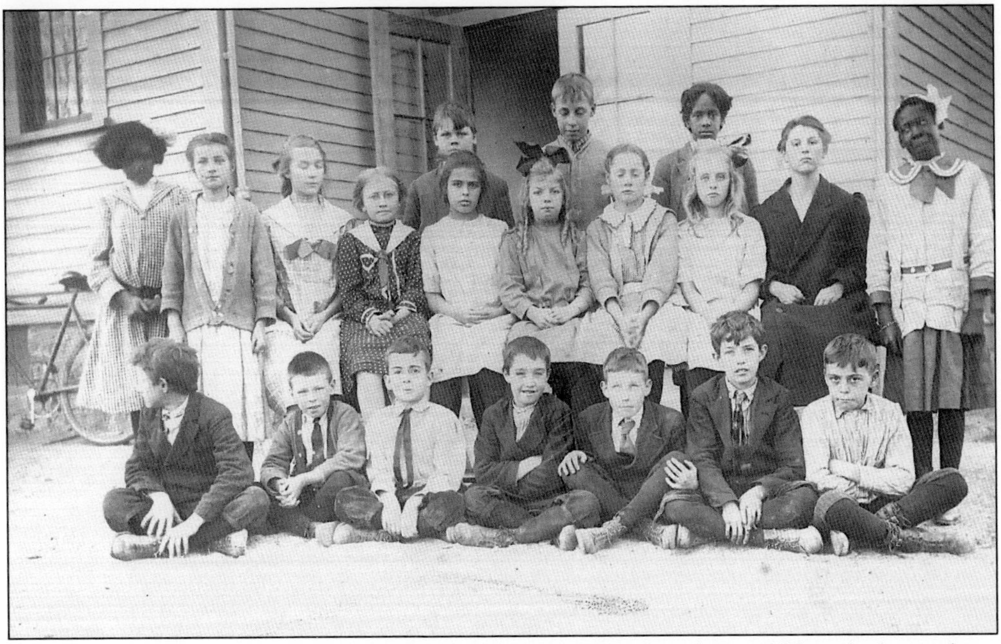

This photograph, c. 1916, shows Kingston Grammar School students. Although the students are not specifically identified, the annual report of the South Kingstown School Committee for 1916 listed as graduates Mary Bailey, Brewer Boardman, Watson Green, and Norman Griffith. Teachers at the four-room school, whose size had been doubled two years before, were O.R. Congdon, Rose Wilsher, Elsie M. Frazier, and Bertha M. Heath. Henry Thomas was the janitor. Those students unable to walk to school were brought by a wagon driven by Ruhamah Nichols. (Courtesy Pettaquamscutt Historical Society.)

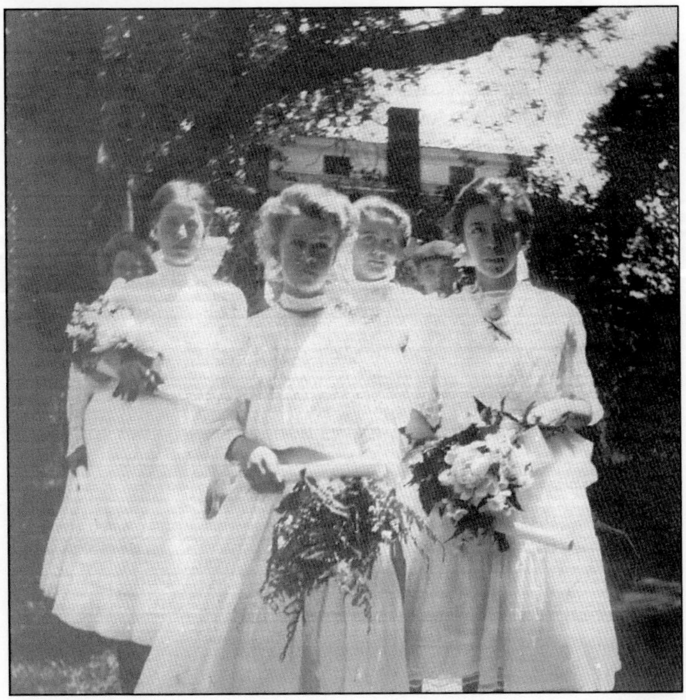

This photograph is said to show Ruhamah Robinson Nichols and Elizabeth Brown Nichols graduating from Kingston Grammar School in 1910. (Courtesy Pettaquamscutt Historical Society.)

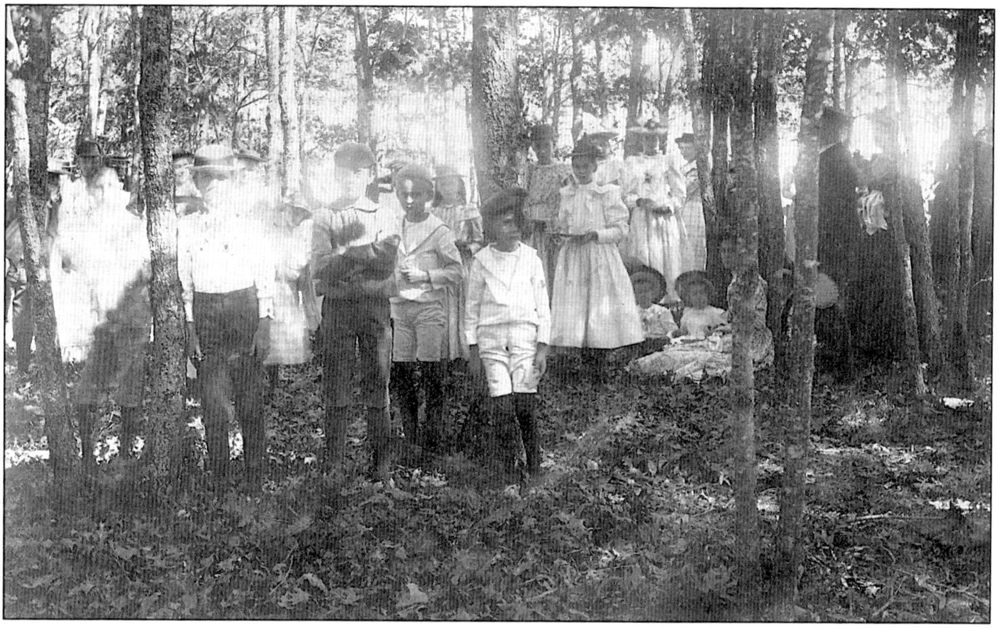

A Sunday school picnic at Laurel Lake Woods, probably near Larkin's Pond, included, from left to right (between the trees), Arthur N. Peckham, unidentified, Thomas P. Wells, John H. Wells, and (in white to John's right) Grace P. Wells. (Courtesy Pettaquamscutt Historical Society.)

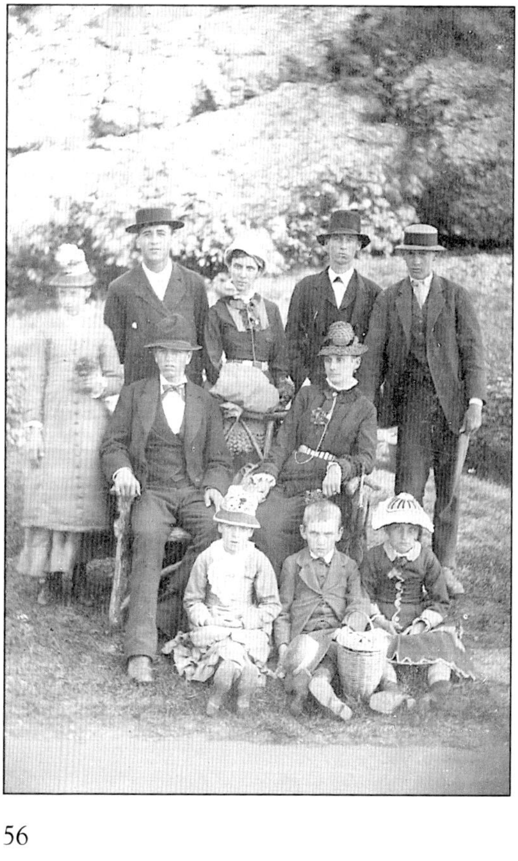

The Mooresfield Sunday School included, from left to right, the following: (front row) Cora Sanderson, Harvey Rodman, and Edith Sanderson; (middle row) Henry Slocum and Abby Rodman; (back row) Lizzie Slocum, Edmund Walker, Almira Rodman, Walter Congdon, and Stephen Lawton. (Courtesy Pettaquamscutt Historical Society.)

Five

Clubs and Organizations

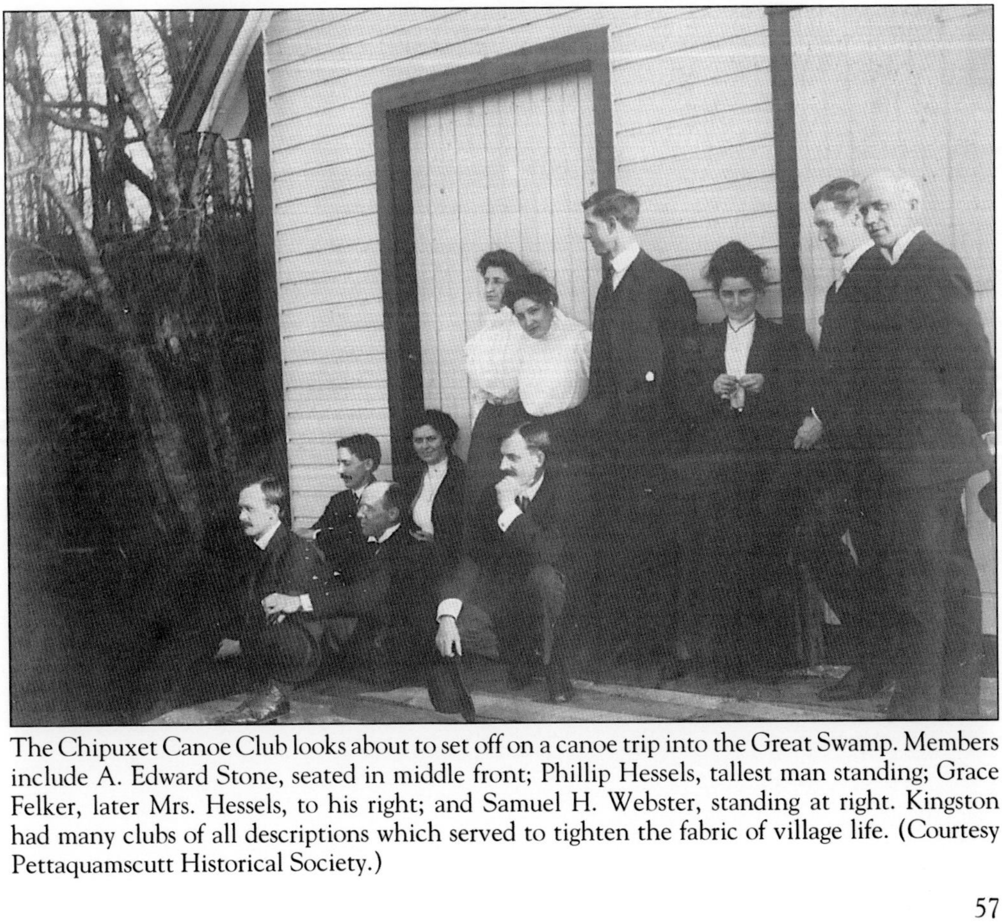

The Chipuxet Canoe Club looks about to set off on a canoe trip into the Great Swamp. Members include A. Edward Stone, seated in middle front; Phillip Hessels, tallest man standing; Grace Felker, later Mrs. Hessels, to his right; and Samuel H. Webster, standing at right. Kingston had many clubs of all descriptions which served to tighten the fabric of village life. (Courtesy Pettaquamscutt Historical Society.)

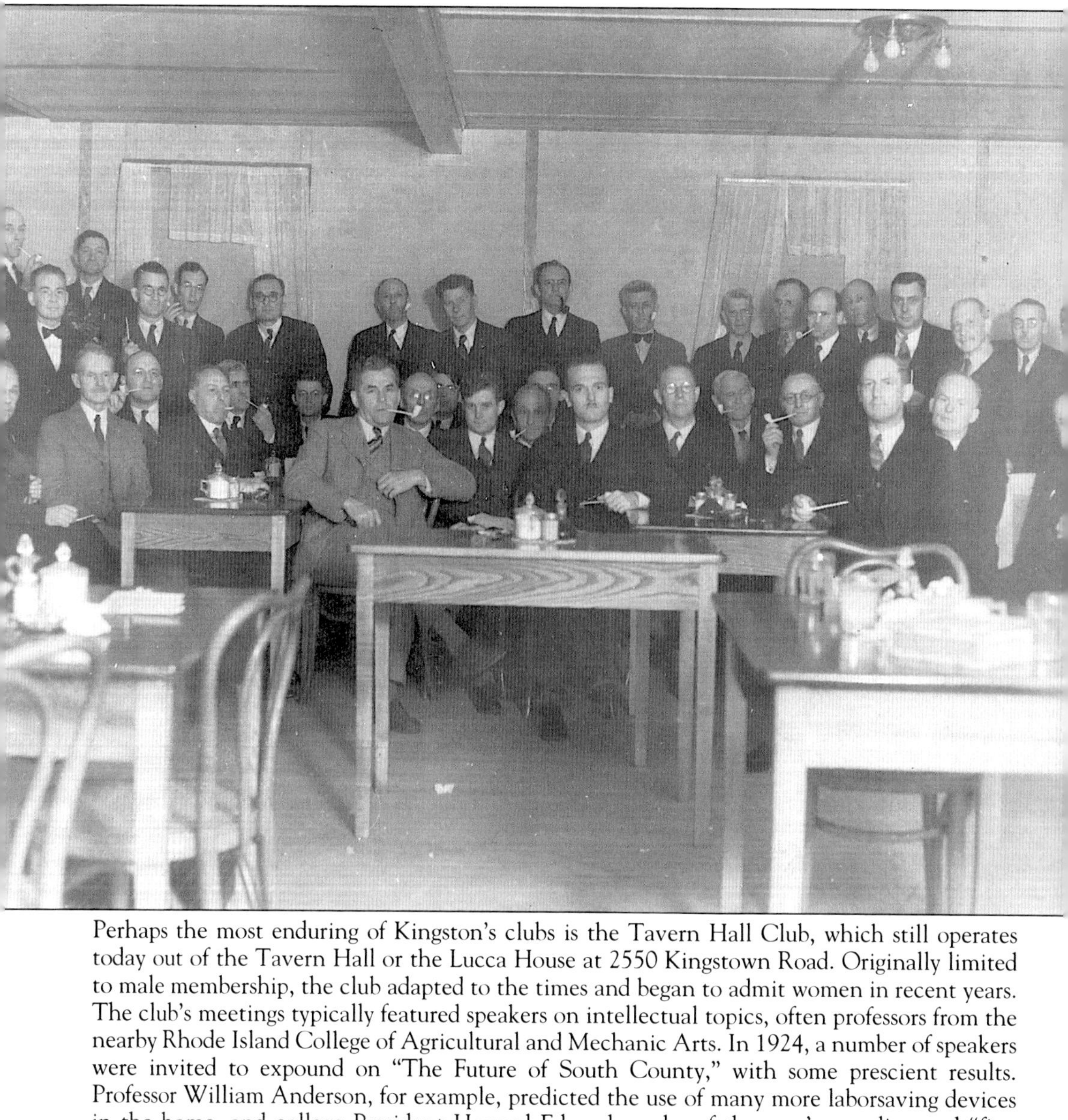

Perhaps the most enduring of Kingston's clubs is the Tavern Hall Club, which still operates today out of the Tavern Hall or the Lucca House at 2550 Kingstown Road. Originally limited to male membership, the club adapted to the times and began to admit women in recent years. The club's meetings typically featured speakers on intellectual topics, often professors from the nearby Rhode Island College of Agricultural and Mechanic Arts. In 1924, a number of speakers were invited to expound on "The Future of South County," with some prescient results. Professor William Anderson, for example, predicted the use of many more laborsaving devices in the home, and college President Howard Edwards spoke of the area's coastline and "fine plant growth" as keys to its future prosperity. Shown in this 1931 photograph of the Tavern Hall Club are, from left to right, the following: (front row) Harry McCready, Lorenzo F. Kinney, John E. Ladd, H. Louis Jackson, Howland Burdick, George B. Durham, R.G. Bressler, A.E. Steve, J.P. Delaplane, Arthur A. Vernon, John Barlow, unidentified, George Parks, Herman Churchill, Samuel C. Damon, E.K. Thomas, Frank H. Bills, Walton H. Scott, and Herbert J. Wells; (back row) John C. Weldin, William J. Champlin, Carroll D. Billings, Fred K. Crandall, Theodore E. Odland, Aden North, Basil E. Gilbert, Frank Roller, William Anderson, Andrew J. Newman, Joseph A. Monahan, Bernon E. Helme, John R. Eldred, Herbert C. Wells, James E. Heap, Albert W. Damon, Nathaniel Helme, Fred R. Pember, and unidentified. (Courtesy Pettaquamscutt Historical Society.)

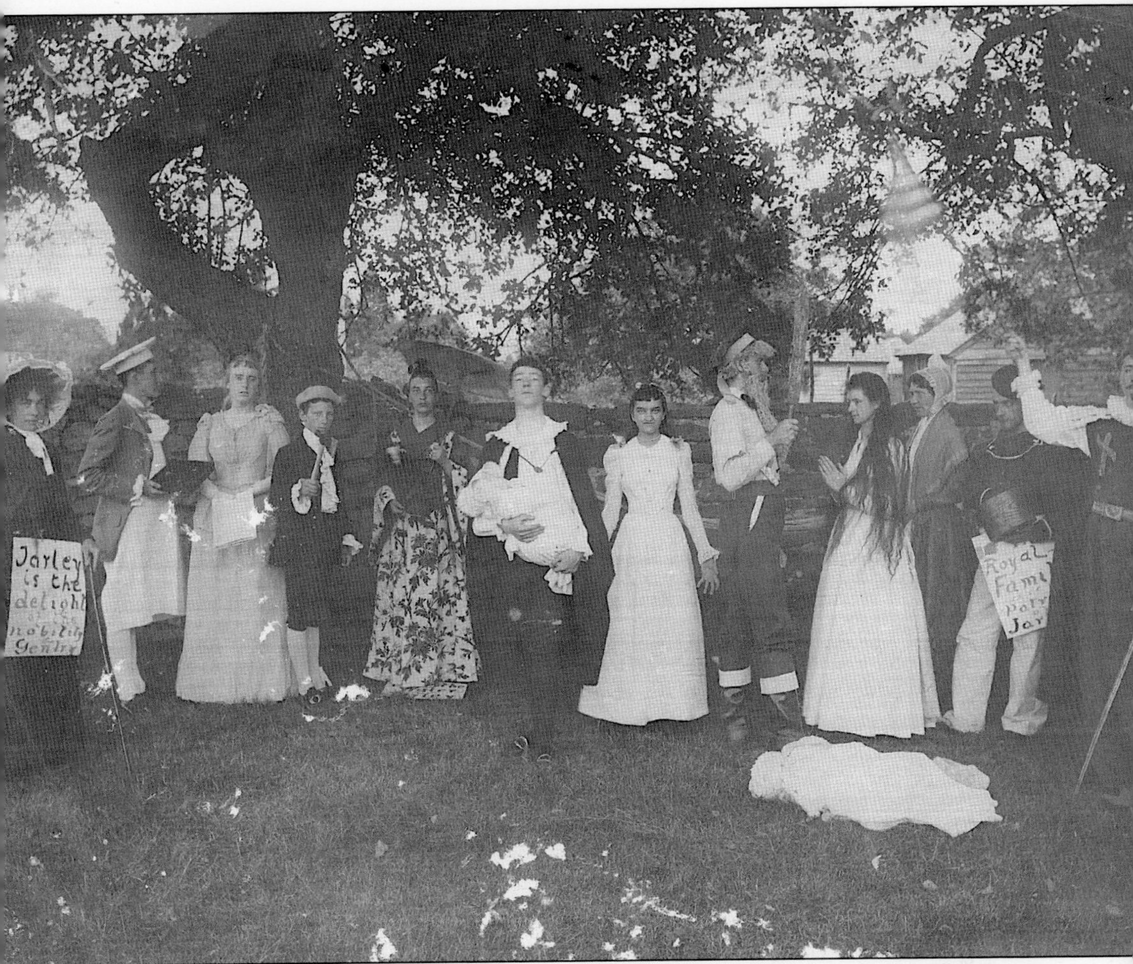

This dramatic presentation, believed to be from the 1890s, was entitled *Miss Jarley's Wax Works*. Kingston residents loved plays and musicales and were forever putting on one production or another on the lawn of the Kingston Free Library or at the home of Miss Robinson next door. There was a Little Rest Dramatic Club, and each August a production was put on to benefit the library. (Courtesy Pettaquamscutt Historical Society.)

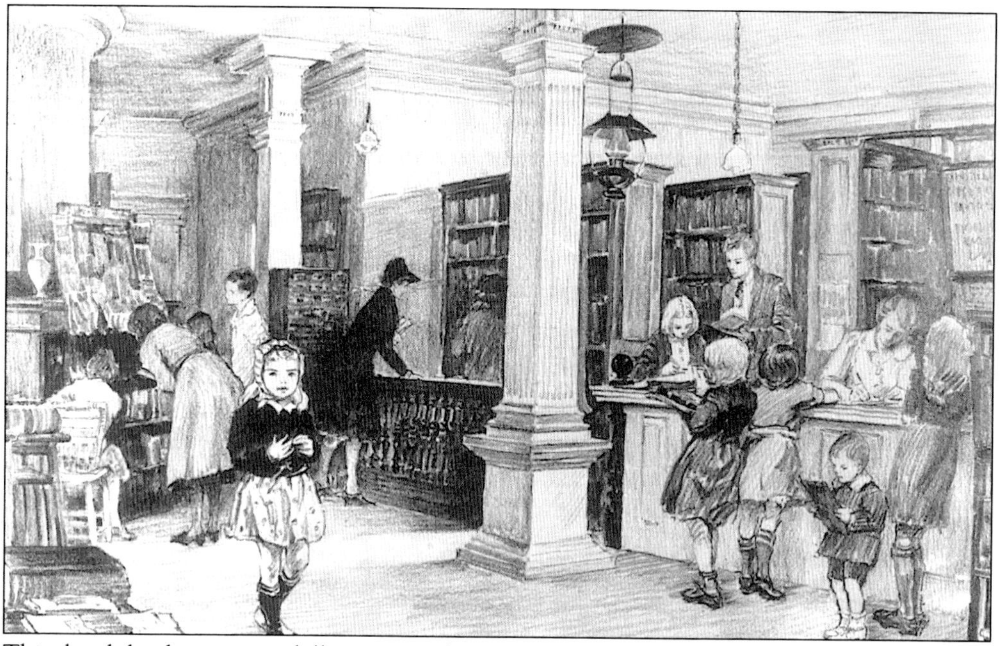

This sketch by the renowned illustrator Helen Mason Grose shows the interior of Kingston Free Library. The artist, who lived in the village from 1938 until her death in 1971, illustrated classic novels and studied art with N.C. Wyeth and Frank W. Benson. She left behind many charming pencil drawings of the village, which are now owned by the library. (Courtesy Diane Smith.)

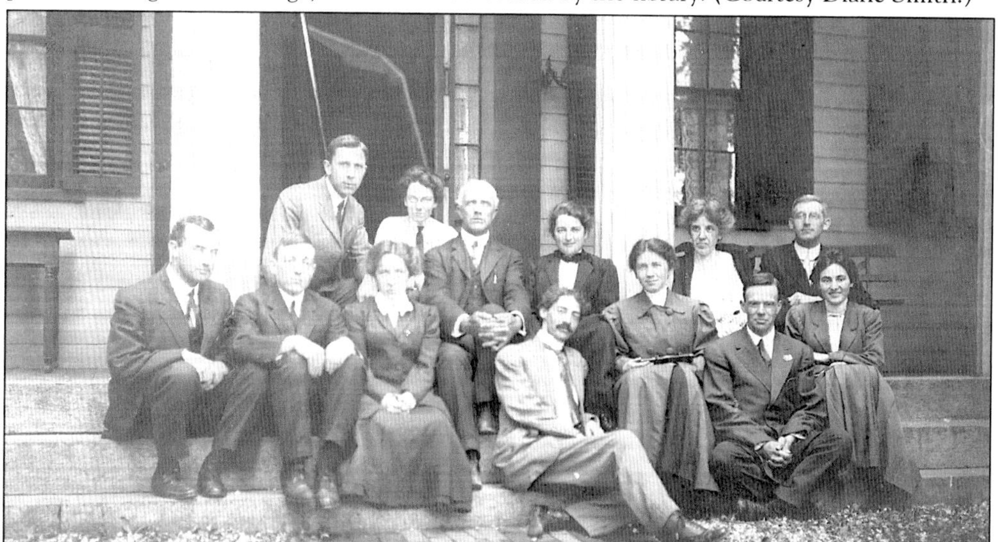

The Johnnycake Club, a musical group, was another of Kingston's organizations. Many of the same people belonged to the same societies, and it seems difficult to imagine how they kept up with the doings of the Ladies Aid Society, the Triangle Club, the Every Tuesday Club, the Little Rest Dramatic Club, not to mention church and library activities. This photograph, c. 1910, shows members who include, from left to right: (front row) L.P. Howard, trombone; Elizabeth Beale, alto; ? Lichtenthaler, organist and tenor; Edith Kennison, alto; and Carroll Magoun, bass; (back row) Grace Felker, alto. (Courtesy Pettaquamscutt Historical Society.)

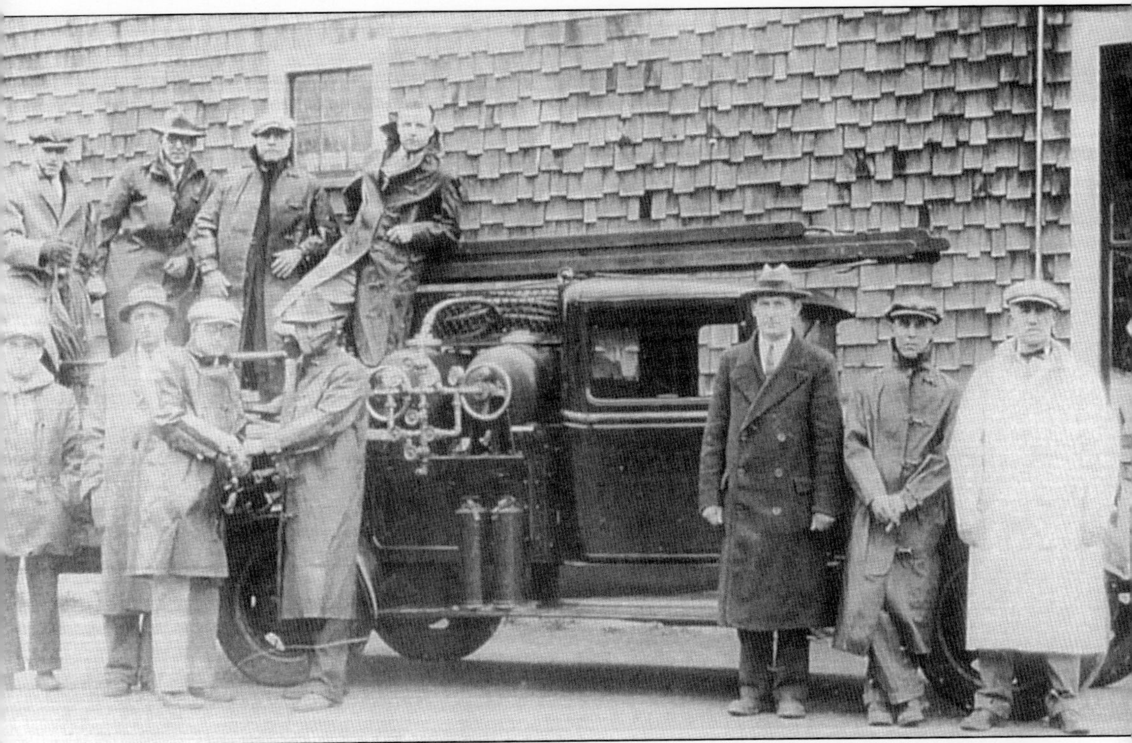

Members of the Kingston Fire District are shown with a chemical hose wagon in 1923. The department served an important function not only in protecting the village but the nearby college as well. (Courtesy Kingston Fire District.)

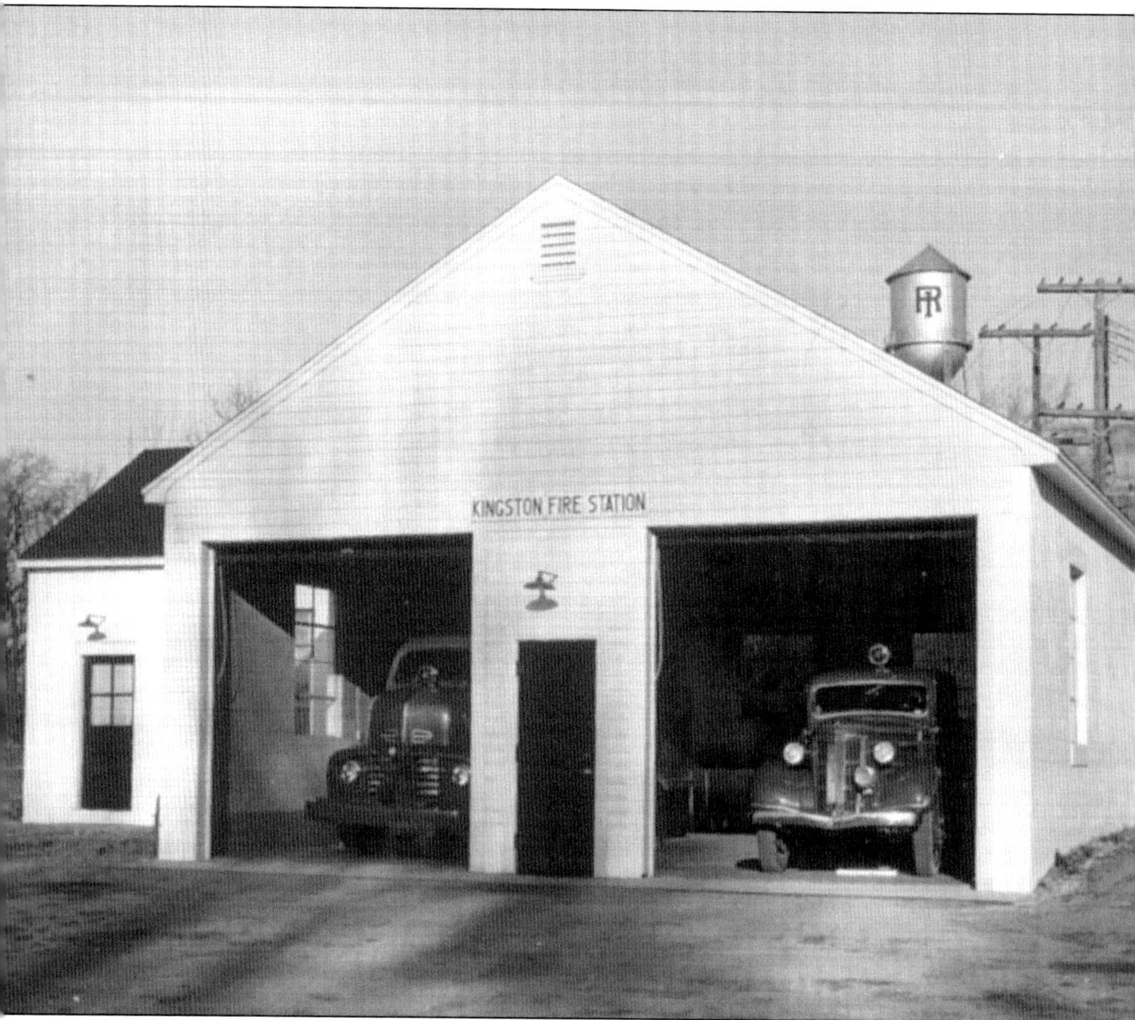

The Kingston Fire Station is shown here on Bills Road, near the University of Rhode Island campus. The college's water tower is visible in the background. (Courtesy Kingston Fire District.)

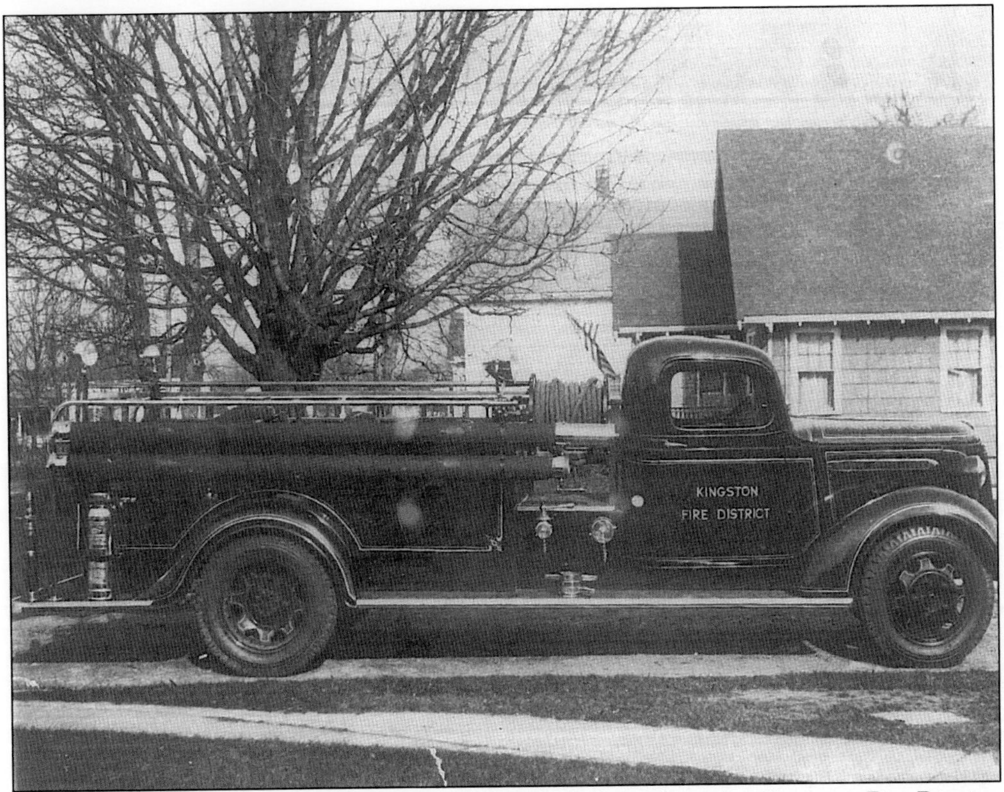

This photograph shows a 1937 pumper truck that belonged to the Kingston Fire District. (Courtesy Kingston Fire District.)

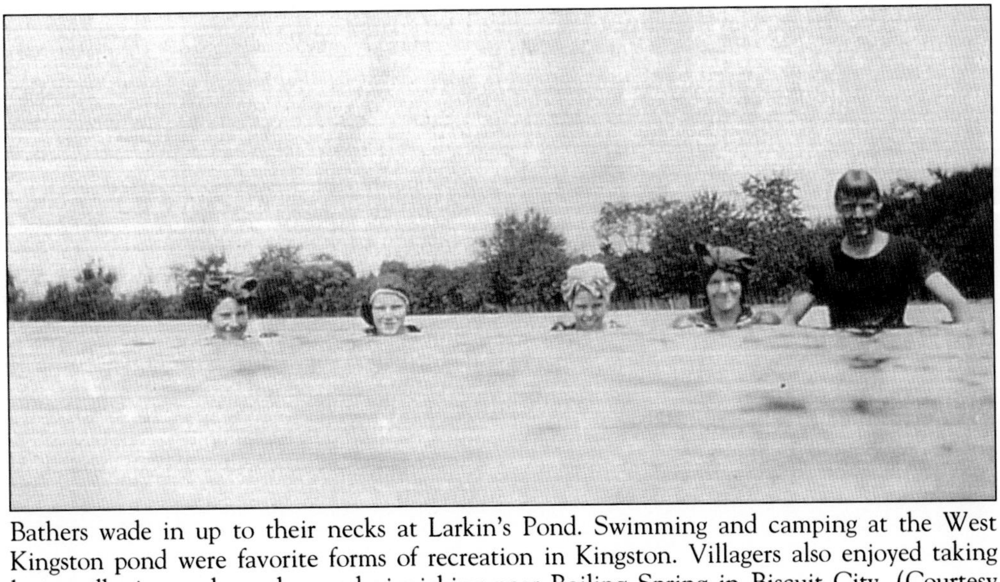

Bathers wade in up to their necks at Larkin's Pond. Swimming and camping at the West Kingston pond were favorite forms of recreation in Kingston. Villagers also enjoyed taking long walks in good weather and picnicking near Boiling Spring in Biscuit City. (Courtesy Betty Faella.)

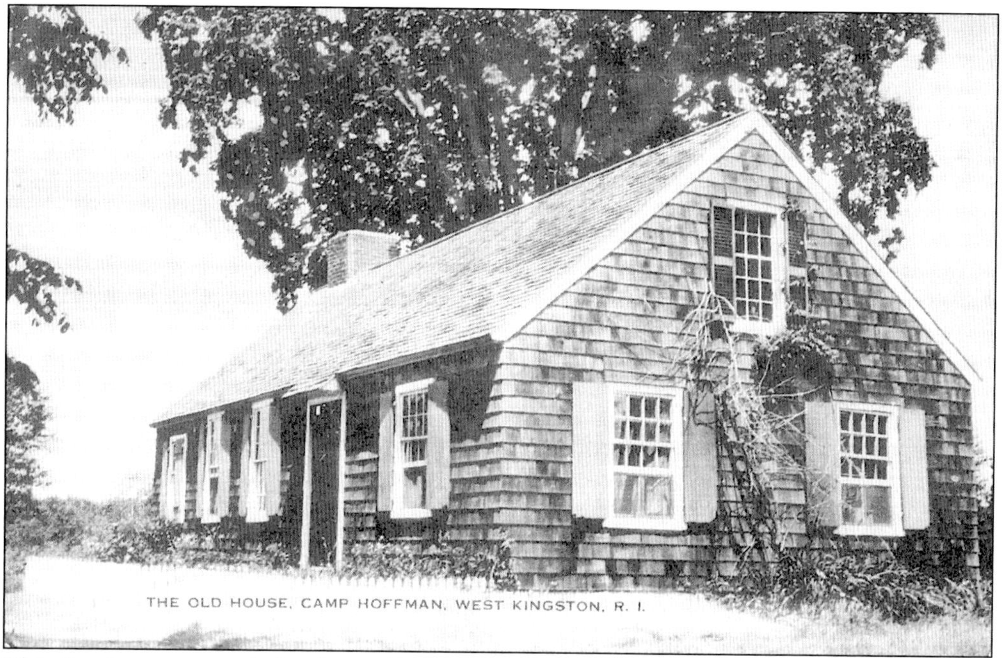

This farmhouse, part of the Sweet Briggs Farm, was established as the Girl Scouts' Camp Hoffman in 1921. The house was remodeled in 1930 and used for winter weekend camp-outs. (Courtesy of Betty Faella.)

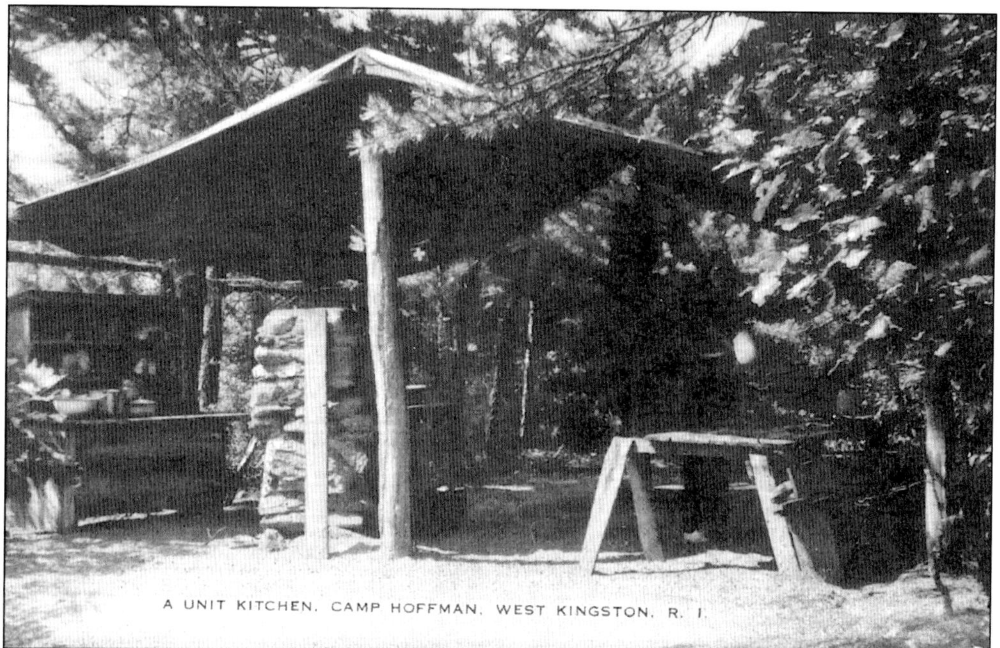

This photograph shows a unit kitchen at Camp Hoffman, which has introduced generations of Rhode Island Girl Scouts to the wonders of nature and the rewards of self-reliance. The camp is located on the shores of Larkin's Pond in West Kingston. (Courtesy of Diane Smith.)

Six

Famous Families

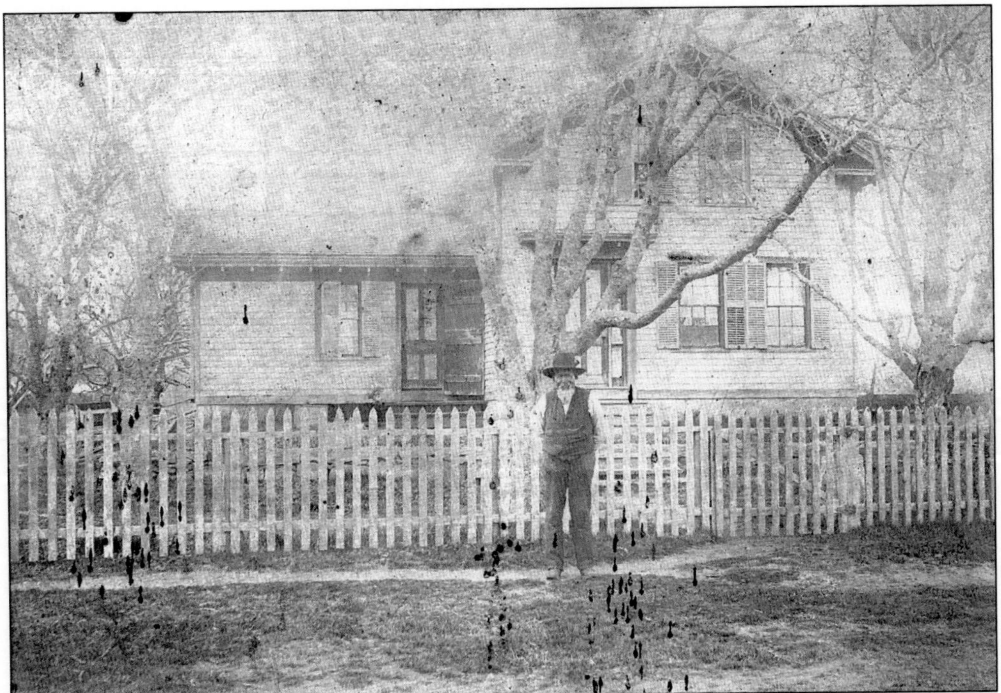

This is James Washington Fayerweather. Descendants of freed slaves, the Fayerweathers, who took their name from the Reverend Samuel Fayerweather, pastor of St. Paul's Episcopal Church in Wickford, became respected members of the Kingston community. George Fayerweather III married Sarah Harris, who had attended Prudence Crandall's school in Canterbury, Connecticut, and with his brother Solomon served the village's blacksmith needs. (Courtesy Pettaquamscutt Historical Society.)

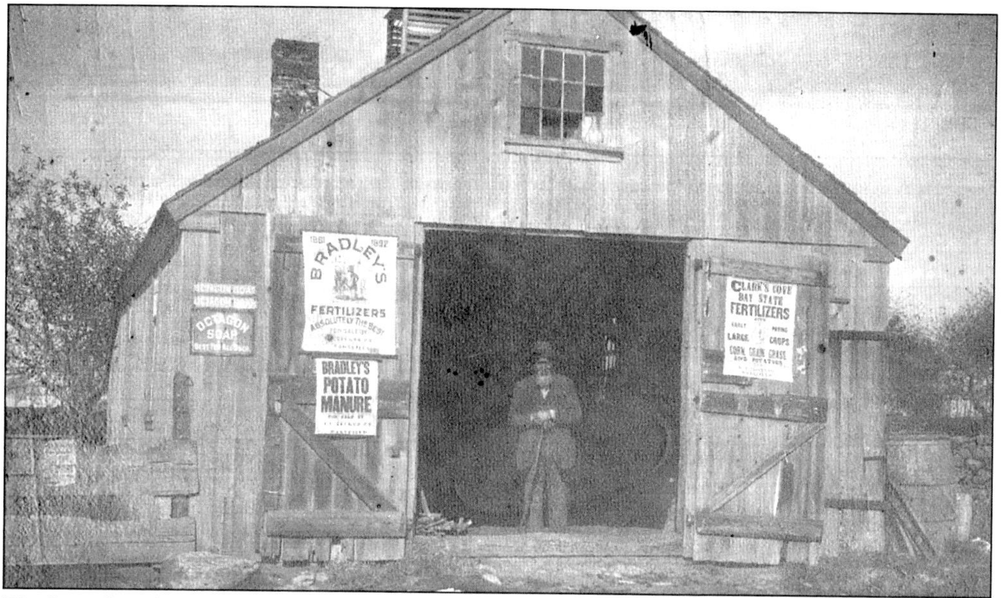

Blacksmith Solomon Fayerweather stands in front of his shop, *c.* 1900. The grandson of a slave, Solomon was the seventh son of George Fayerweather. In his reminiscences, the Reverend J. Hagadorn Wells remembers the shop for its "scenes of useful toil, accompanied by good-natured jollity." Phillip Kittredge Taylor, writing in 1903, described the shop as a "rare museum of metal odds and ends" that was a "rich mine for searchers after antique andirons, fire shovels, tongs, and all the impediments of an old-fashioned fireplace." (Courtesy Pettaquamscutt Historical Society.)

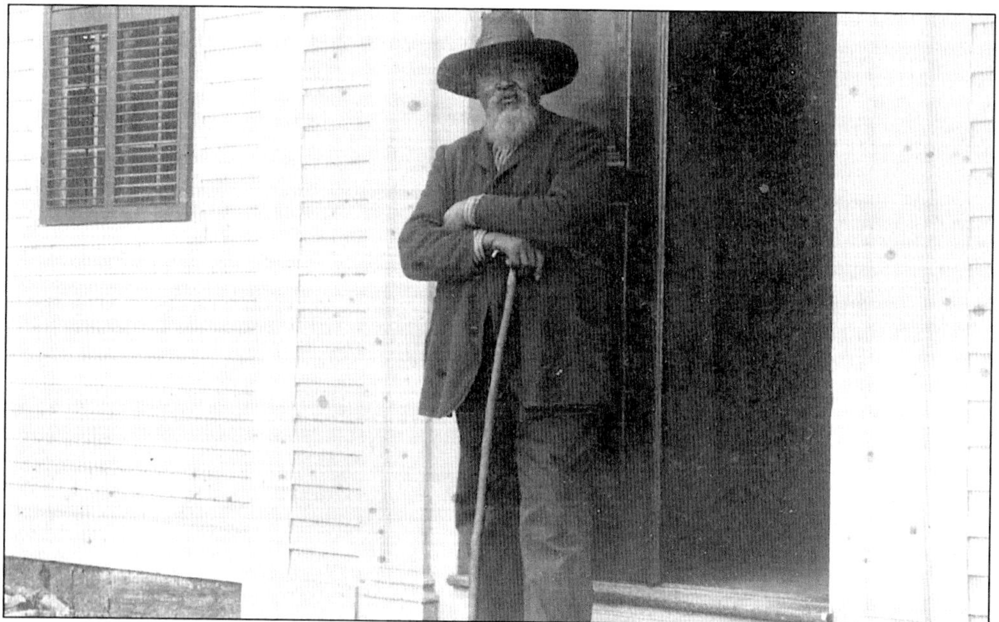

Solomon Fayerweather served as the sexton of the Kingston Congregational Church. "Since his day no one has so skillfully rung the sweet-toned bell that hangs in the village spire to warn the people to dress for meeting, to gather at the service, or to 'toll the preacher into church,' " recalled Philip Kittredge Taylor. (Courtesy Pettaquamscutt Historical Society.)

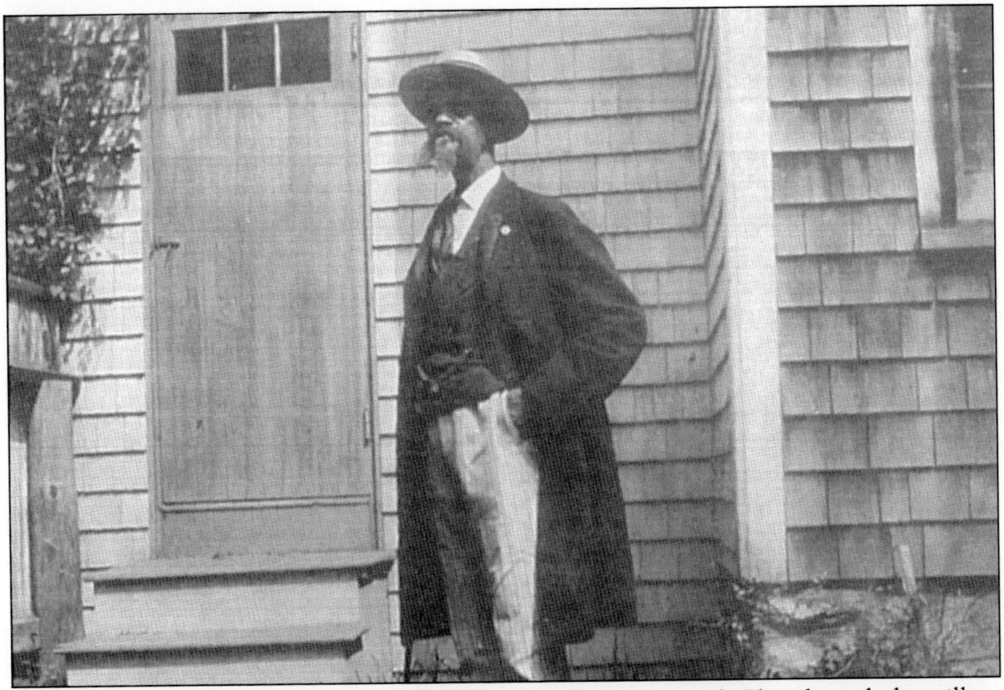

Henry Thomas was the janitor at the Kingston Congregational Church and the village lamplighter and handyman. (Courtesy Betty Faella.)

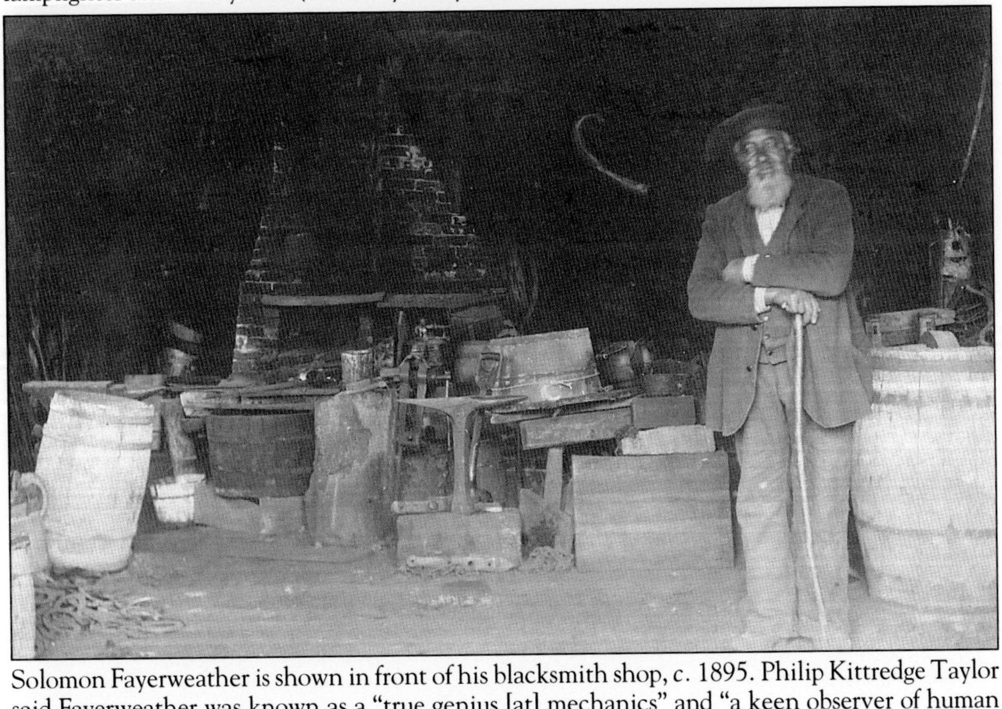

Solomon Fayerweather is shown in front of his blacksmith shop, c. 1895. Philip Kittredge Taylor said Fayerweather was known as a "true genius [at] mechanics" and "a keen observer of human nature." One can imagine Taylor visiting Fayerweather's shop as much for conversation as for a piece of metalwork. Today, the Fayerweathers' house on Route 138 is home to the Fayerweather Craft Guild. (Courtesy Pettaquamscutt Historical Society.)

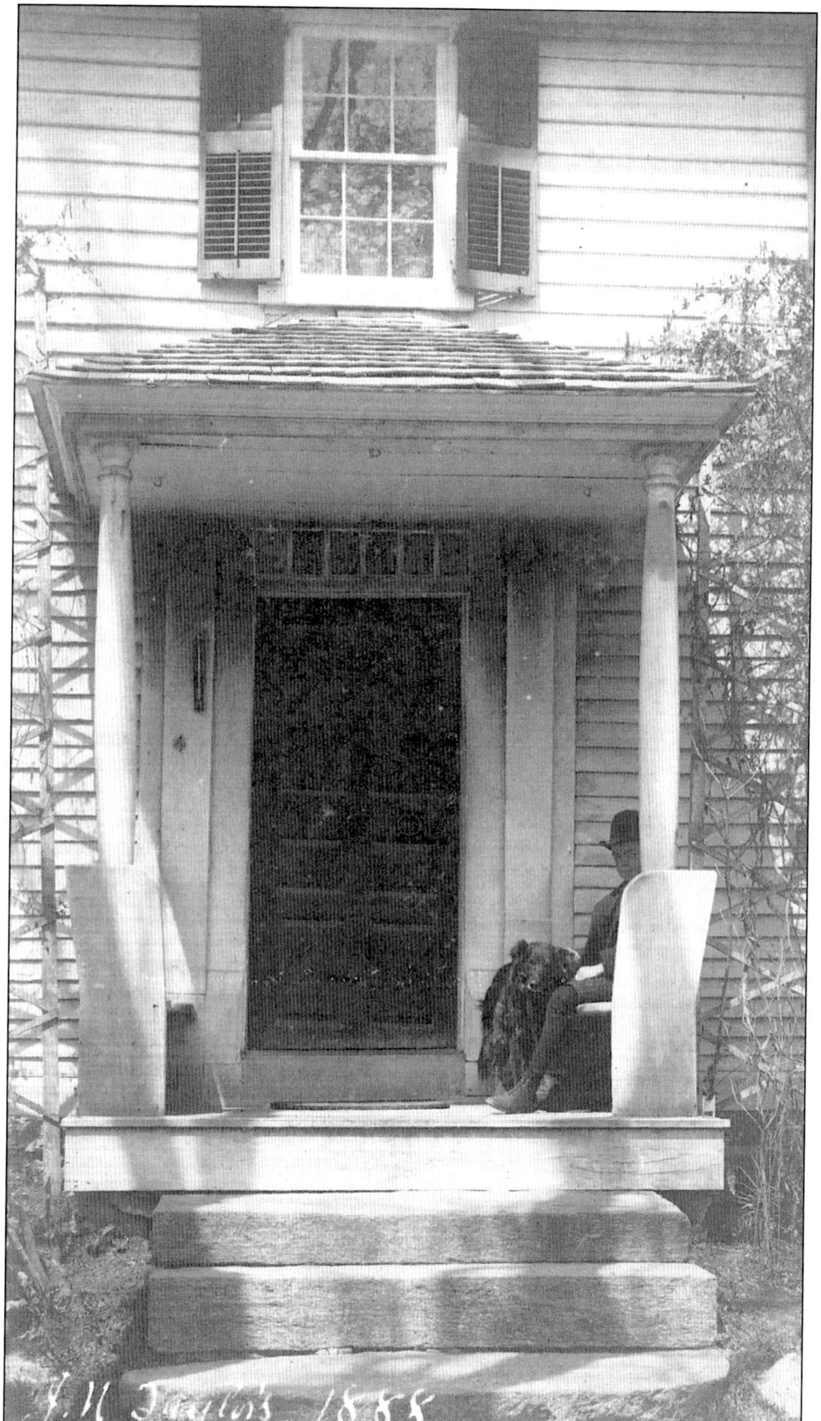

This photograph shows an unidentified boy at J.H. Taylor's Tavern in 1888. The tavern was a place for the men of the village to gather for conversation and was immortalized in Shepherd Tom Hazard's "Jonny-Cake Papers." (Courtesy Pettaquamscutt Historical Society.)

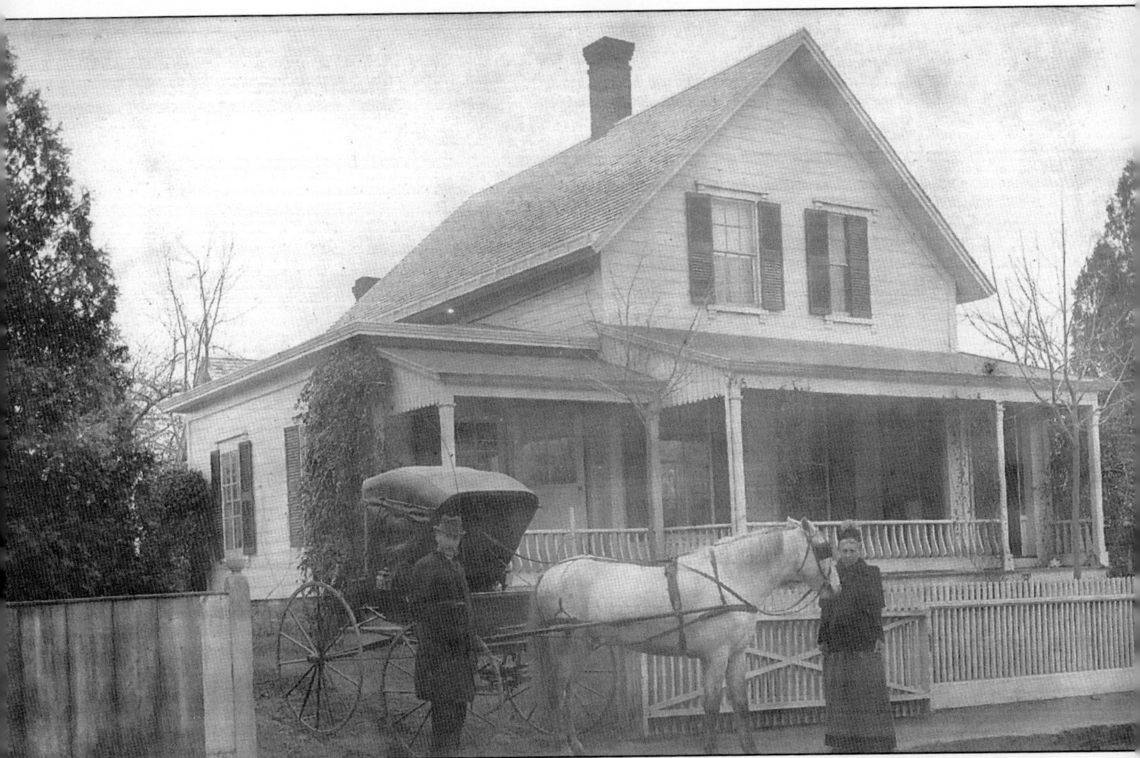

Dr. Hartwell's house on Upper College Road (also pictured on page 42) probably belonged to Burt L. Hartwell, the director of the Experiment Station at the Rhode Island College of Agricultural and Mechanic Arts. Hartwell became entangled in a power struggle with college President Howard Edwards and left the college in 1928. The man next to the buggy shows a strong resemblance to Hartwell. (Courtesy Pettaquamscutt Historical Society.)

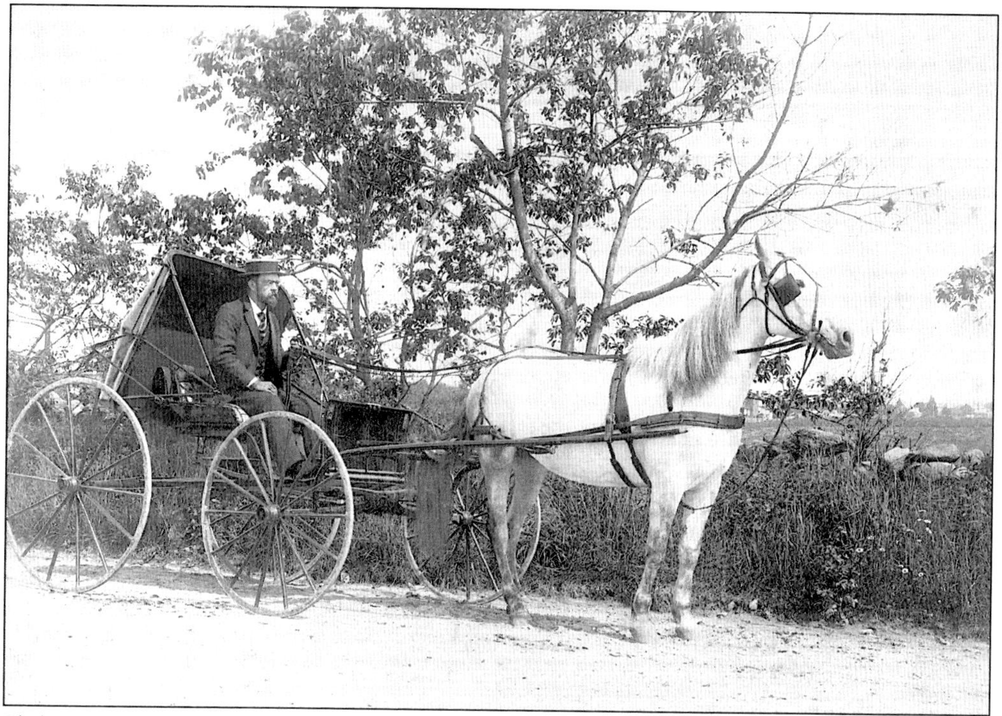

Philip Kittredge Taylor is shown with his horse and buggy in 1889. Taylor wrote a piece for the *New England Magazine* in 1903 that captured valuable aspects of the village's history. He apparently left Kingston in 1910, for the Kingston Free Library and Reading Room replaced him as a library trustee that year "on account of his removal from the village" and praised him as "one of its most loyal members," the *Narragansett Times* reported. A physician, Taylor apparently had left the village many times before to work on steamers. The *Narragansett Times* reported his departure for New York in 1898 to catch a steamer bound for Rio de Janeiro, "on his usual trip, as steamer physician." (Courtesy Pettaquamscutt Historical Society.)

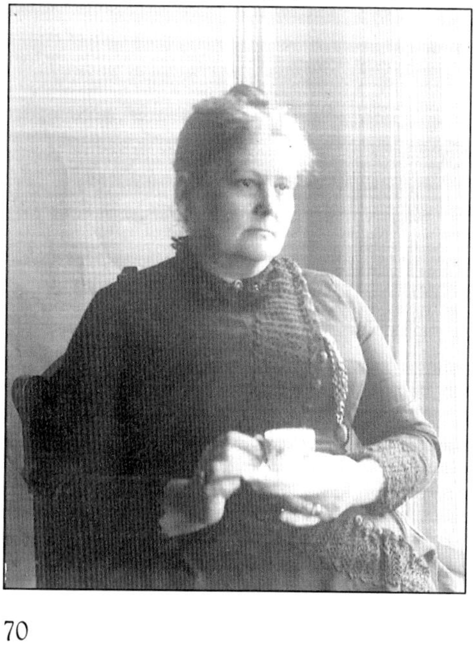

"A good picture—a cause for Thanksgiving" wrote Kate Taylor about this 1898 portrait of herself. (Courtesy Pettaquamscutt Historical Society.)

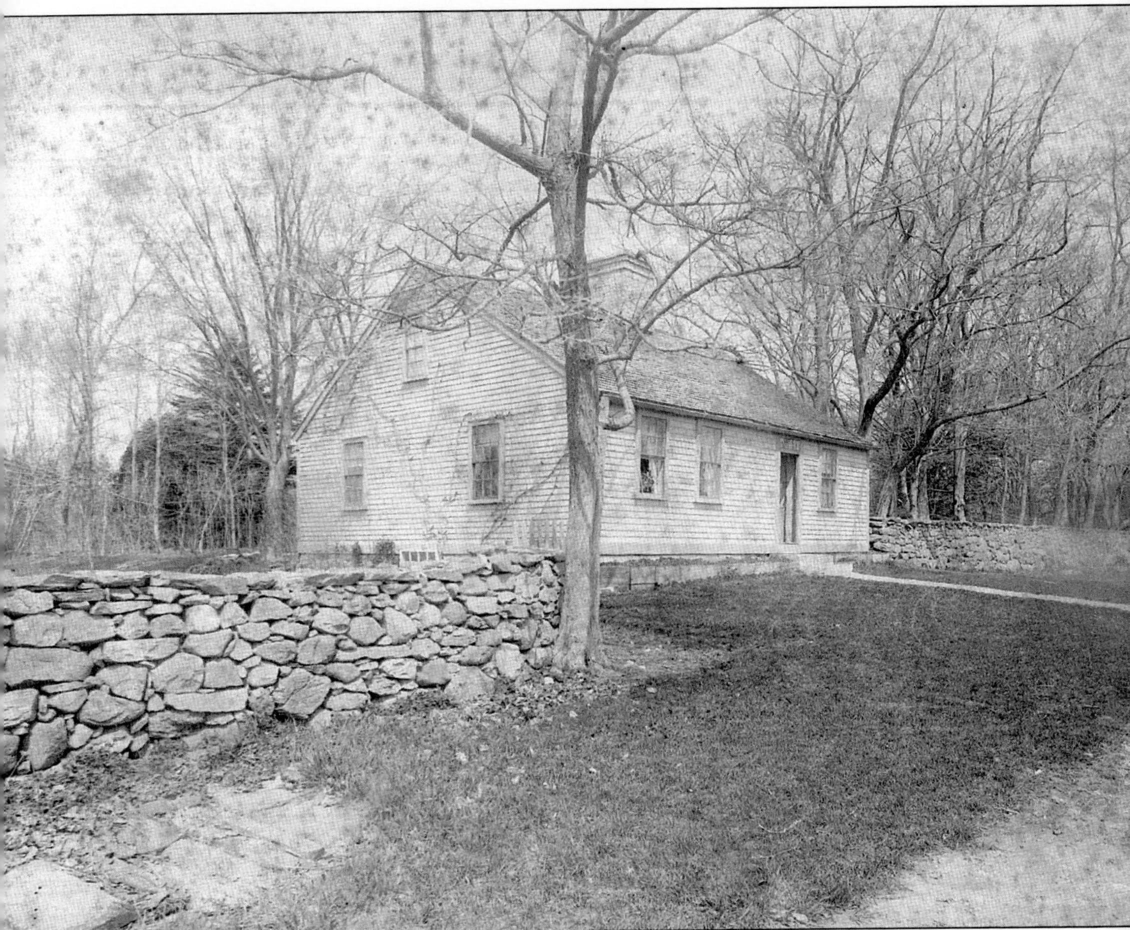

This house on South Road, which is still standing, was the home of baker Stephen Greene, whose delicious gingerbread gained a fame that long outlived him. In his "Jonny-Cake Papers," Shepherd Tom Hazard expounded on the gingerbread's virtues. "Don't I remember it!" he exclaimed. "Baked in fluted cards some eight inches square. Ninepence for a whole card and four-pence-half-penny for half a card! Oh, how unlike the vile stuff now sold at bakers' and restaurants," he wrote in 1915. (Courtesy Pettaquamscutt Historical Society.)

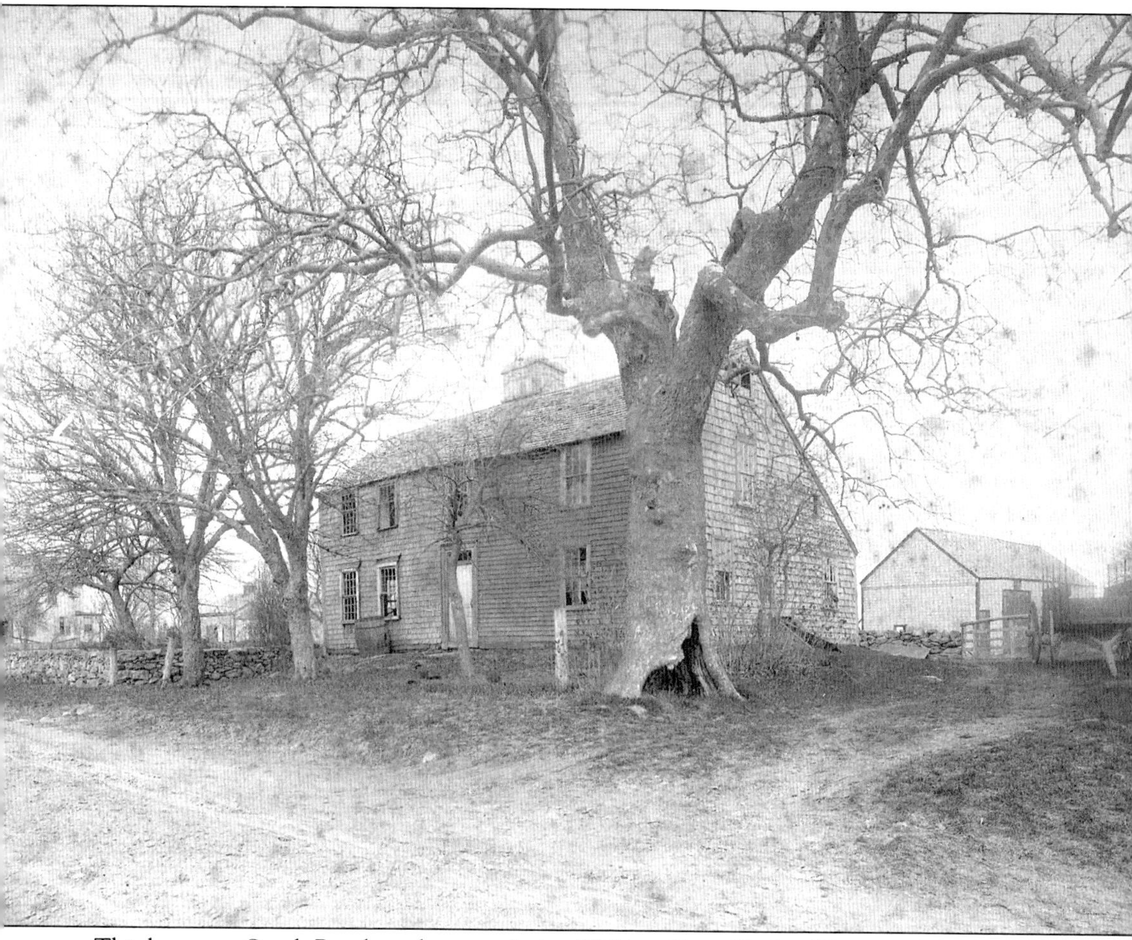

This house on South Road was home to Judge William Case Clarke. (Courtesy Pettaquamscutt Historical Society.)

This William Case Clarke (1841–1902) was son of Col. George C. Clarke. A major in the Pettaquamscutt Infantry, he served in the Civil War and returned home to become president of the Sea View Railroad Company. (Courtesy Pettaquamscutt Historical Society.)

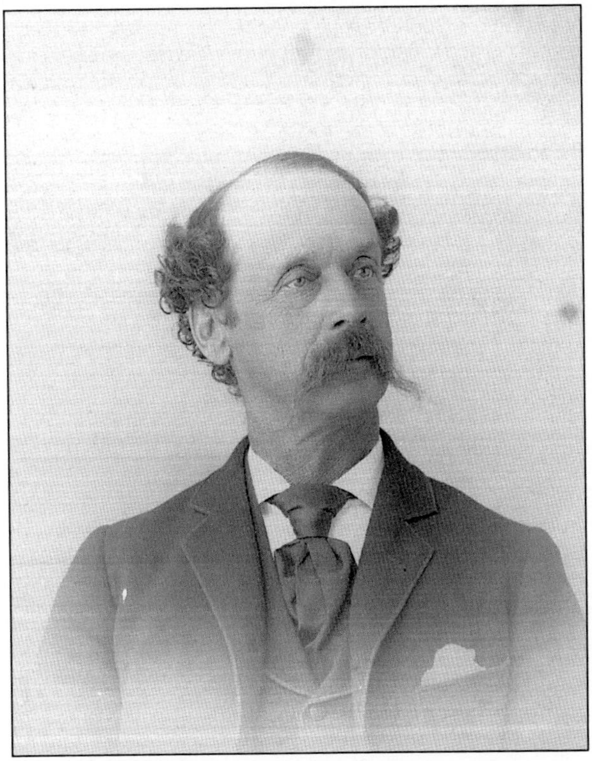

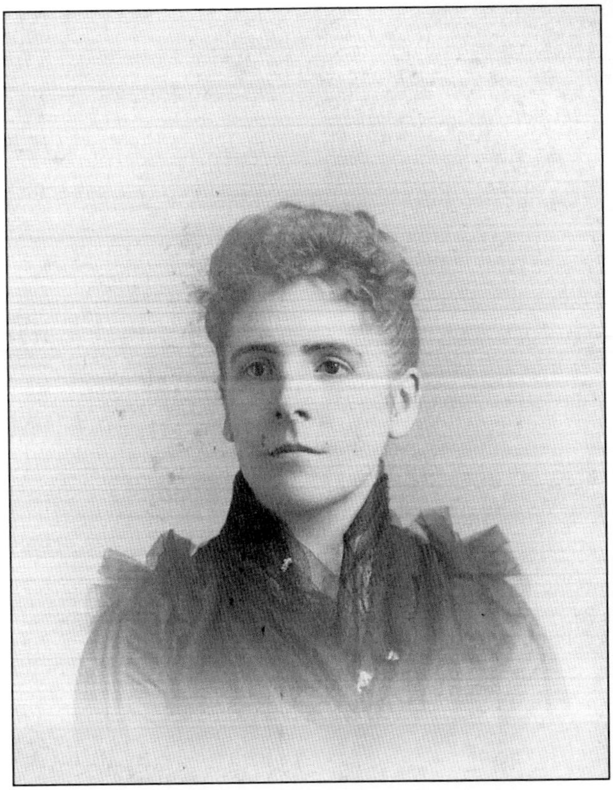

Mary Reynolds Clark was daughter of Rowse Clark, M.D. (Courtesy Pettaquamscutt Historical Society.)

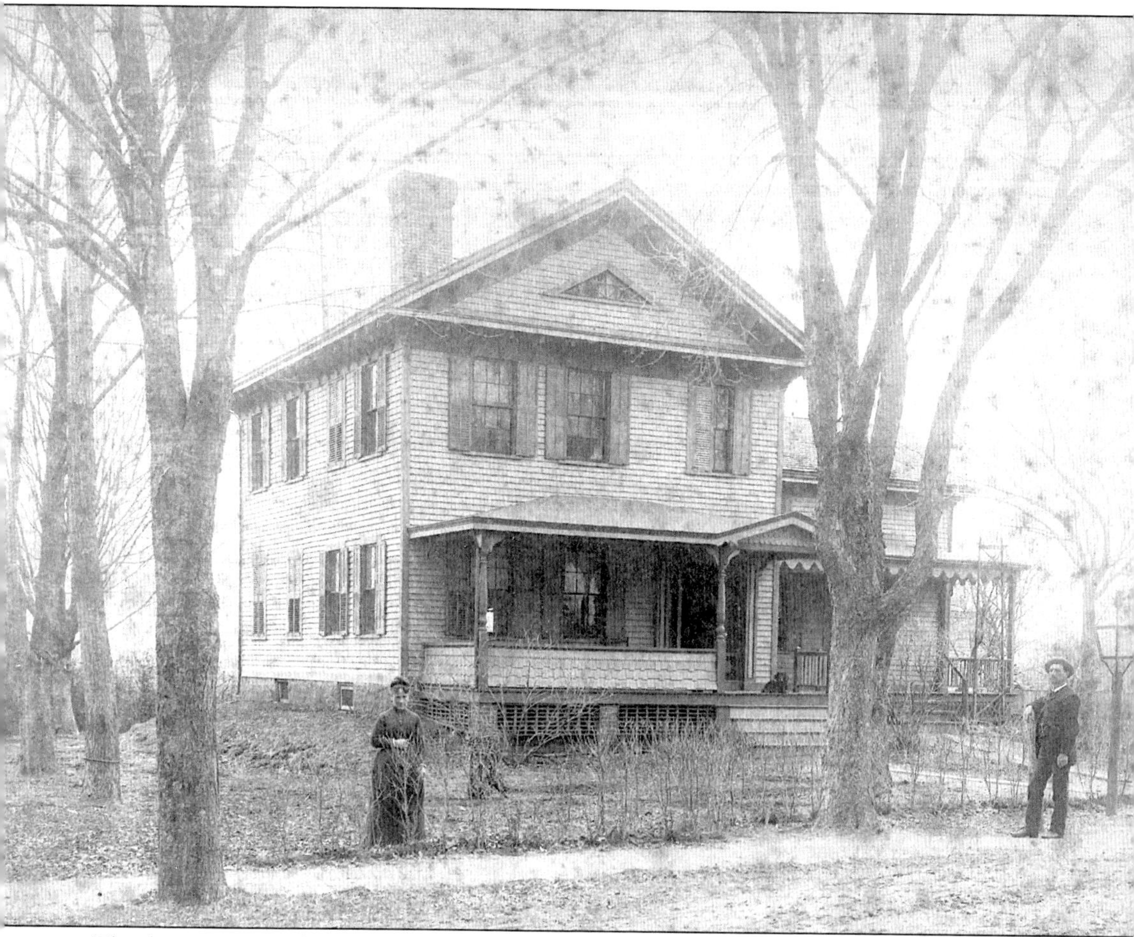

This house on South Road was built by George C. Clarke. Shown standing at right is Elisha C. Clarke, with a woman who is believed to be either his wife or his sister-in-law. (Courtesy Pettaquamscutt Historical Society.)

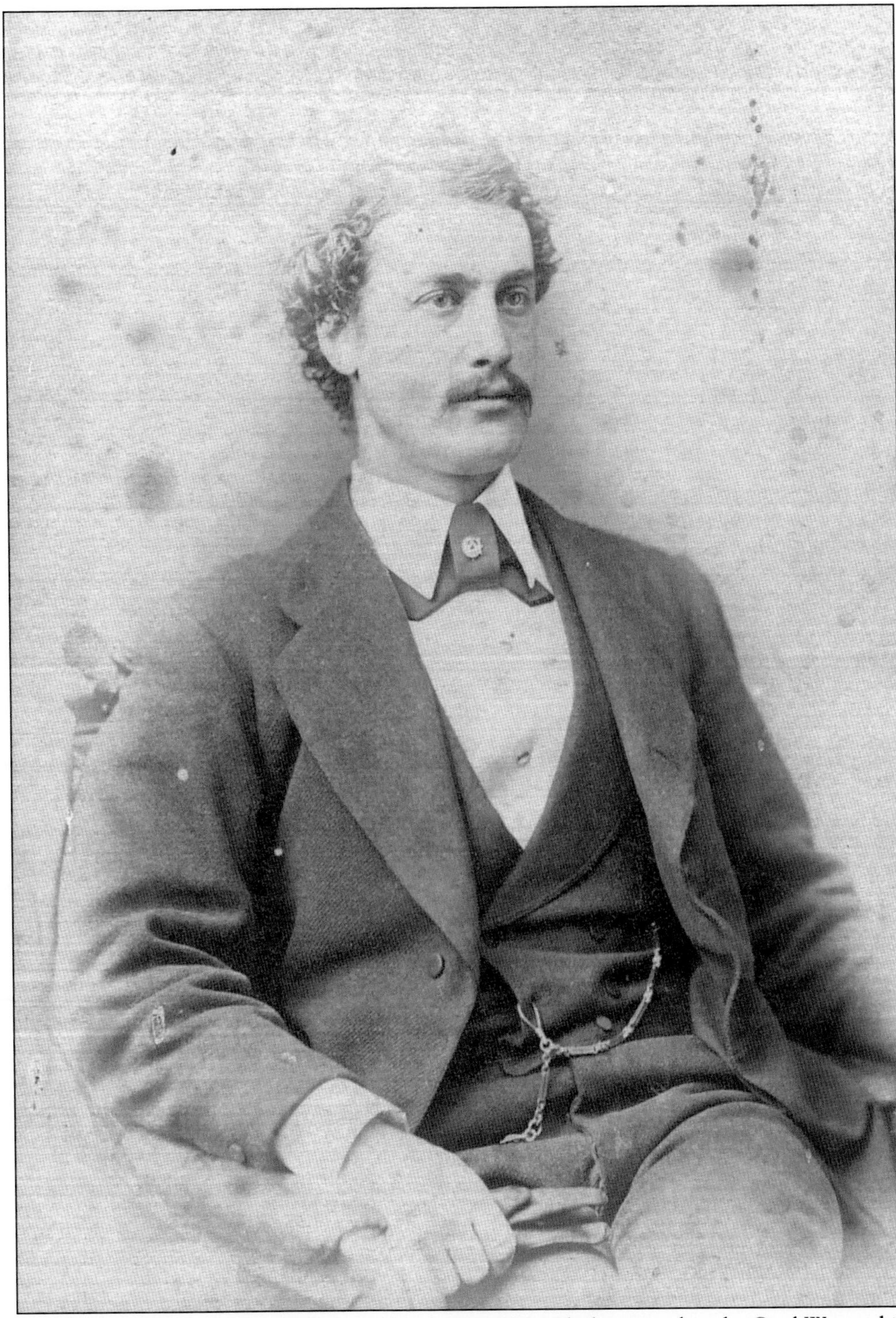

Joseph Case Clarke (1845–1877), son of Col. George C. Clarke, served in the Civil War and is buried in Riverside Cemetery in Wakefield. This photograph was taken by the famed Civil War photographer Mathew B. Brady. (Courtesy Pettaquamscutt Historical Society.)

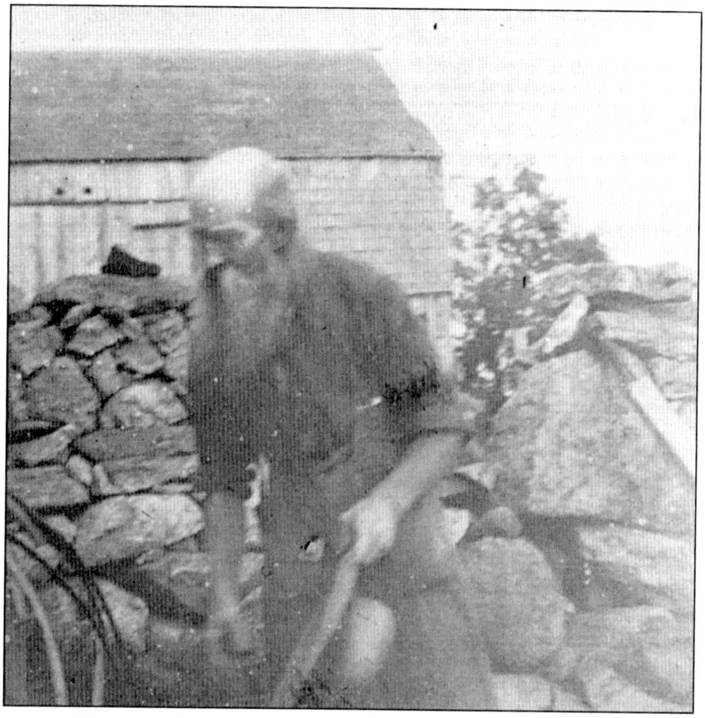

William Henry Harrison Rose (1839–1913), known variously as "Quaker Billy Rose" or "Weaver Rose," is captured in a rare photograph in 1910. Rose was famed for his handweaving, a Colonial art he continued long after textile mills had begun to replace the itinerant weaver. He learned to weave from his grandfather Robert Northup; his grandmother Mary Northup taught weaving in Kingston. (Courtesy Pettaquamscutt Historical Society.)

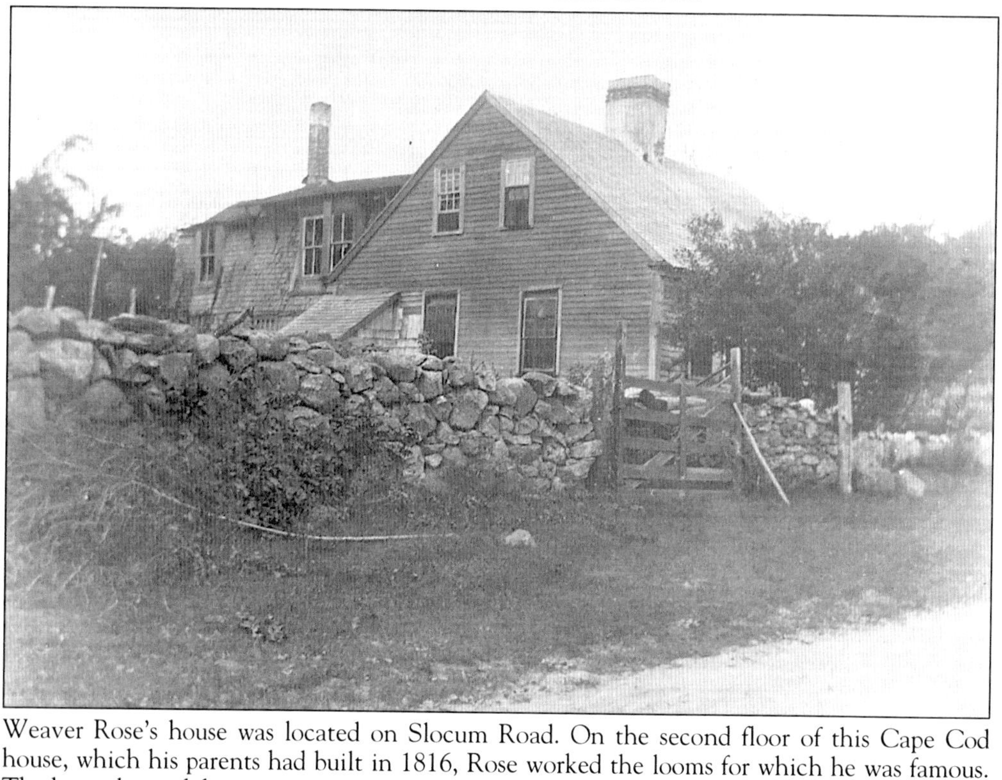

Weaver Rose's house was located on Slocum Road. On the second floor of this Cape Cod house, which his parents had built in 1816, Rose worked the looms for which he was famous. The house burned down in 1926. Rose is believed to be buried in an unmarked grave across the street. (Courtesy Pettaquamscutt Historical Society.)

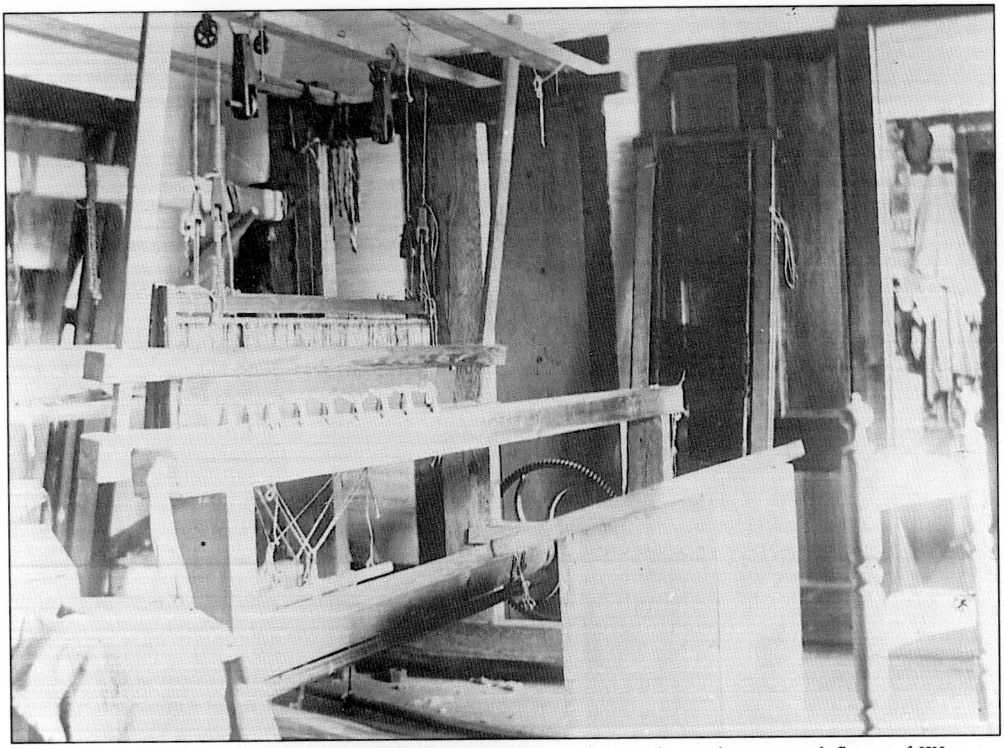

This is believed to be a Swedish-style loom that was located on the second floor of Weaver Rose's house. (Courtesy Pettaquamscutt Historical Society.)

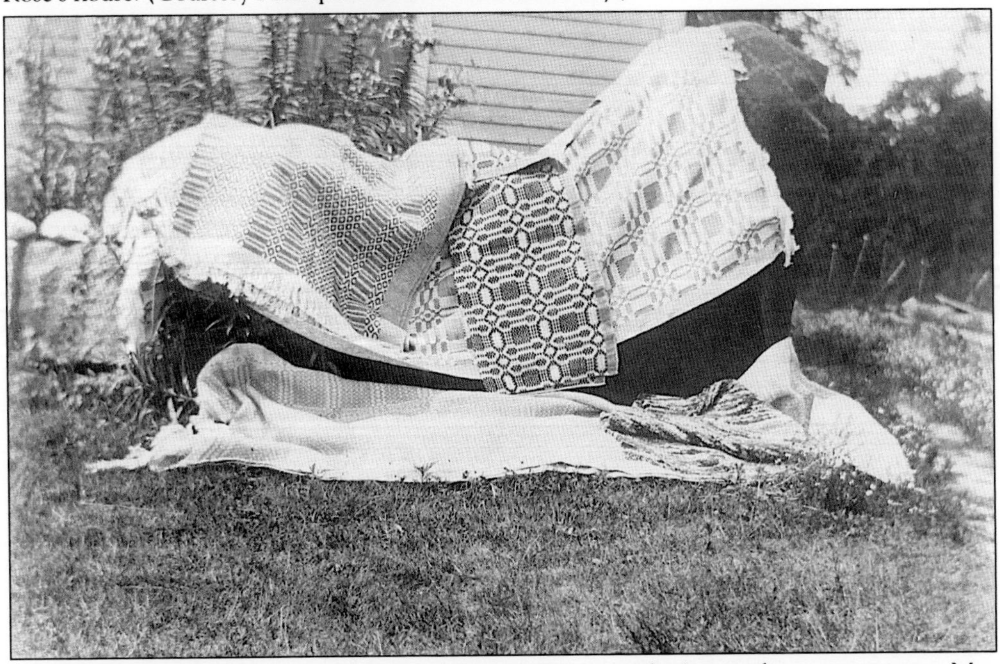

This photograph shows some examples of Weaver Rose's work. Among his customers was Mrs. Theodore Roosevelt, who is believed to have ordered carpets from him. An autographed picture of the president hung in the Rose home. (Courtesy Pettaquamscutt Historical Society.)

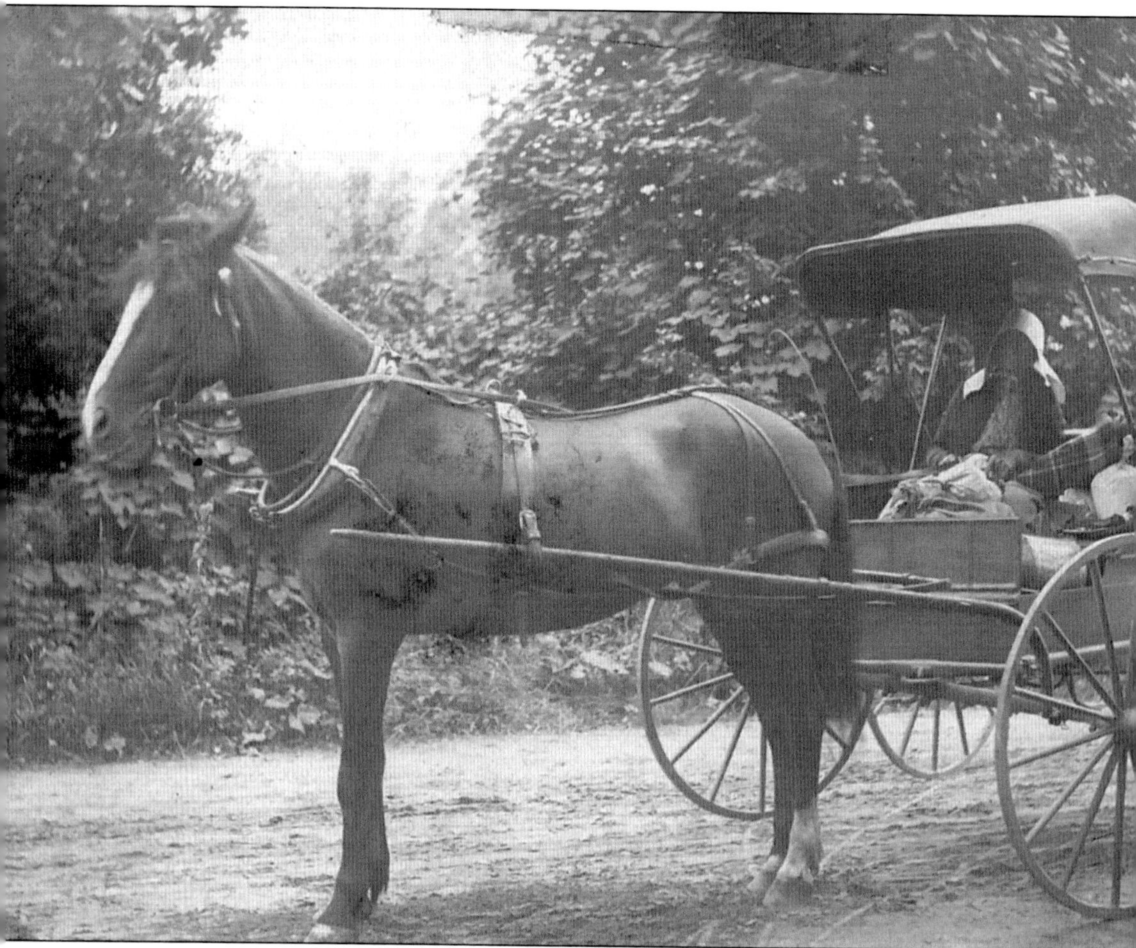

Elsie Rose, sister of Weaver Billy Rose, is shown in her buggy, c. 1900. Although her brother gained fame for his weaving, Elsie probably wove some of the work that he sold as his own. The two shared the family home on Slocum Road, where she kept rose gardens and took care of the animals. (Courtesy Pettaquamscutt Historical Society.)

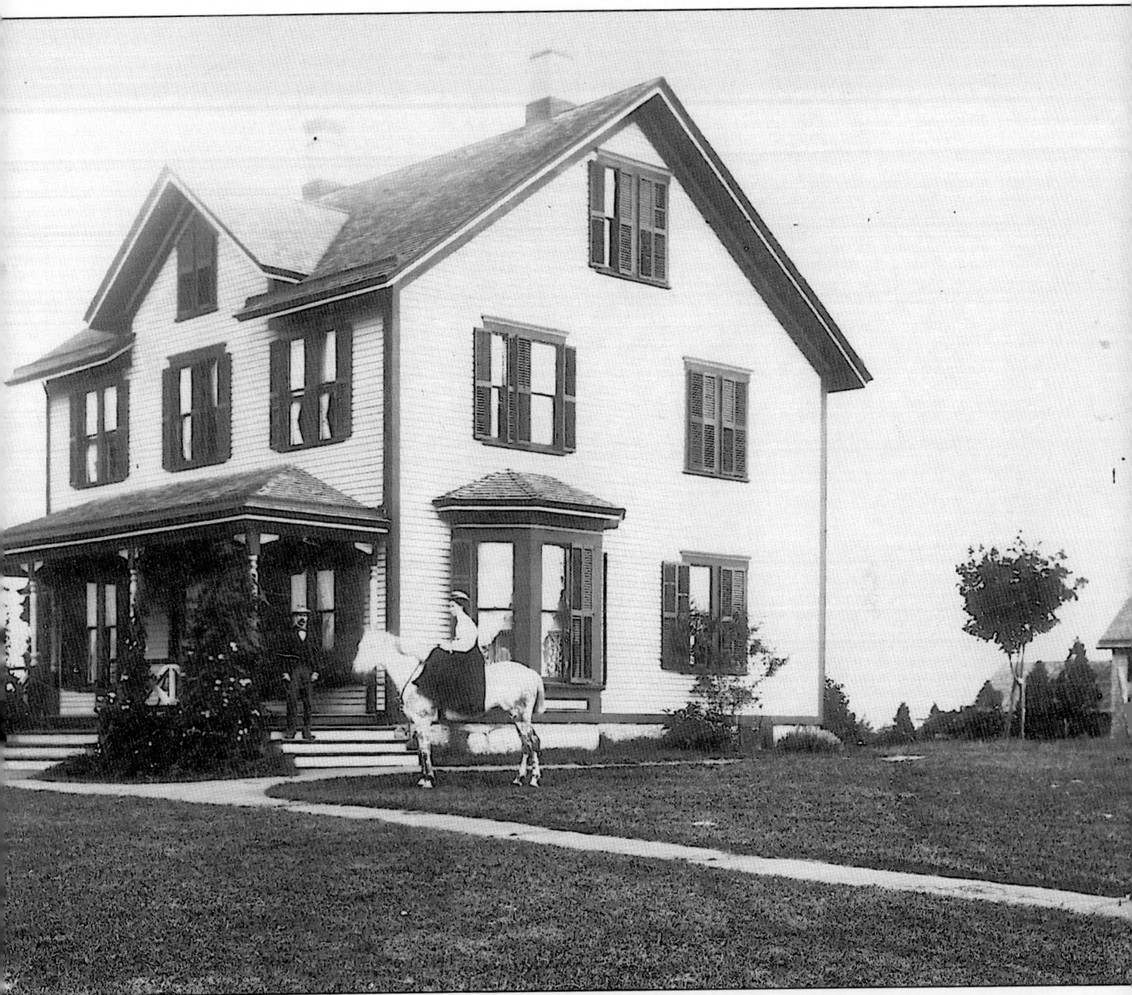

This house, variously called the Tefft house and the Jackson property, was located near the intersection of Lower College Road and Kingstown Road. It is shown here, c. 1896. The University of Rhode Island acquired the property and demolished the house. (Courtesy Pettaquamscutt Historical Society.)

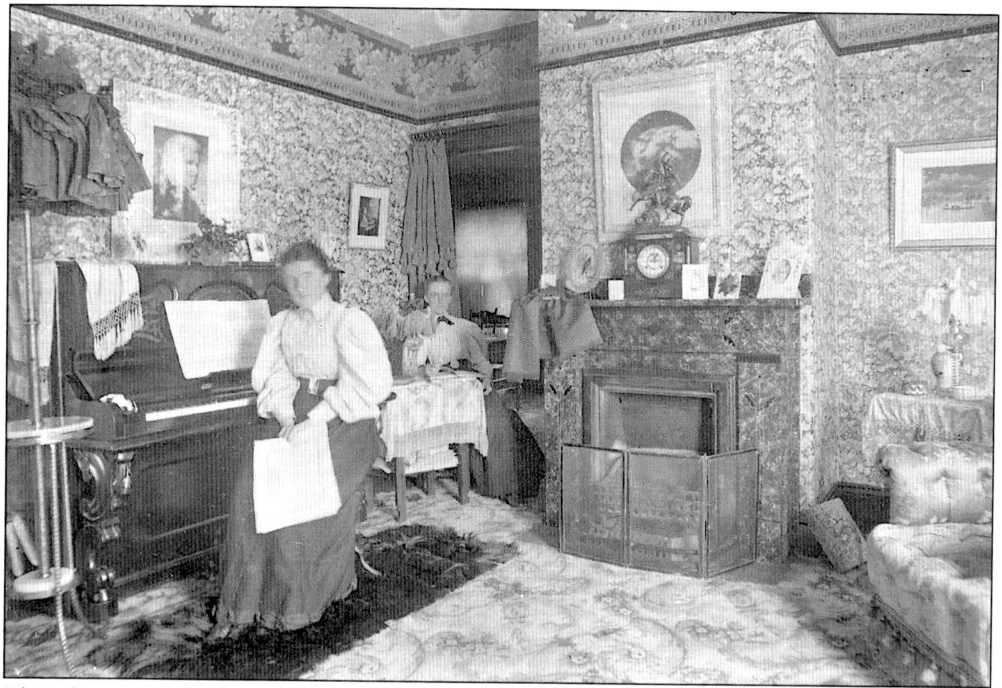

This photograph shows the ornate Victorian interior of the Tefft house on Kingstown Road. Some believe the people pictured are Mr. and Mrs. Millard Fillmore Perry, whose wedding was recounted on page 51. (Courtesy Pettaquamscutt Historical Society.)

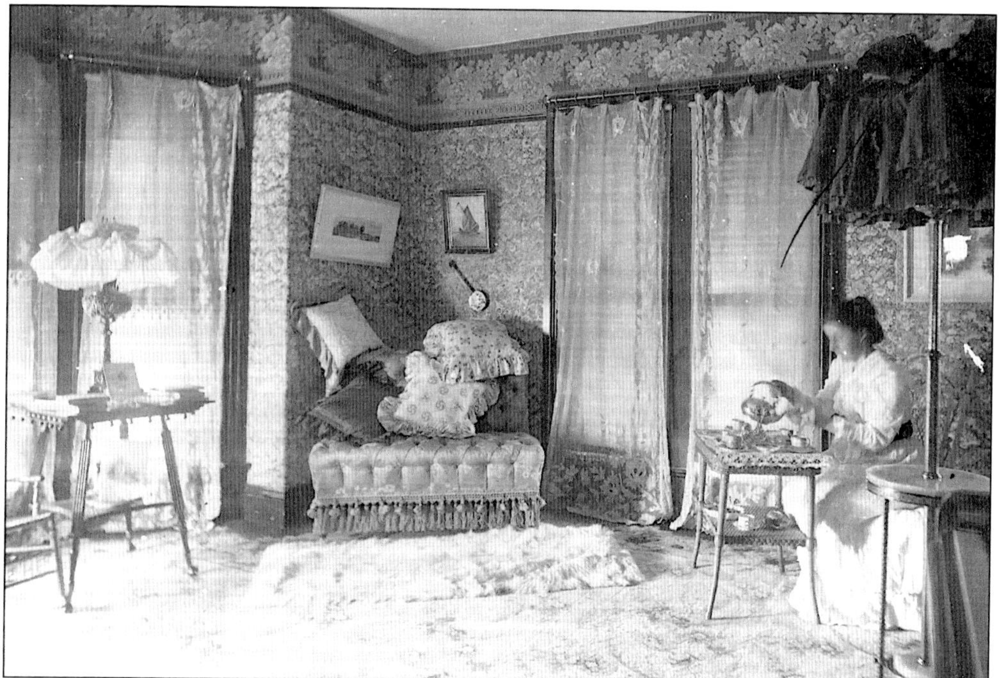

A woman pours tea in the Tefft house on Kingstown Road. Note the fancy wallpaper, the carpets, and the draperies. (Courtesy Pettaquamscutt Historical Society.)

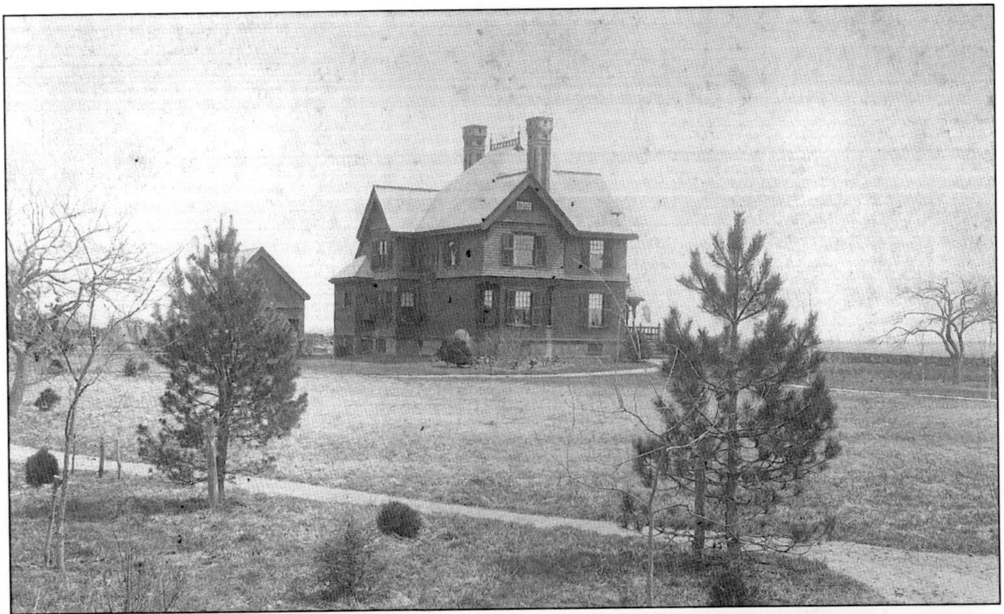

Sherwell, today known as the Crossways, is the name of this Victorian house built in 1893 at the eastern end of the village by Herbert J. Wells. He was president of Hospital Trust Bank from 1884 until 1919. Note how open the landscape is in this picture; today, the house is barely visible from the road. (Courtesy Pettaquamscutt Historical Society.)

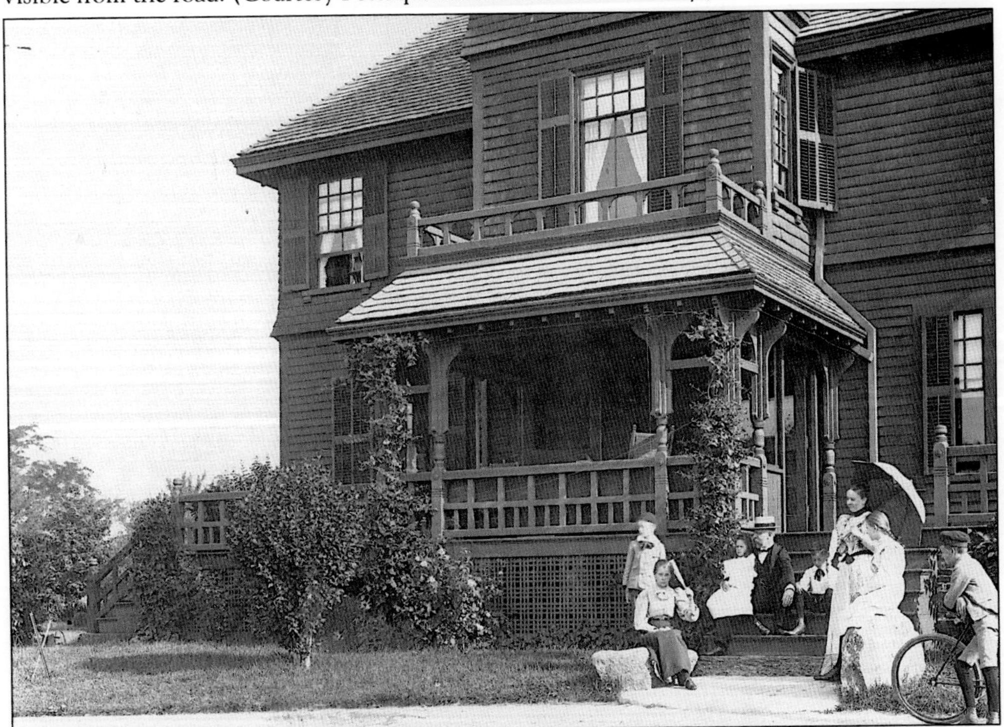

The Herbert J. Wells family relaxes on the porch of Sherwell, c. 1896. They include Thomas, Grace, Elizabeth, on the knee of father Herbert J. Wells, John, Emily (Perry) Wells (wife and mother), daughter Emily, and Herbert C. Wells. (Courtesy Pettaquamscutt Historical Society.)

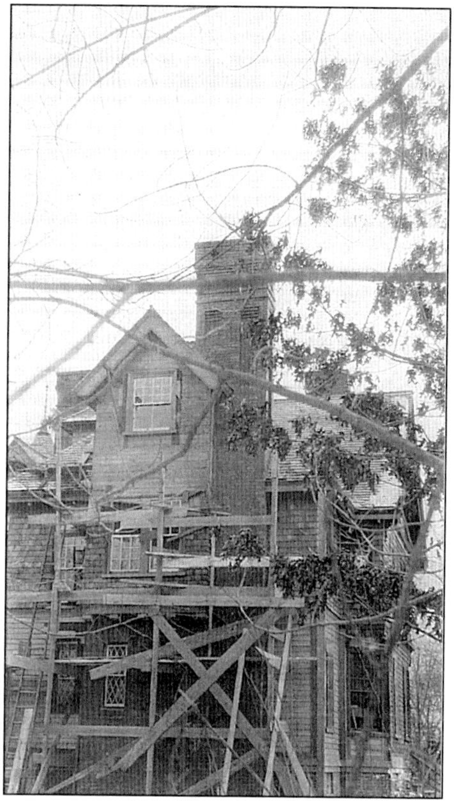

Sherwell, or the Crossways, is being added onto in this undated photograph. (Courtesy Betty Faella.)

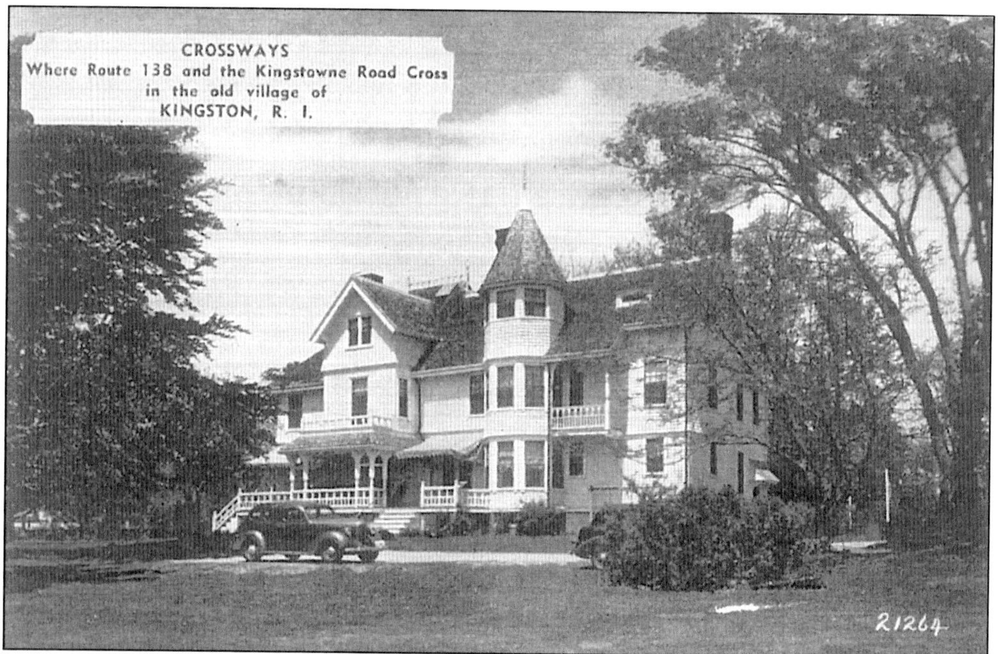

This is a more contemporary view of Sherwell, after its name had been changed to the Crossways. It is now rented as apartments. (Courtesy Elaine Pereira.)

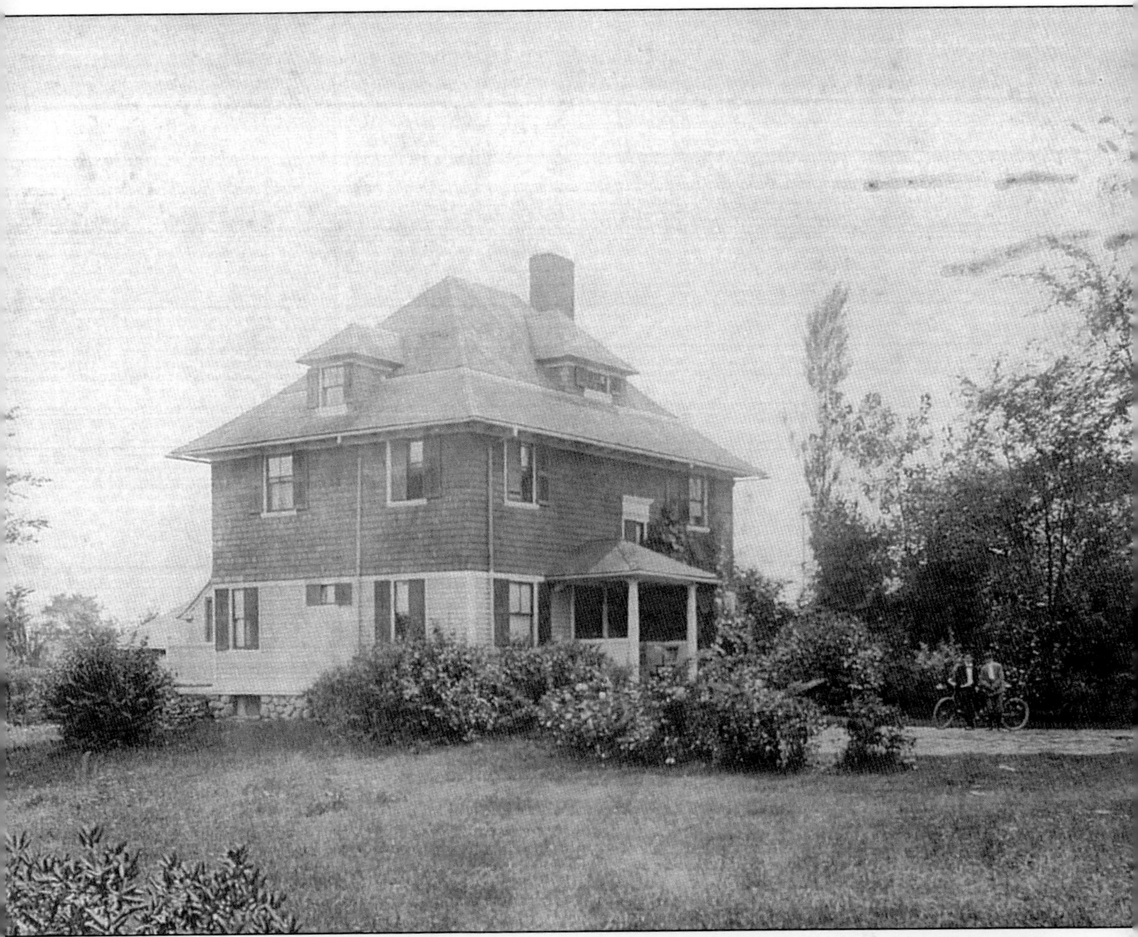

Called the Rhododendrons, this house was built behind the Crossways as a home for Helen May Wells and her husband, Lorenzo Kinney Sr. Kinney was the first professor hired at the new Rhode Island College of Agricultural and Mechanic Arts, where he taught horticulture and helped run the Experiment Station. His future wife was hired as an instructor in freehand drawing in 1891. Kinney stayed for about a decade before resigning to pursue his own horticultural business. The professor began growing rhododendrons, bringing them from a lot in the Great Swamp he had purchased for this purpose. The plants were carried by train to New York, Newport, and Philadelphia as landscaping for the big estates that had emerged in the country's golden age. (Courtesy Betty Faella.)

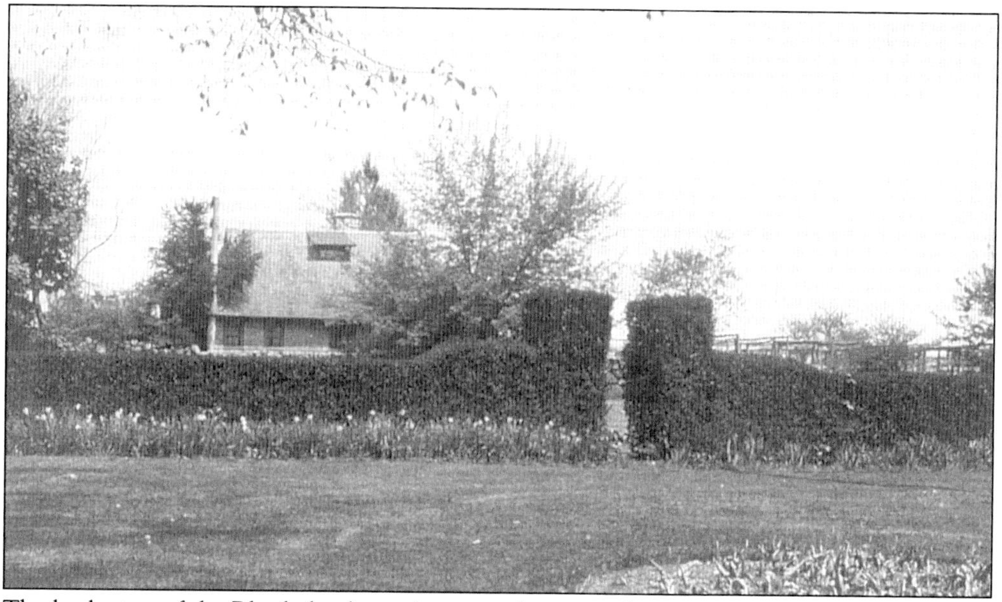

The back view of the Rhododendrons shows, at the rear right, frames used for propagating the bushes that gave the estate its name. (Courtesy Betty Faella.)

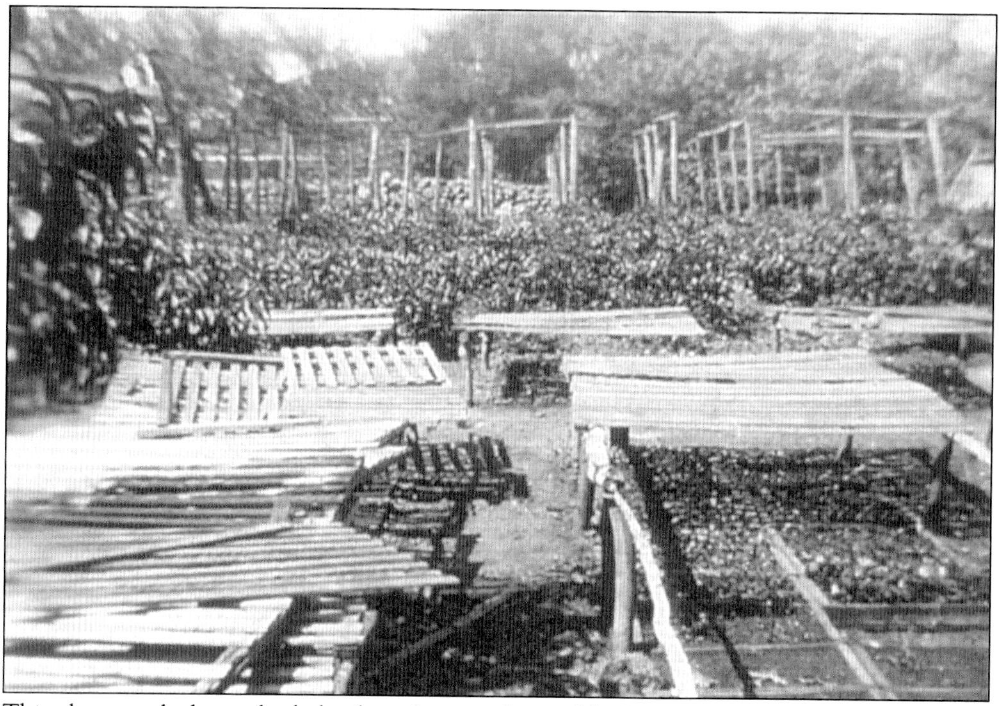

This photograph shows rhododendrons being cultivated by Lorenzo Kinney Sr. at his home off Mooresfield Road. Kinney continued his business of selling the plants to big estates until the stock market crashed in 1929. In his later years, Kinney ran a greenhouse for the Potter family on South Road. He died in 1944. (Courtesy Betty Faella.)

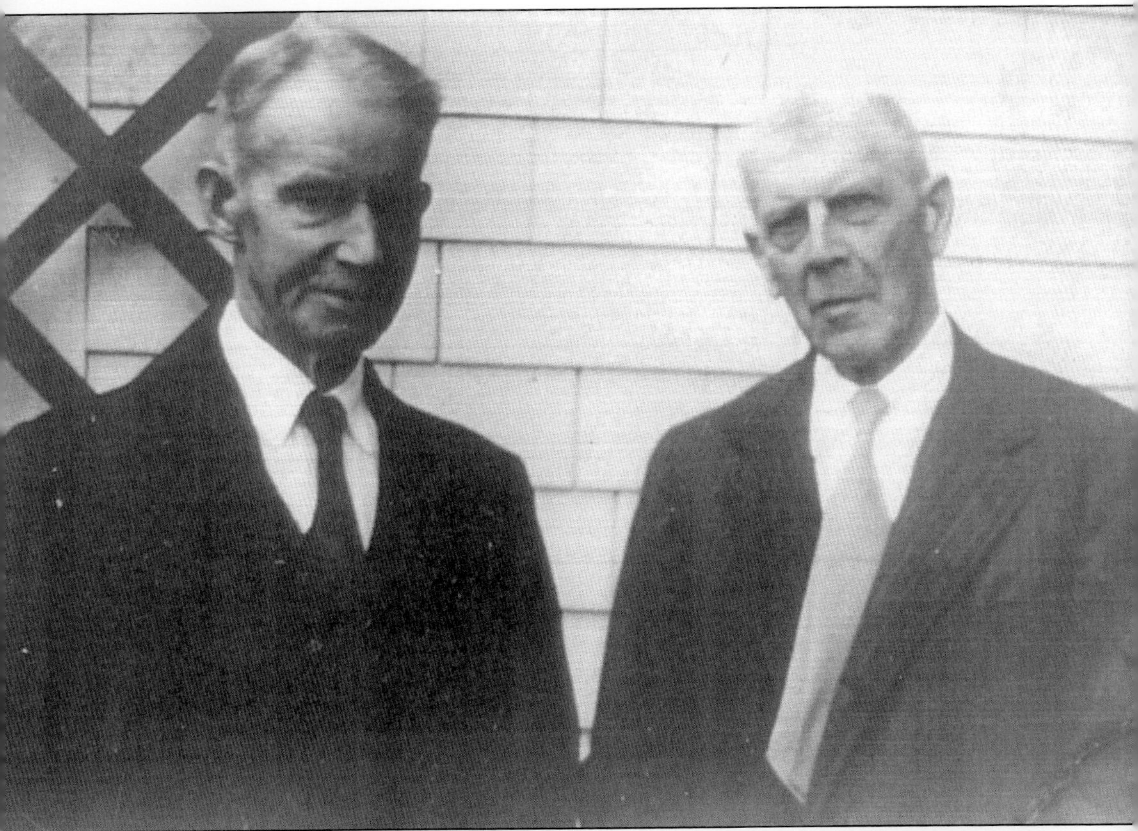

Lorenzo Kinney Sr., on the left, and Bernon E. Helme, two distinguished gentlemen of Kingston, are captured in a moment together by Kinney's son Lorenzo Kinney Jr. Helme is credited with the idea of locating an Experiment Station and agricultural school in Kingston, which led to today's University of Rhode Island. A merchant and prominent actor in village affairs, Helme spent a great deal of time lobbying the legislature in Providence for his idea. The Reverend J. Hagadorn Wells, in his memoirs, claims the idea came to Helme while he was vigorously sweeping the wooden floor of his store on Kingstown Road. Long after the college had become a reality, Helme remained interested in its affairs. In 1910, he testified before a state property committee against a college proposal to sell some of its land so that faculty members could build houses. Helme was convinced that enough private land already existed for this purpose, and he brought a map along to prove his point. Kinney was the first professor hired by the college, although he left after ten years to cultivate rhododendrons. At the time of this photograph, c. 1935, Kinney was working in the Potter greenhouse on South Road. (Courtesy Betty Faella.)

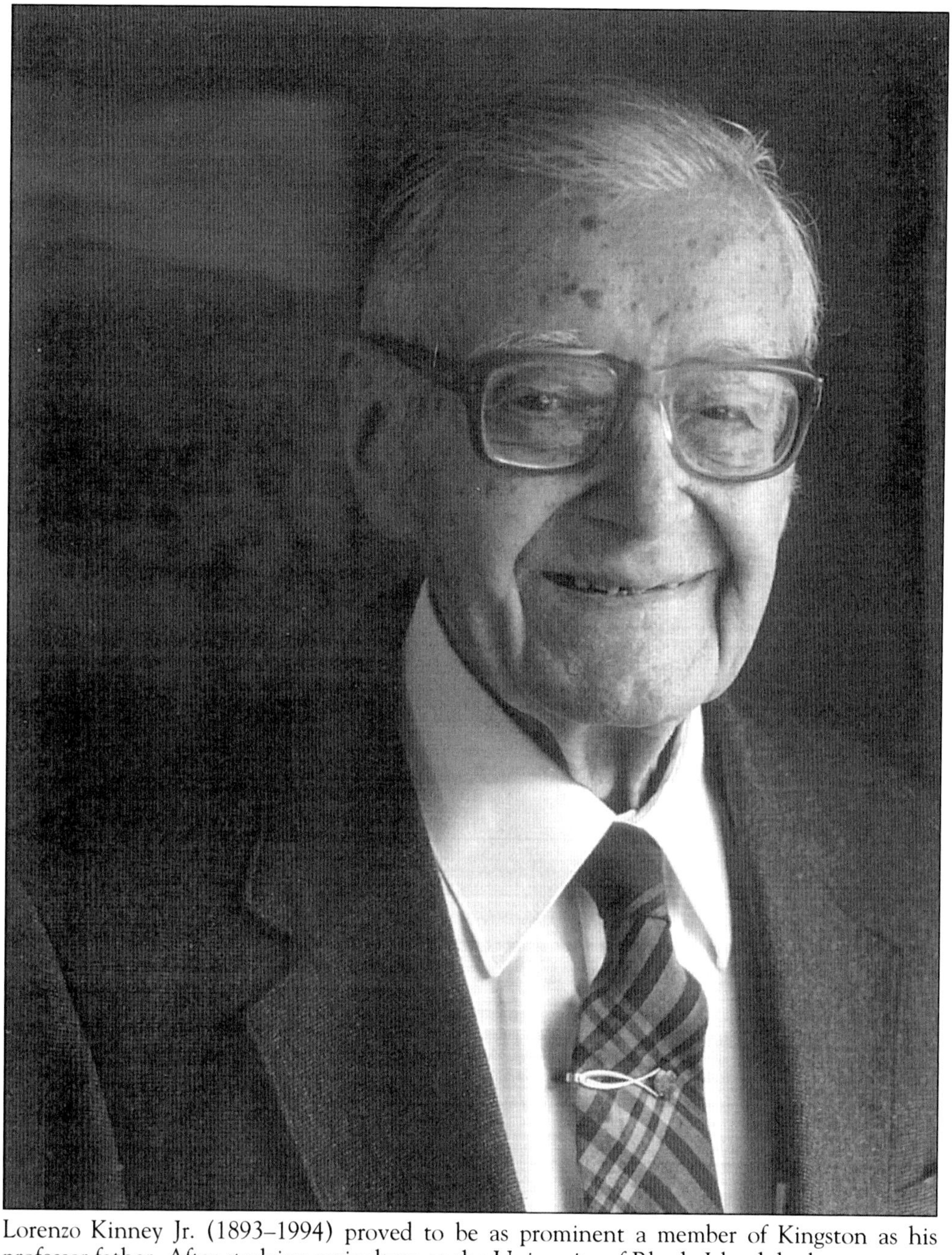

Lorenzo Kinney Jr. (1893–1994) proved to be as prominent a member of Kingston as his professor father. After studying agriculture at the University of Rhode Island, he became state 4-H club leader, a job he held for 38 years, retiring in the mid-1950s. But the second part of his life was to be a true renaissance. Interested in painting, photography, and horticulture, the younger Kinney began to cultivate azaleas south of the Rhododendrons estate at a home he and his wife, Elizabeth, had built before their 1927 marriage. Today, the 7-acre estate includes hundreds of his plants, many of them varieties that he developed himself. The grounds of his home are open to the public year-round. Kinney also left behind paintings and thousands of photographs, which he took daily and referred to as his diary. (Courtesy Betty Faella.)

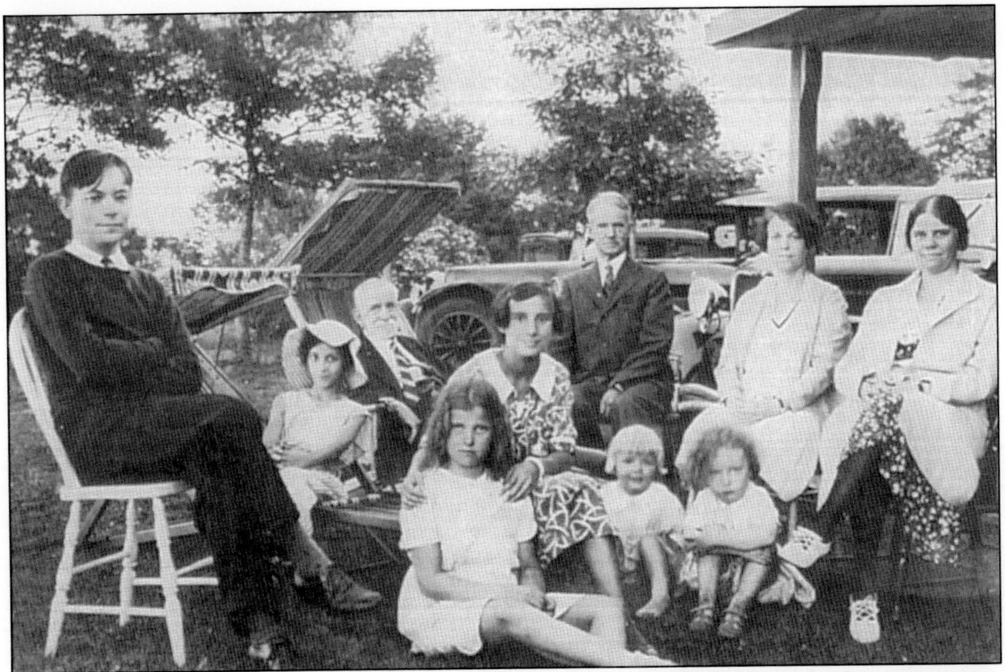

Members of the Wells and Kinney families enjoy a picnic at Larkin's Pond in West Kingston. They include, from left to right, Wells Coleman, an unidentified girl, Herbert J. Wells (the older gentleman in the back), Sally Wells (now Bechtold), an unidentified girl, Lorenzo Kinney Sr., Betty Kinney (now Faella), Peggy Gilbert, Elizabeth Kinney (wife of Lorenzo Kinney Jr. and mother of Betty), and Elizabeth Wells. The two unidentified girls were city children visiting the family through a sunshine program. (Courtesy Betty Faella.)

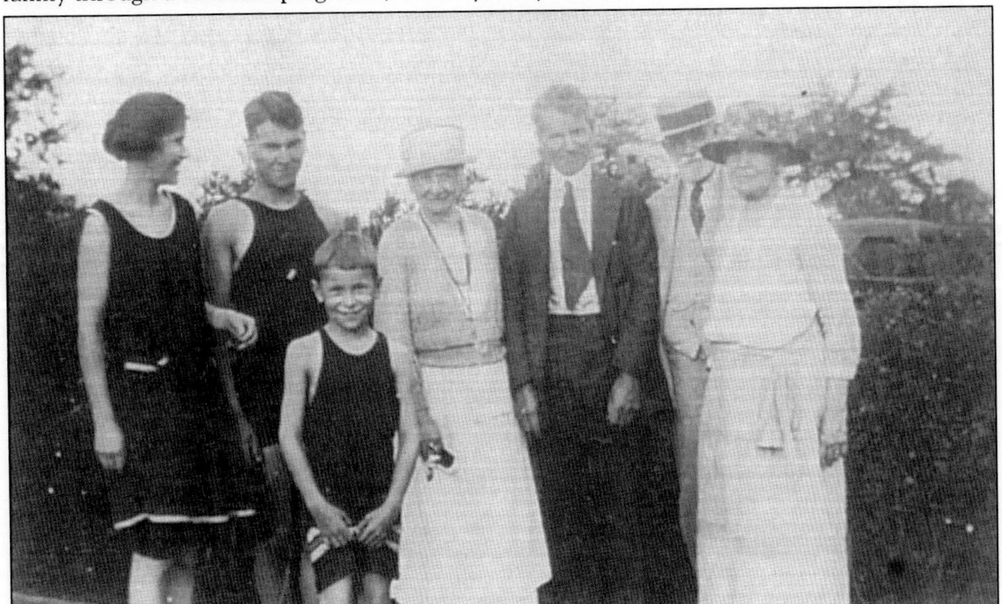

Some people in this 1923 picture appear ready to take a dip into Larkin's Pond. On hand for the picnic were Galen Kinney, second from left; Herbert and Emma Wells, at right; and Robert Kinney, third from right. (Courtesy Betty Faella.)

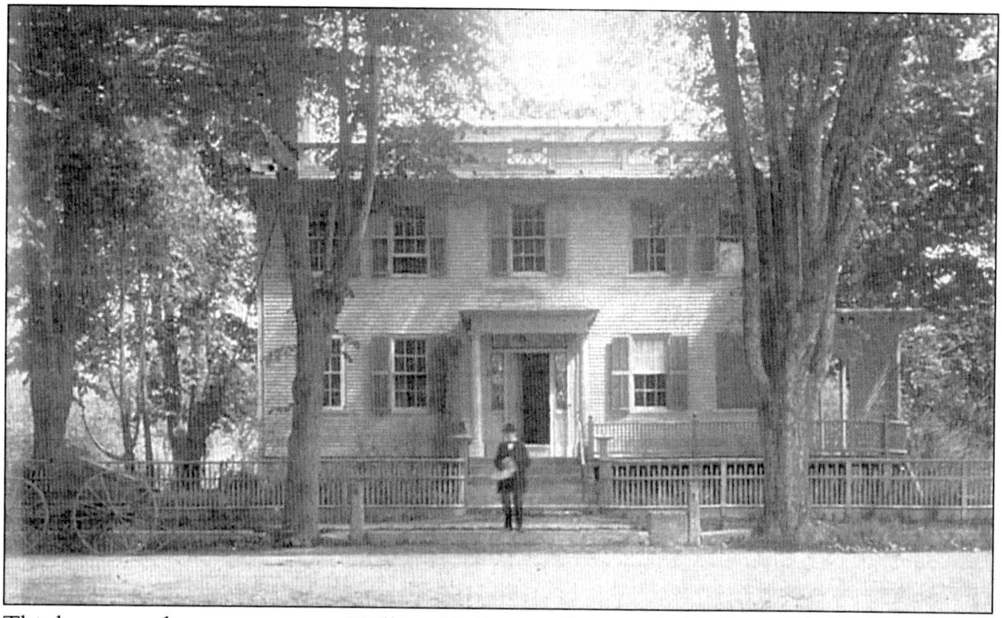

This house was home to attorney William H. Potter, who is probably the gentleman standing at the gate. (Courtesy Pettaquamscutt Historical Society.)

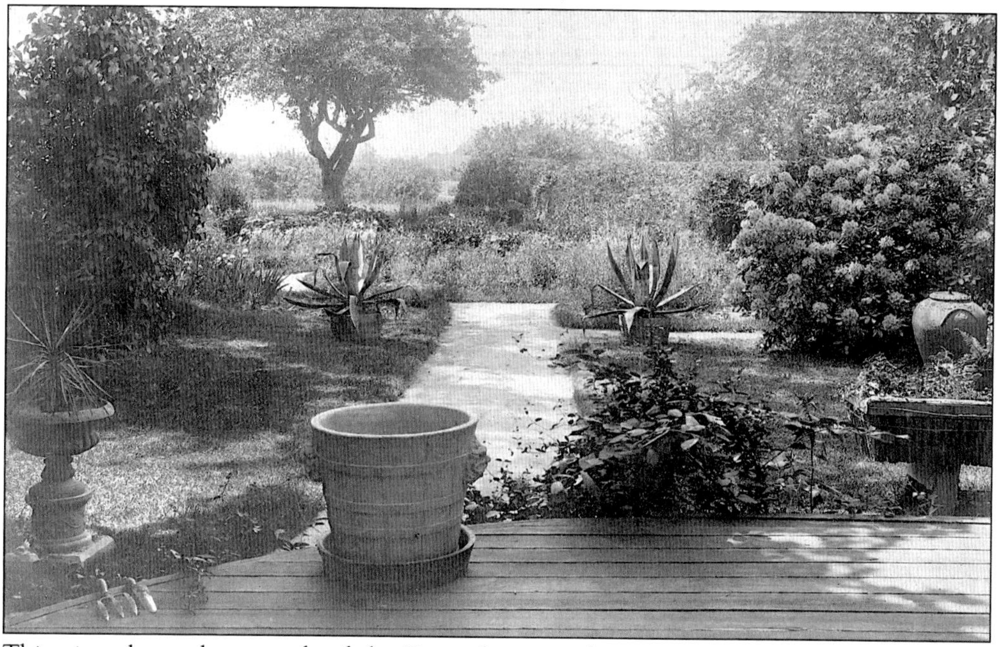

This view shows the grounds of the Potter homestead on Potter Lane, home to Elisha R. Potter Jr. (1811–1882) and other Potter family members. The landscaping is testimony to the prominence of the Potter family. Elisha Jr. was an author, lawyer, State Supreme Court judge, adjutant general, and member of Congress. He wrote *The Early History of Narragansett*, as well as other historical tracts, including studies of paper money in Rhode Island and early French settlements. Elisha R. Potter Sr., also a congressman, built the homestead, which later became home to Elisha Jr.'s brother William, who willed it to his niece Mary LeMoine Potter. (Courtesy Pettaquamscutt Historical Society.)

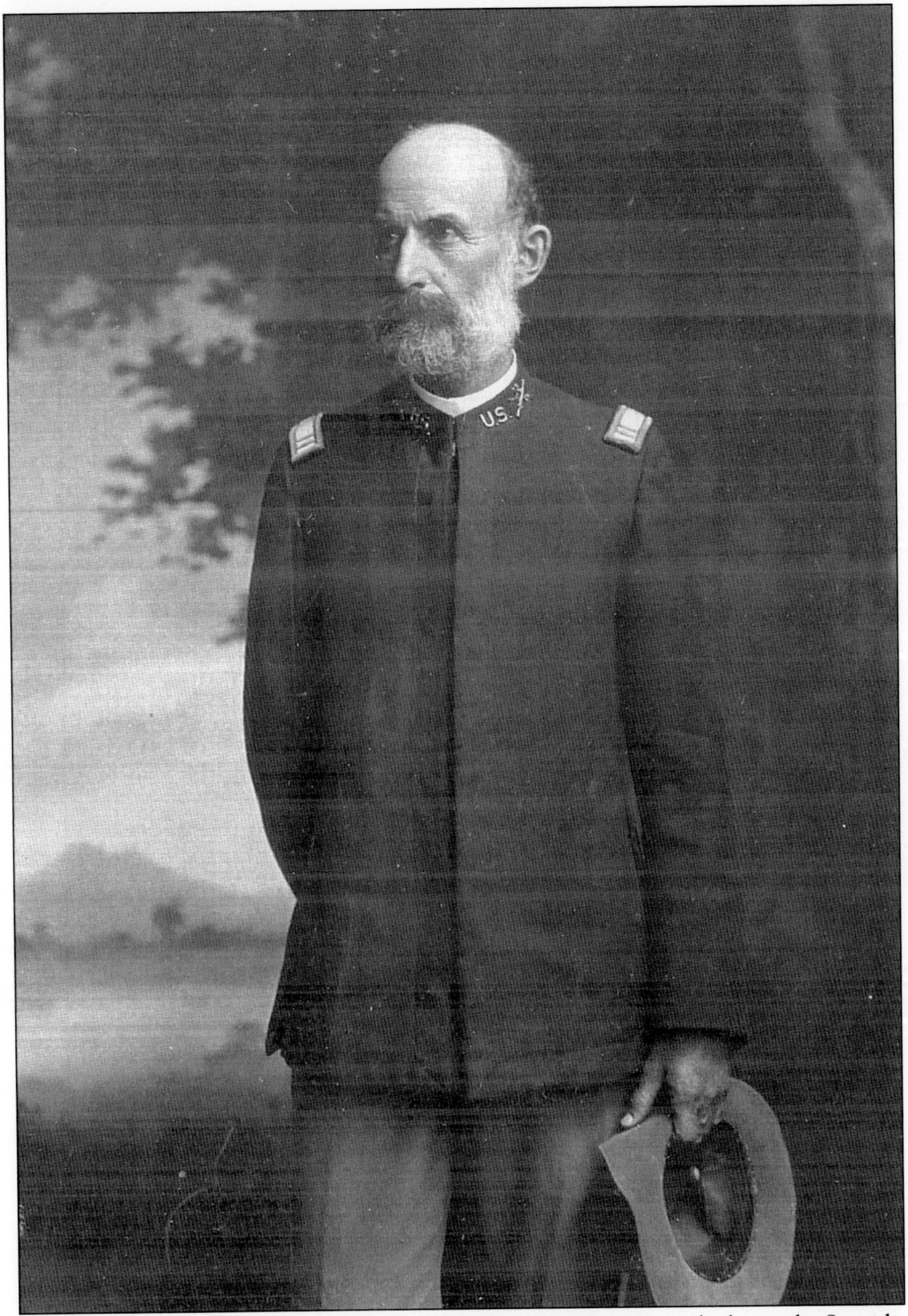

This photograph purports to show Maj. C.H. Potter at Manila, apparently during the Spanish-American War, although the photographer was from San Francisco. (Courtesy Pettaquamscutt Historical Society.)

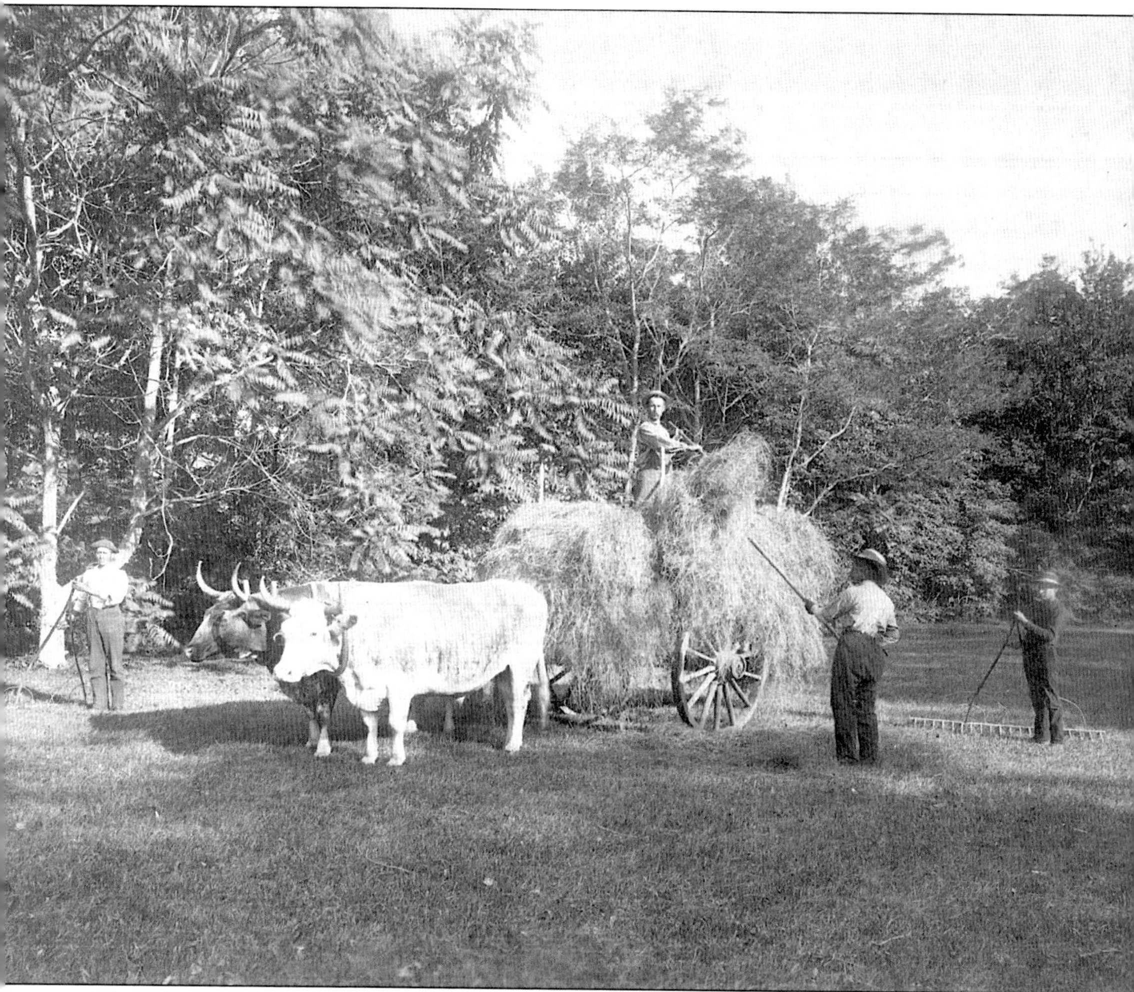

This photograph shows haying time at the Potter homestead on Potter Lane. The Potters employed a retinue of servants, chauffeurs, and farmhands and were among the wealthiest residents of Kingston. (Courtesy Pettaquamscutt Historical Society.)

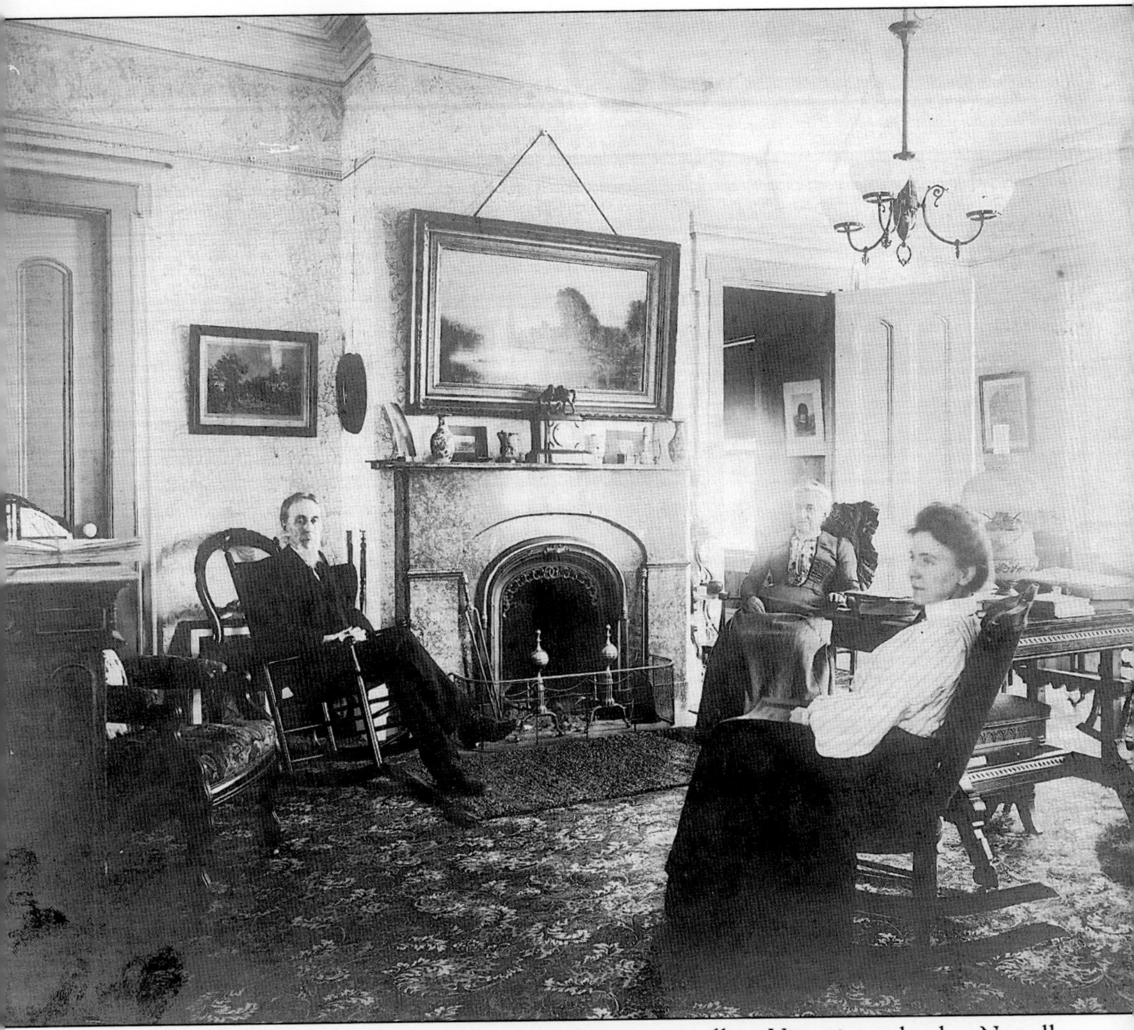

This is an interior of the Potter homestead in Kingston, in all its Victorian splendor. Not all of the living room occupants are identified, but the gentleman is either Judge Elisha Potter Jr. or his younger brother William H. Potter. The latter acquired the property after his brother's death in 1882. (Courtesy Pettaquamscutt Historical Society.)

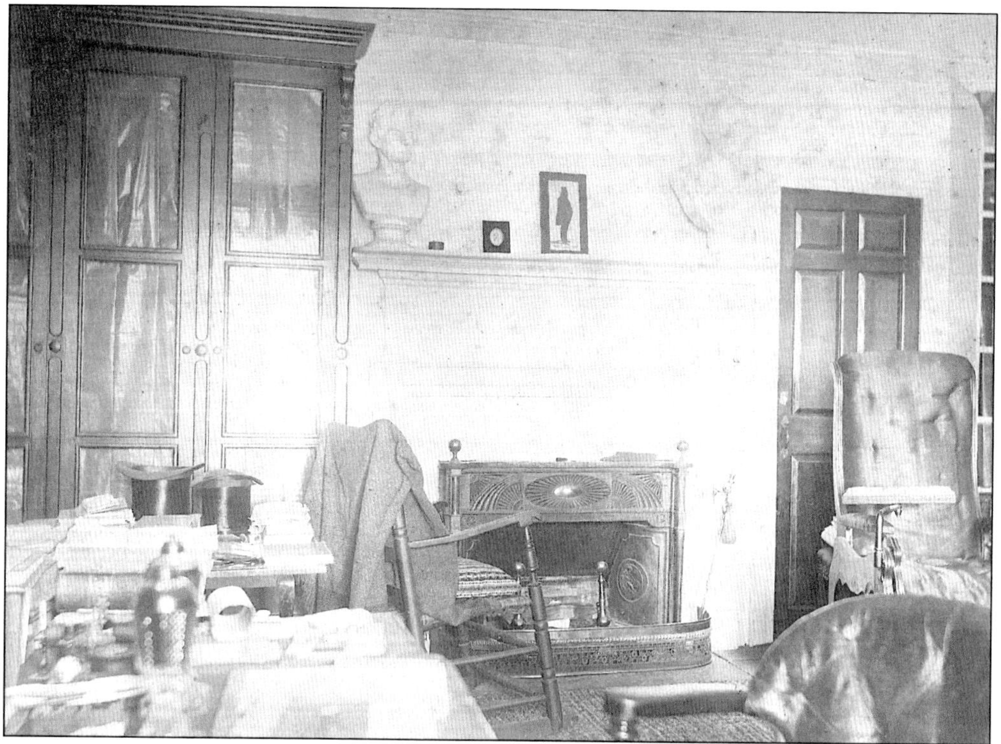

This photograph shows an interior view of the Potter homestead. Built in 1809, the Federal-style home includes all the accoutrements of Victorian living, such as the Morris chair on the right. Note the top hats left casually on the table and the jacket draped over the chair on the left. (Courtesy Pettaquamscutt Historical Society.)

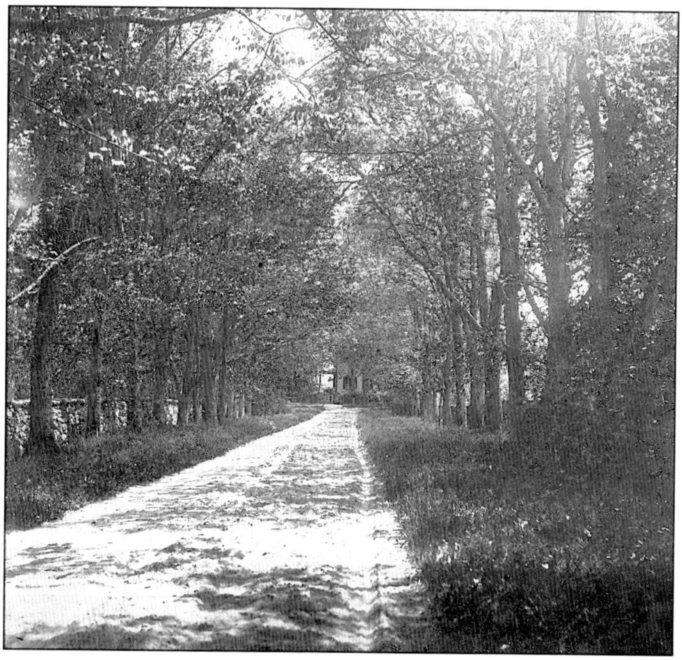

This is Potter Lane, the private drive that leads from Kingstown Road to the Potter homestead. (Courtesy Pettaquamscutt Historical Society.)

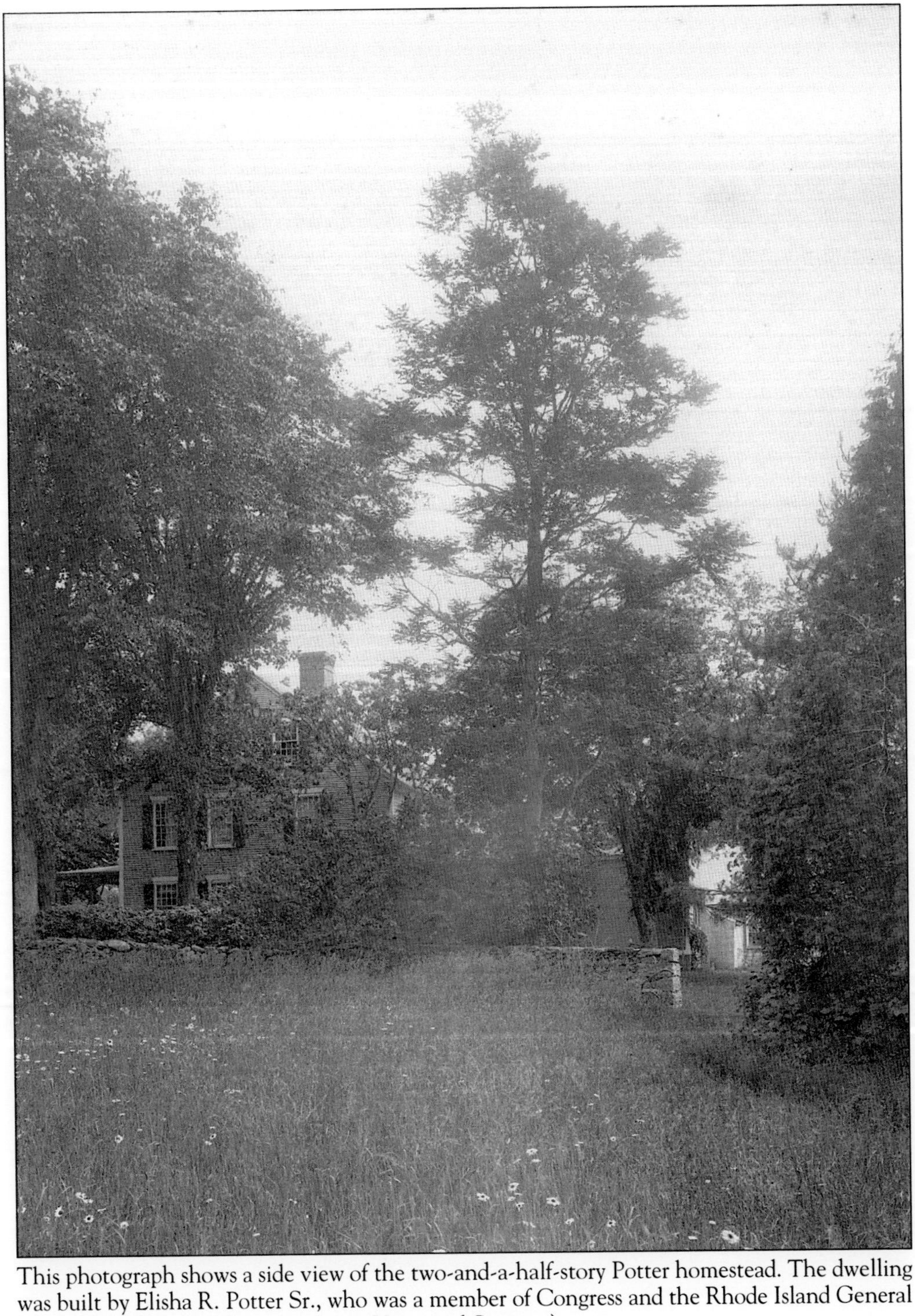

This photograph shows a side view of the two-and-a-half-story Potter homestead. The dwelling was built by Elisha R. Potter Sr., who was a member of Congress and the Rhode Island General Assembly. (Courtesy Pettaquamscutt Historical Society.)

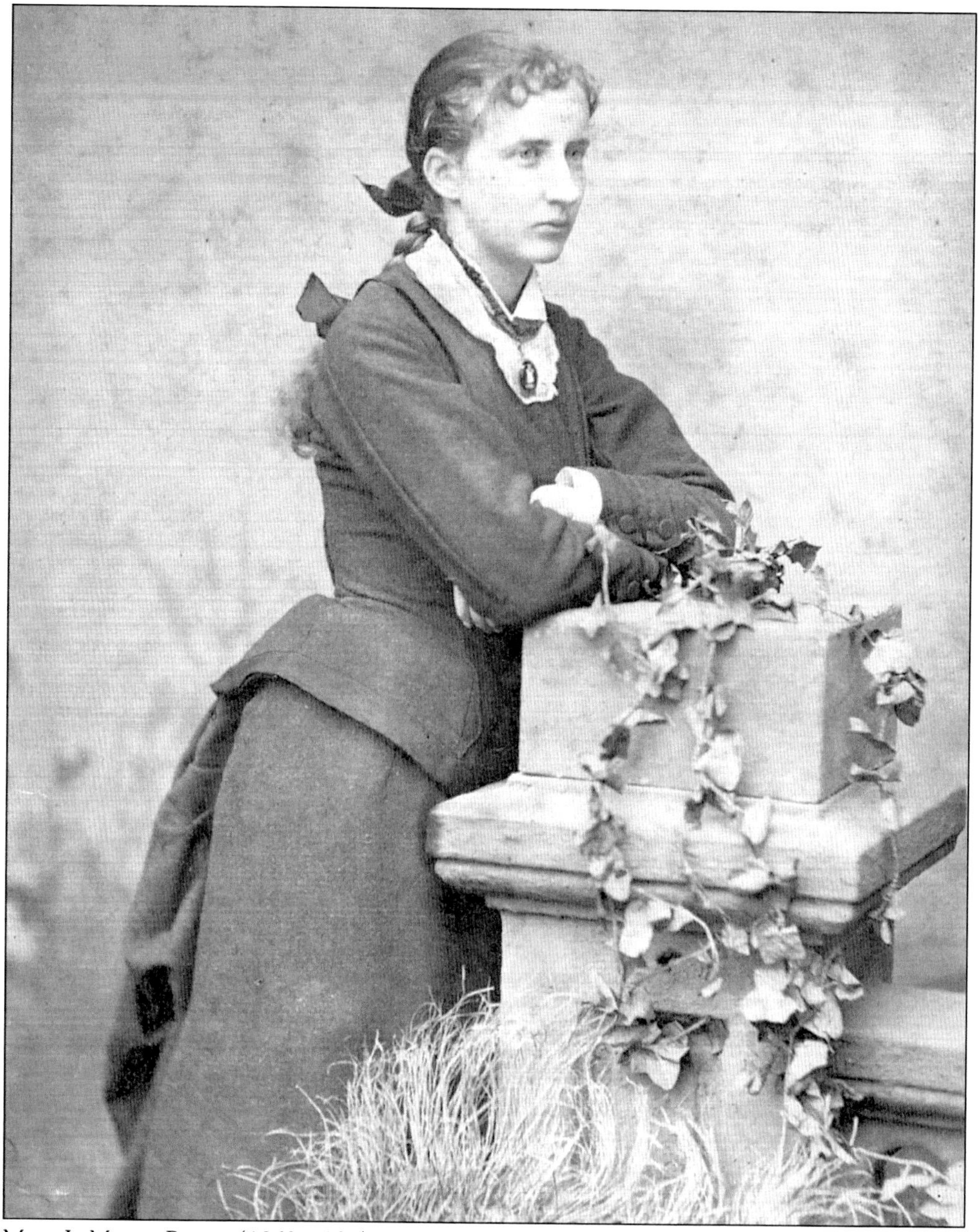

Mary LeMoine Potter (1860–1938) was the last member of the Potter family to live in the homestead on Potter Lane. She was the daughter of Col. James B.M. Potter, who was a paymaster for the army. Her father was with President Abraham Lincoln at his assassination in Ford's Theatre and helped take Mrs. Lincoln away from the box—a story that Miss Potter told the Every Tuesday Club many years later. Miss Potter left many bequests to Kingston charities at her death, including Potter Woods off South Road, which now belongs to the Kingston Improvement Association and contains a ballfield, basketball court, playground, and hiking trails. She also gave property to the Girl Scouts and financial bequests to the South County Hospital, the Kingston Free Library, and the Kingston Congregational Church, among others. (Courtesy Pettaquamscutt Historical Society.)

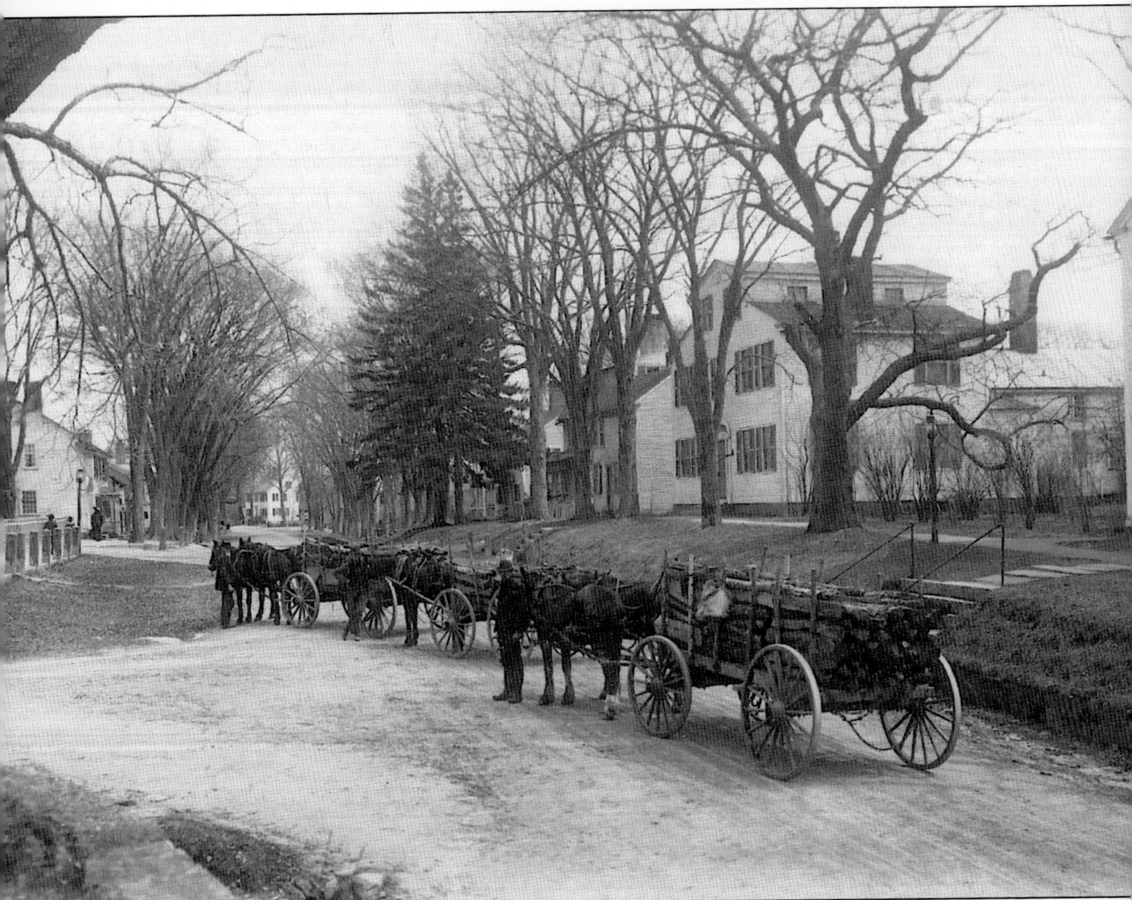

Drivers carry cordwood up Kingston Hill. The Kingston Congregational Church is on right, and the view is looking east. (Courtesy Pettaquamscutt Historical Society.)

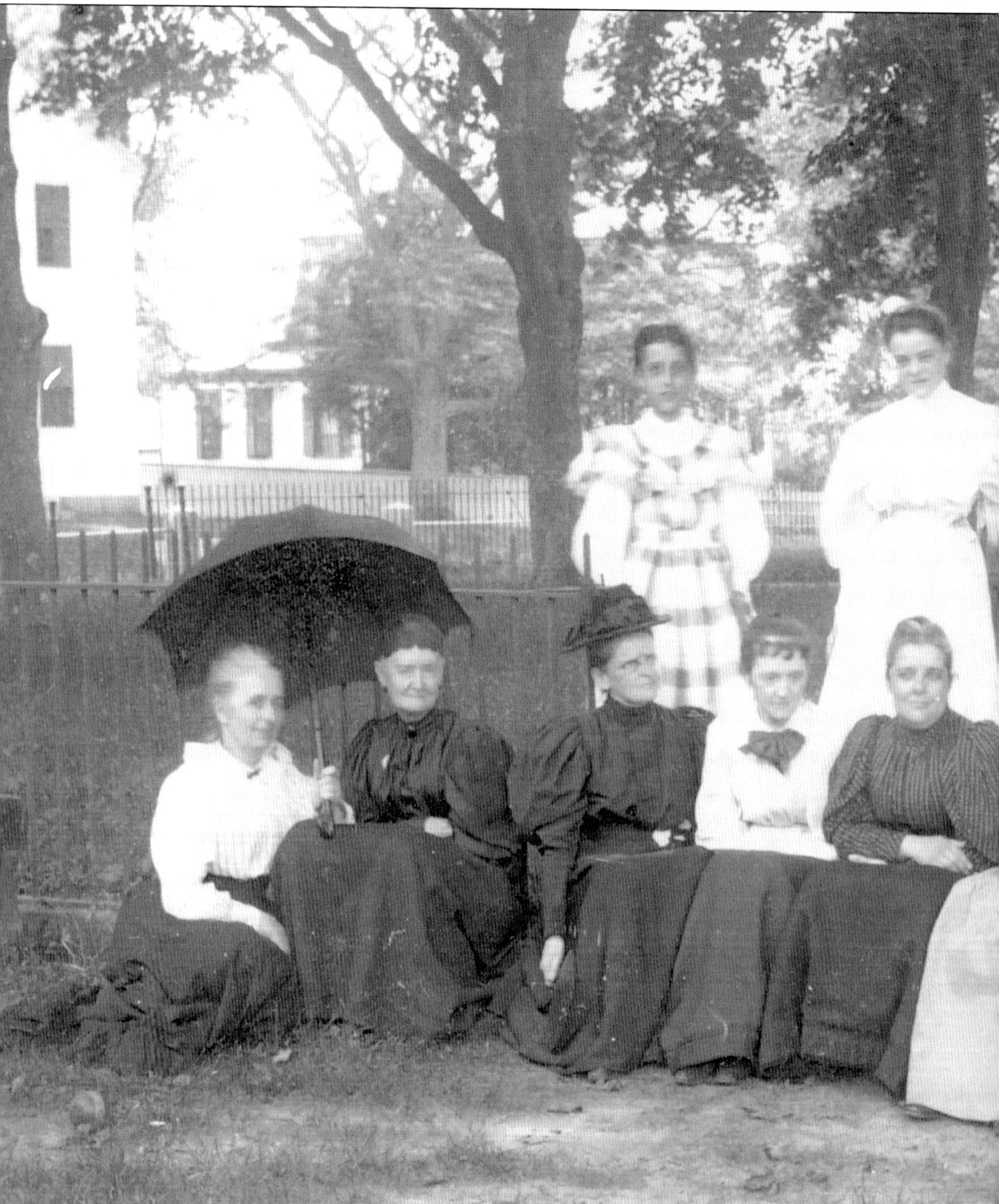

In the side yard of the Timothy Peckham house in Kingston, the Robinson family and friends gather for a picture. The buildings in this photograph are the Kingston Free Library, at far right on page 97, and, on the far left, the Kingston Congregational Church. Peckham built the house as a tavern *c.* 1820. Later, Dr. Daniel Watson used the house for his business and doctor's office. After Watson moved to Newport, the firm of Robinson and Anthony acquired it for use as a store and living quarters. The Reverend J. Hagadorn Wells recalled that the two "carried on a

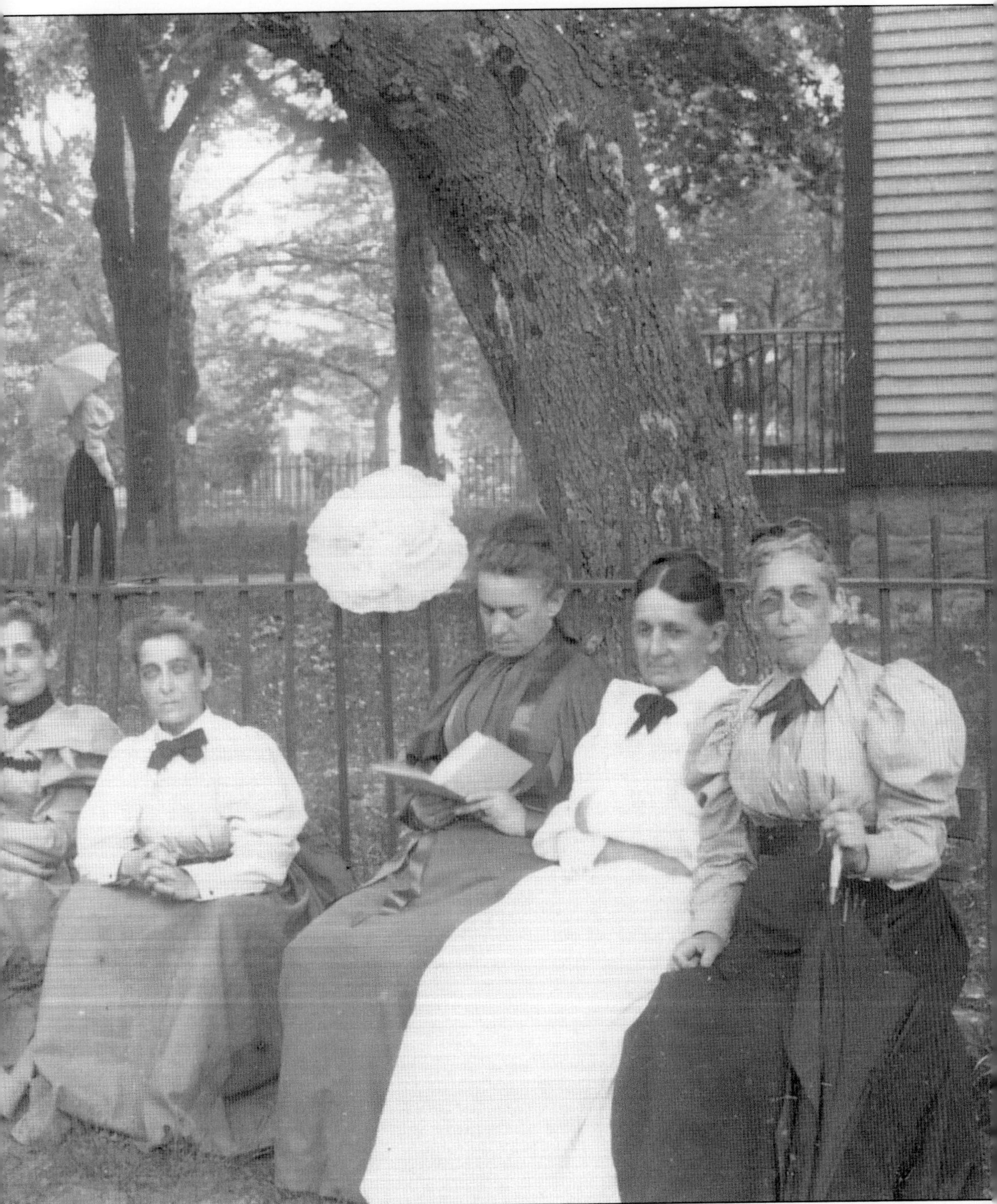

brisk trade in a store standing in the northwest corner of the house, corner to corner." George B. Robinson then became sole owner, and the store eventually was moved off site. Shown in this 1895 photograph are, from left to right, Hannah Robinson, who lived in the home; Mrs. Newcomb; unidentified; Virginia Wheaton; Mary Newcomb; two unidentified persons; Mrs. Wheaton or possibly Mrs. J. Adams Brown; two unidentified persons; Lizzie Robinson; and Isabel Knight, perhaps. (Courtesy Pettaquamscutt Historical Society.)

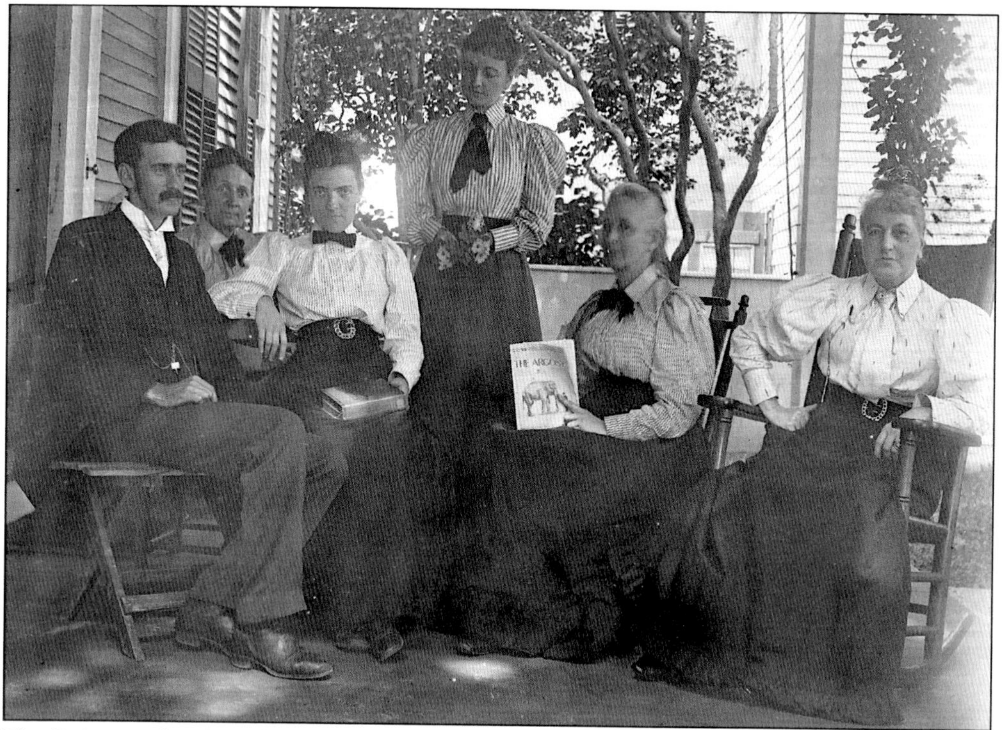

The Robinson family and friends enjoy a spell on the porch of their house on Kingstown Road. Hannah Robinson, second from right, holds a copy of *Argosy* magazine. Others are, from left to right, Mr. Lee, Elizabeth Robinson, Jennie Hagadorn, Mary Newcomb, and Mary Brine. (Courtesy Pettaquamscutt Historical Society.)

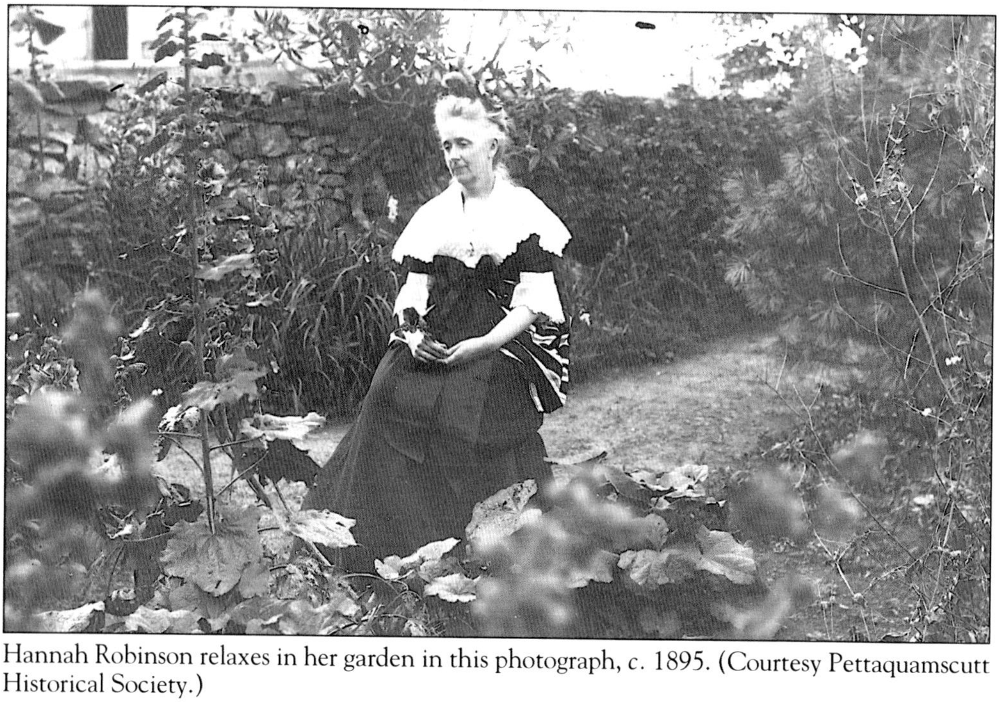

Hannah Robinson relaxes in her garden in this photograph, *c.* 1895. (Courtesy Pettaquamscutt Historical Society.)

Seven

Town and Gown

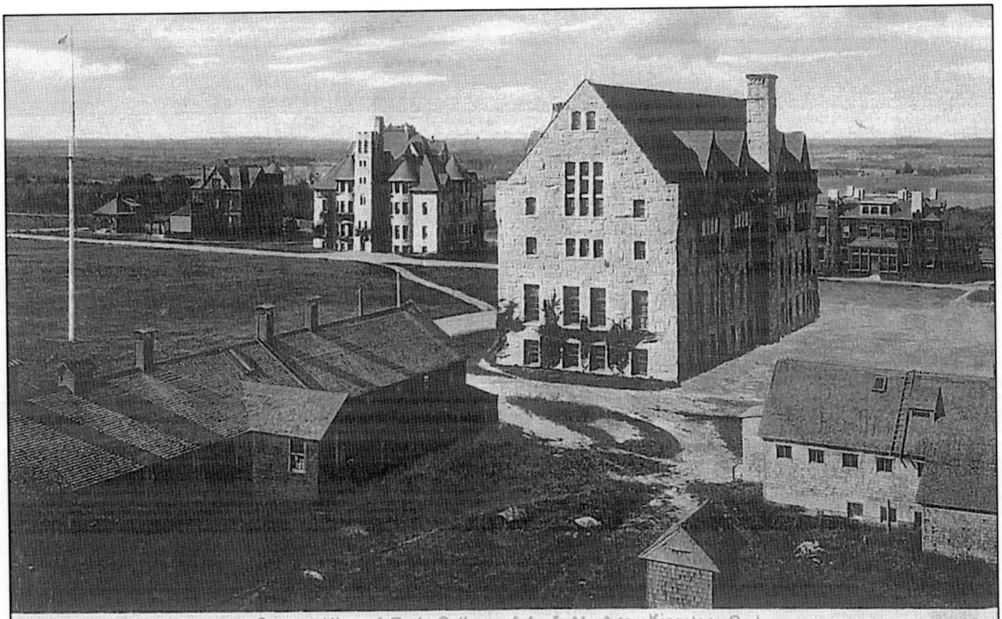

This post-1897 postcard shows a sweeping view of the campus quadrangle at the Rhode Island College of Agricultural and Mechanic Arts. When the first students arrived in 1890, some of the buildings were only half completed. The driving force behind the establishment of the college and Experiment Station in Kingston was Bernon E. Helme, a village merchant and postmaster who was a skilled and tireless lobbyist on behalf of locating the college at the 140-acre Oliver Watson Farm, north of the village center. (Courtesy Pettaquamscutt Historical Society.)

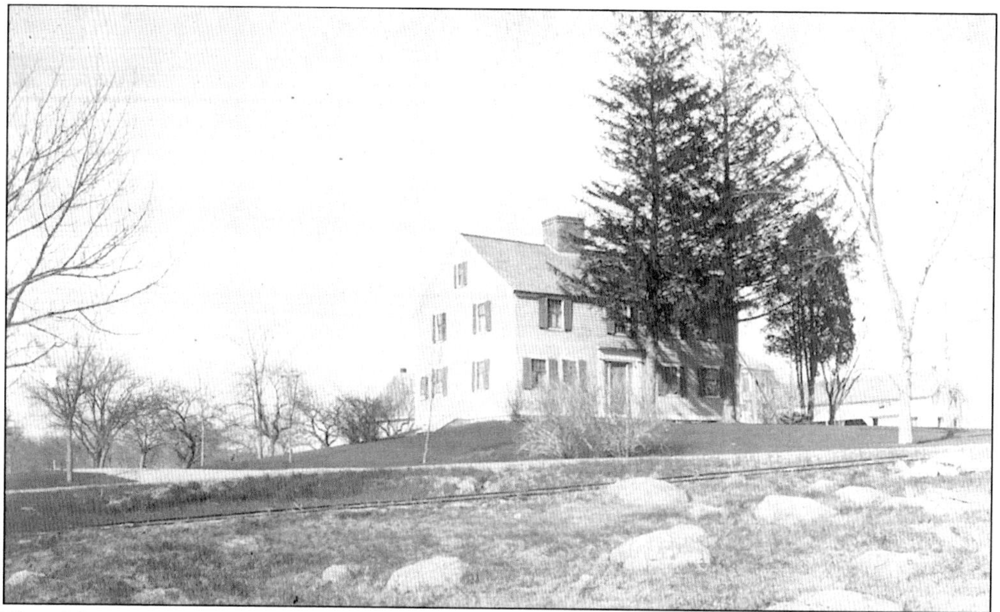

The Oliver Watson-Tefft farm was for sale for $5,000 when a group of South Kingstown residents, spurred on by merchant Bernon E. Helme, approached the Rhode Island General Assembly about locating an agricultural school there. Helme had raised about $2,000 in the village, and Jeremiah Peckham Jr. had convinced the South Kingstown Town Council to contribute the same amount toward the purchase. The house, barn, and outbuildings were said to be dilapidated, but enthusiastic village supporters cited the farm's clean air and good soil in their arguments. This photograph of the farmhouse was taken *c.* 1898. (Courtesy Pettaquamscutt Historical Society.)

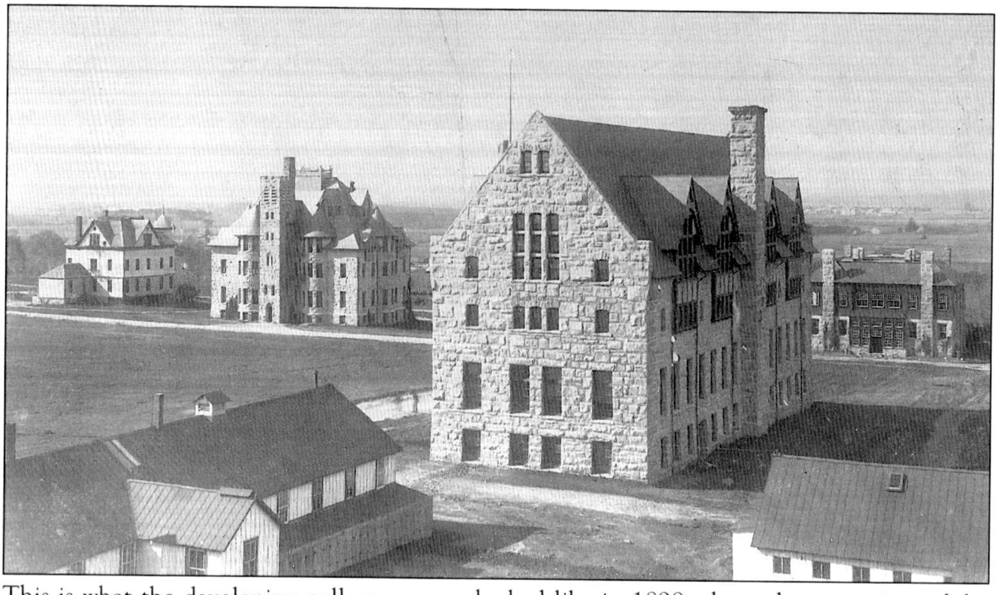

This is what the developing college campus looked like in 1898, about the same time of the top photo. In the foreground is Lippitt Hall, with Davis Hall to its left. The top photo shows the rails by which quarried granite was hauled to build Lippitt. (Courtesy Pettaquamscutt Historical Society.)

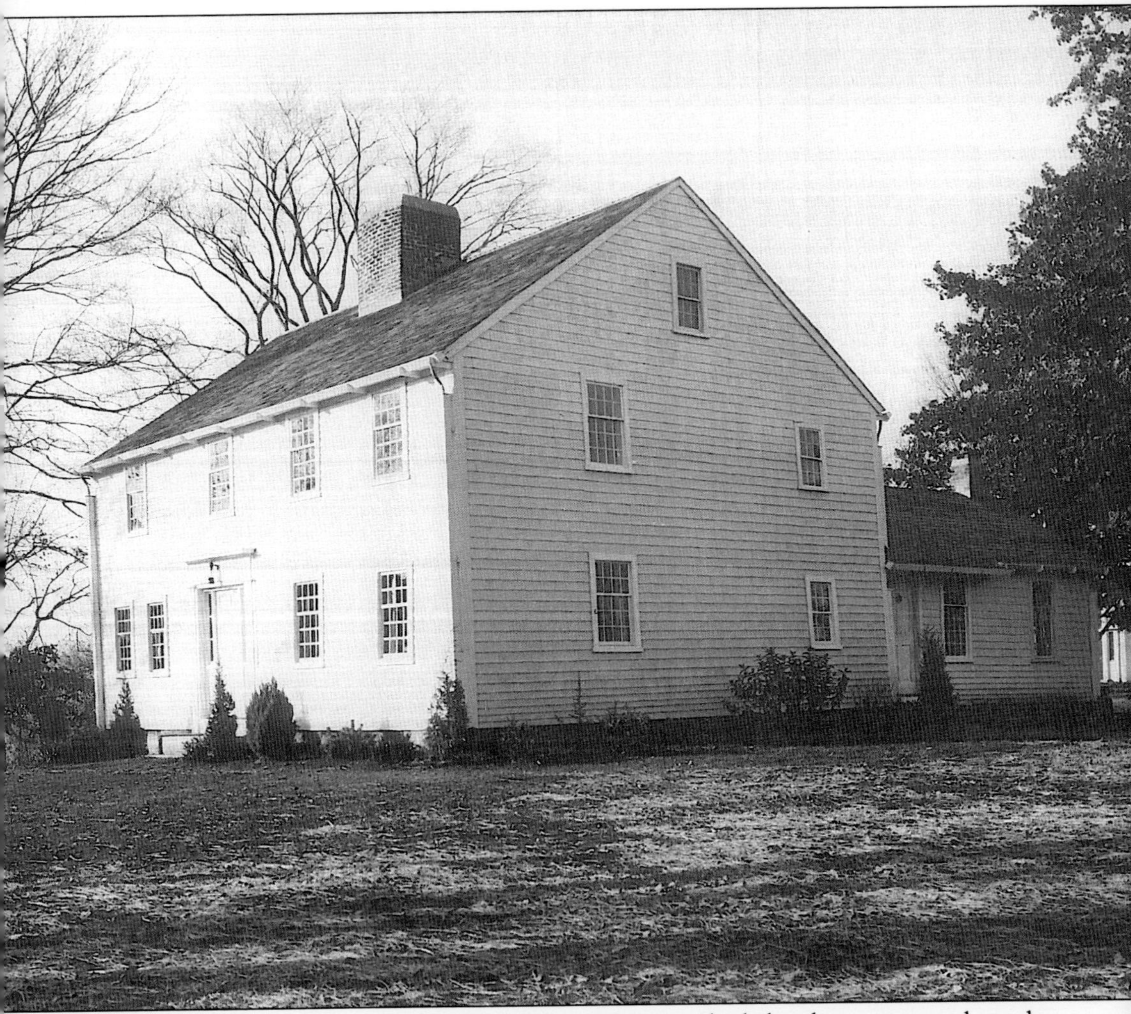

This is a more recent view of the Oliver Watson house, which has been preserved on the University of Rhode Island campus. The farmhouse was built in 1792 to replace a house belonging to Nathaniel Niles, which had burned. Oliver Watson and John H. Tefft were later occupants. The state continued to lease out the farm after the college was established, and it was restored in the 1960s and made into a museum. Everett Hopkins remembers his father, an electrician, rewiring the building at that time. (Courtesy Everett J. Hopkins.)

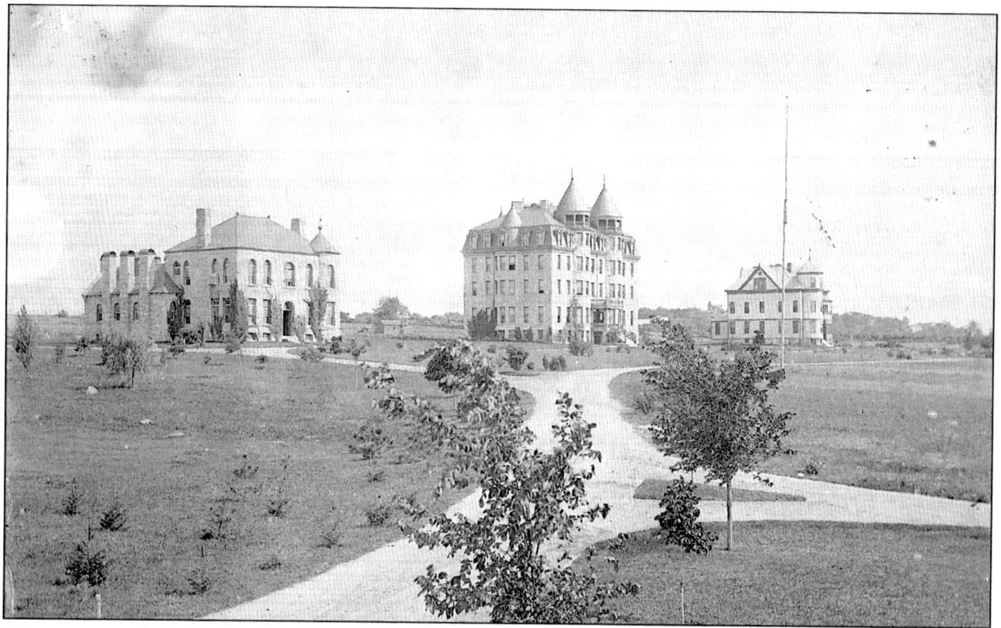

These were, from left to right, the first three buildings of the state college: Taft Laboratory, built for the Experiment Station; College Hall, which served as a dormitory, chapel, library, office, and academic center for the new college; and Boarding Hall, a dormitory. (Courtesy Pettaquamscutt Historical Society.)

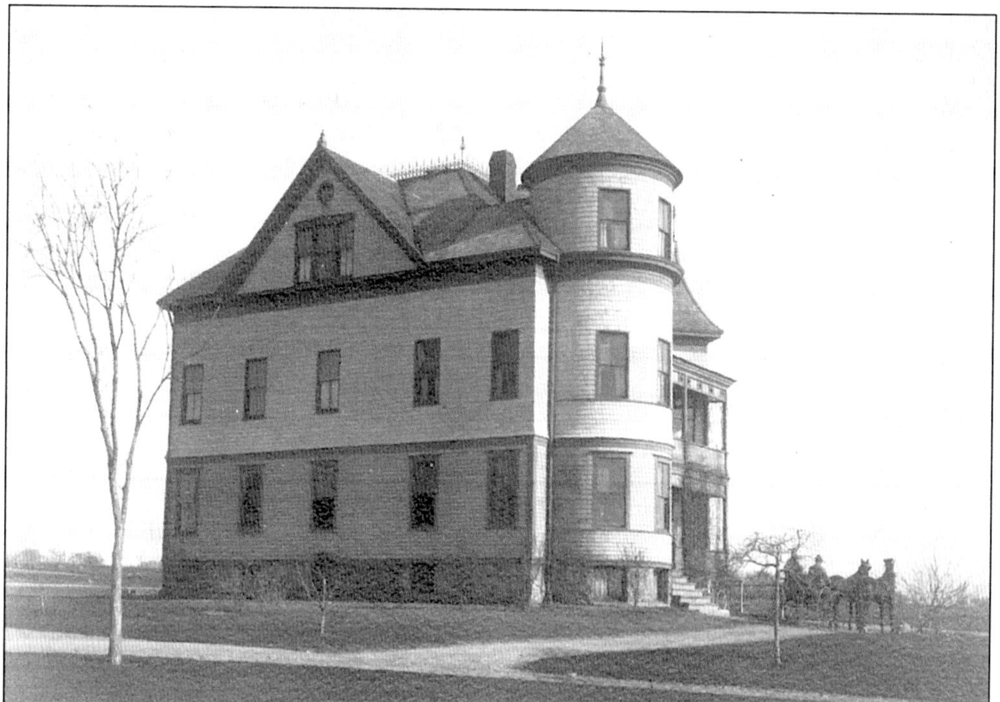

Boarding Hall, later called South Hall and at one time home to Rho Iota Kappa, opened to students on December 6, 1890. It stood where the campus administration building is now. (Courtesy Pettaquamscutt Historical Society.)

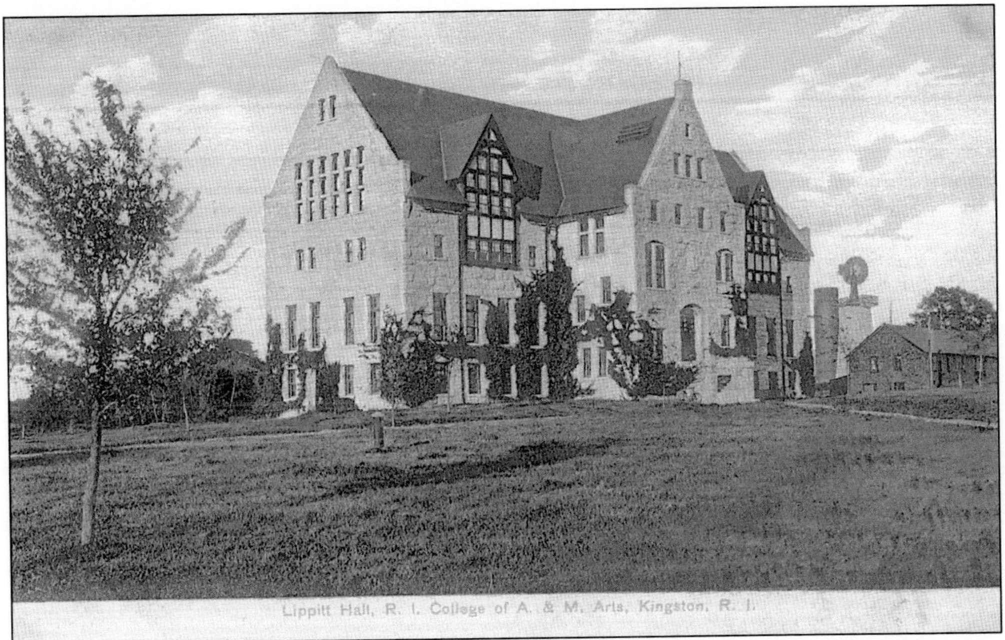

Lippitt Hall was built in 1897–98 and was named for Gov. Charles W. Lippitt. Originally, it was designed to be a drill hall and gymnasium, but those functions were eventually moved so that Lippitt could house the college's burgeoning engineering program. The engineering program became part of the curriculum the same year that Lippitt was built. (Courtesy Diane Smith.)

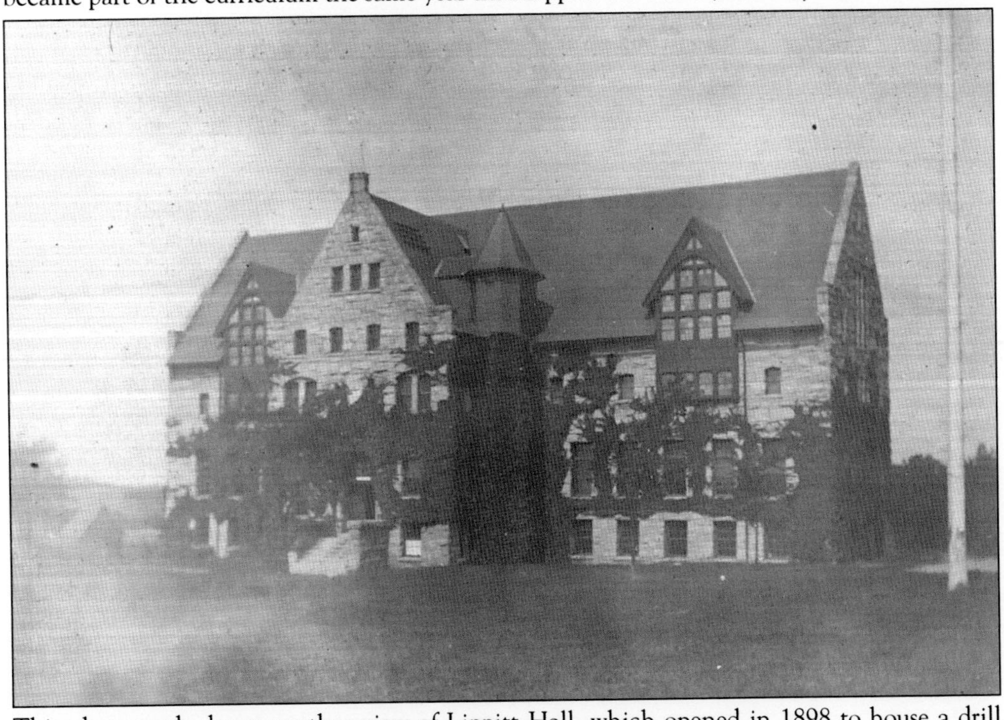

This photograph shows another view of Lippitt Hall, which opened in 1898 to house a drill hall, laboratories, classrooms, recitation rooms, a chapel, library, reading room, and a study for female commuter students. (Courtesy Pettaquamscutt Historical Society.)

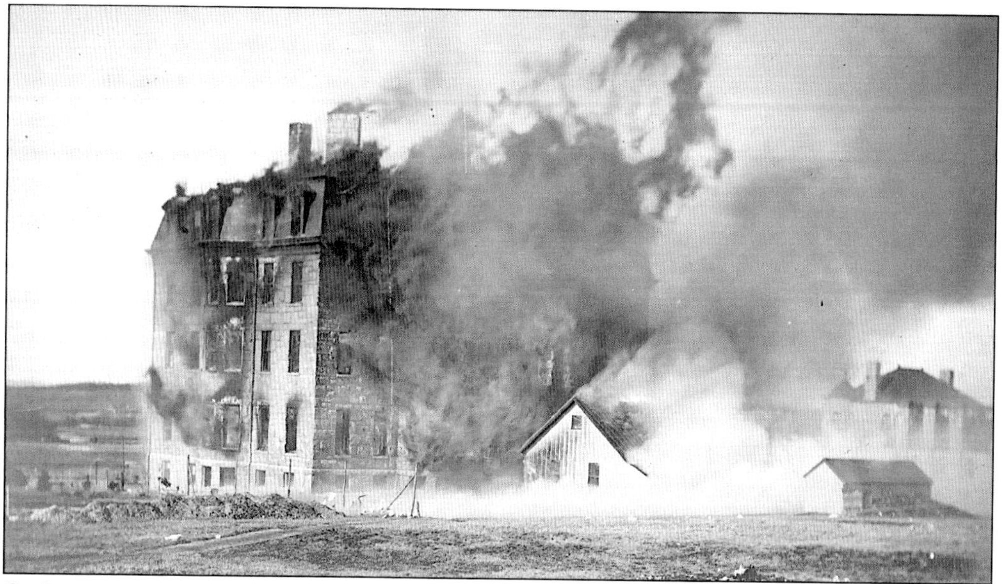

On January 27, 1895, most of the college's students were attending the Kingston Congregational Church when a fire broke out in College Hall. The fire started in a closet near a chimney. Within an hour it destroyed the building, while onlookers watched helplessly. Kingston had no fire department. The fledgling college had no insurance, and $12,000 worth of equipment was lost in the fire. The college quickly rebounded from the setback. Villagers opened their homes to students. Classes were held in the courthouse. By October of that year, College Hall had been rebuilt—renamed this time for Gov. John W. Davis. (Courtesy Pettaquamscutt Historical Society.)

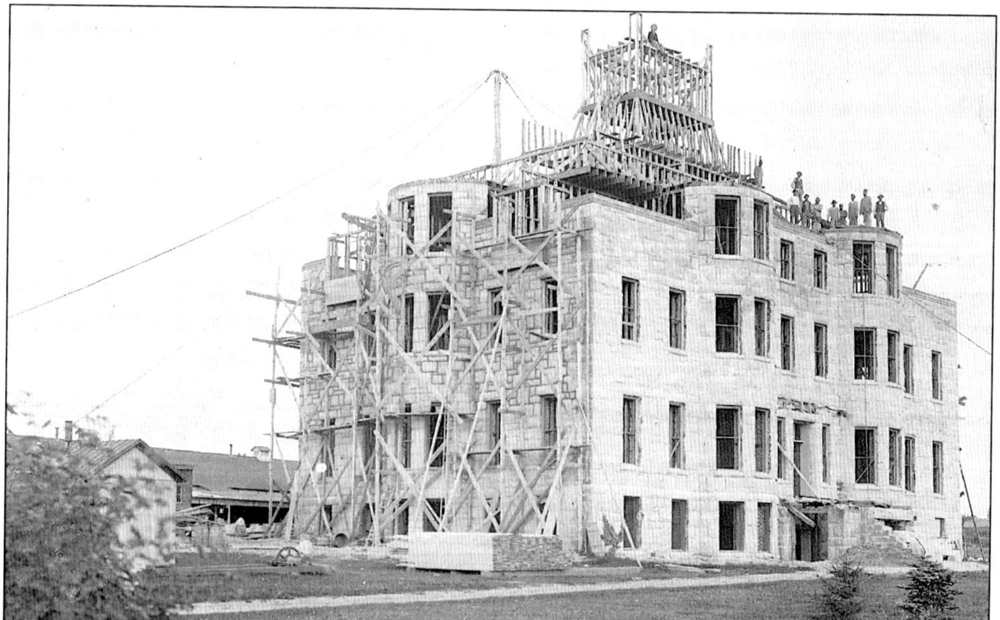

College Hall is shown during its reconstruction after the 1895 fire that destroyed the original building. The new building, named Davis Hall, had a slightly less elaborate, although no less attractive, design. (Courtesy Pettaquamscutt Historical Society.)

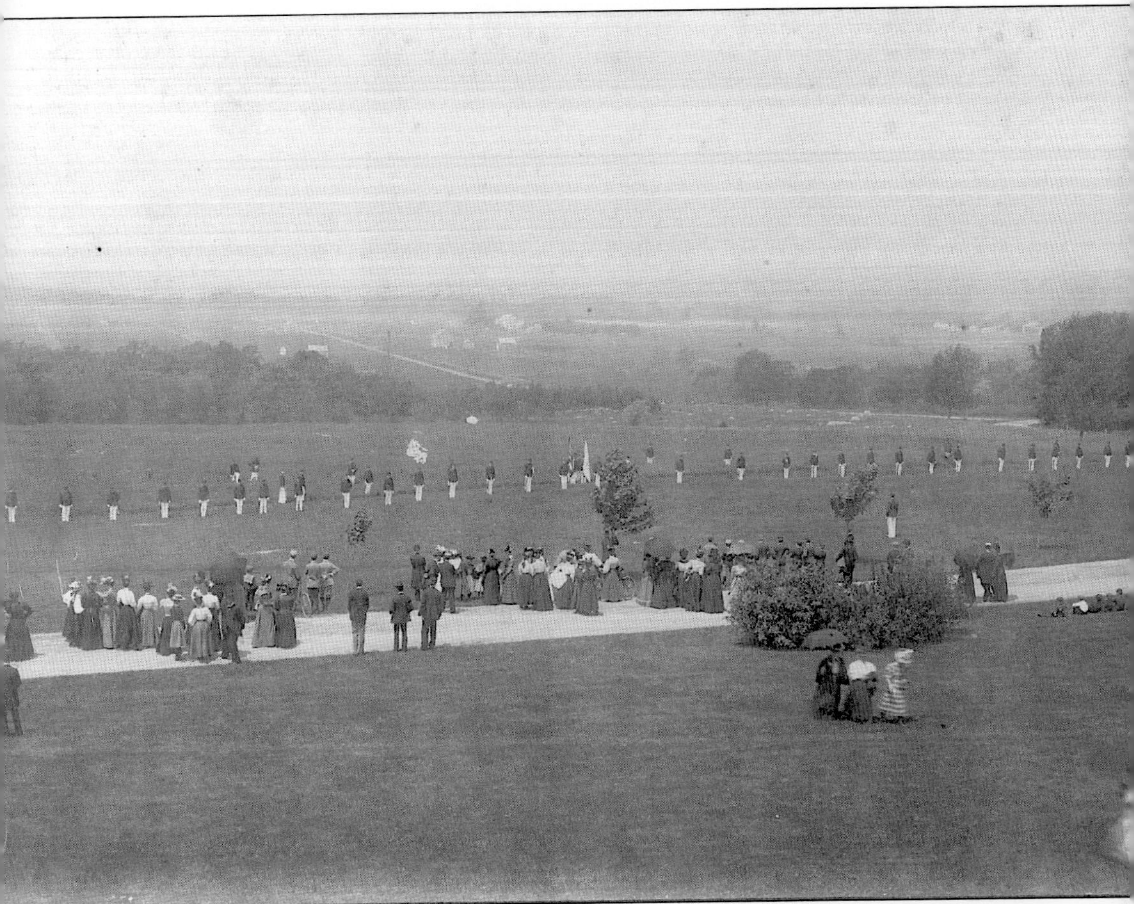

This photograph shows a military drill at the college, *c.* 1898. The view is looking west from Davis Hall. Most notable is the derrick that can be seen in the far center. From this site the quarry stones used to build College Hall, Davis Hall, Taft Hall, and Lippitt Hall were obtained. Oxen were used to haul the granite stones up the hill on a narrow-gauge track. (Courtesy Pettaquamscutt Historical Society.)

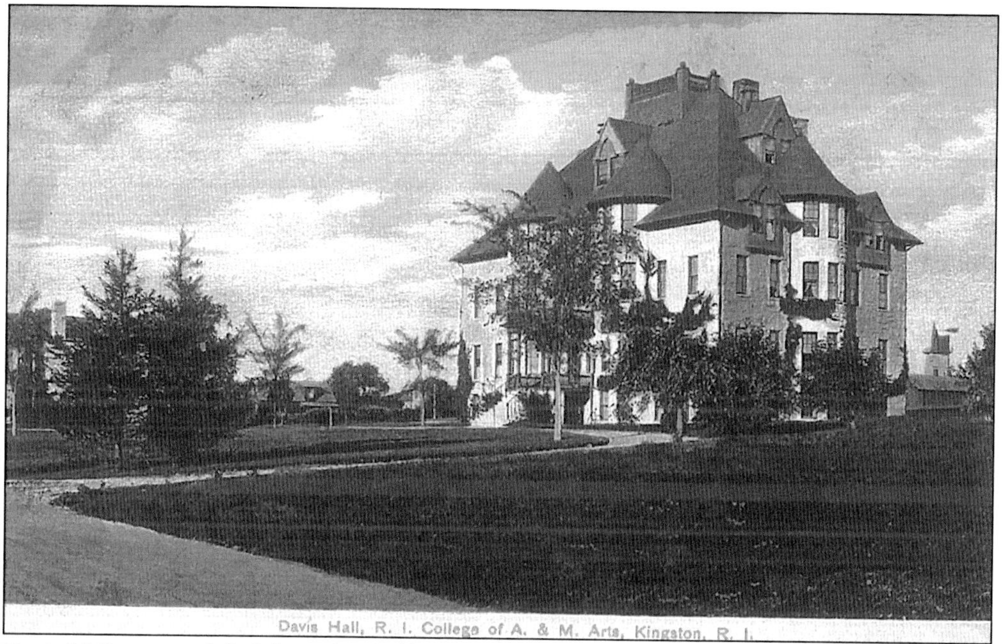

Davis Hall was modified from the College Hall design of Stone, Carpenter, and Willson and renovated in 1959 according to designs by Robinson, Green, and Beretta. It is one of the campus' most magnificent buildings. (Courtesy Pettaquamscutt Historical Society.)

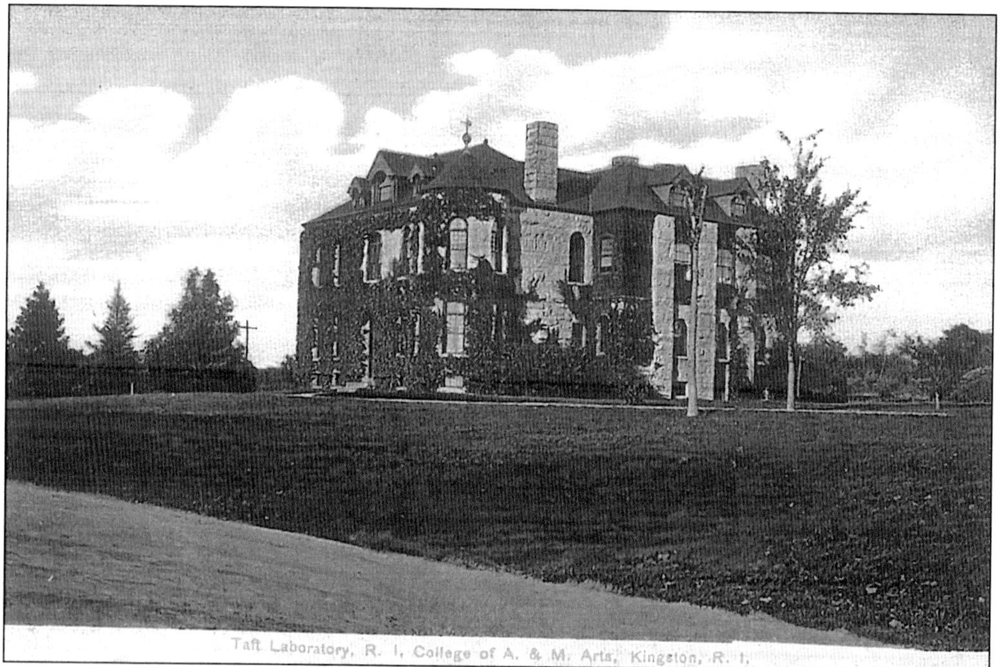

Taft Laboratory, built in 1889, was also designed by Stone, Carpenter, and Willson and was built with granite quarried from a ledge on the campus. (Courtesy Pettaquamscutt Historical Society.)

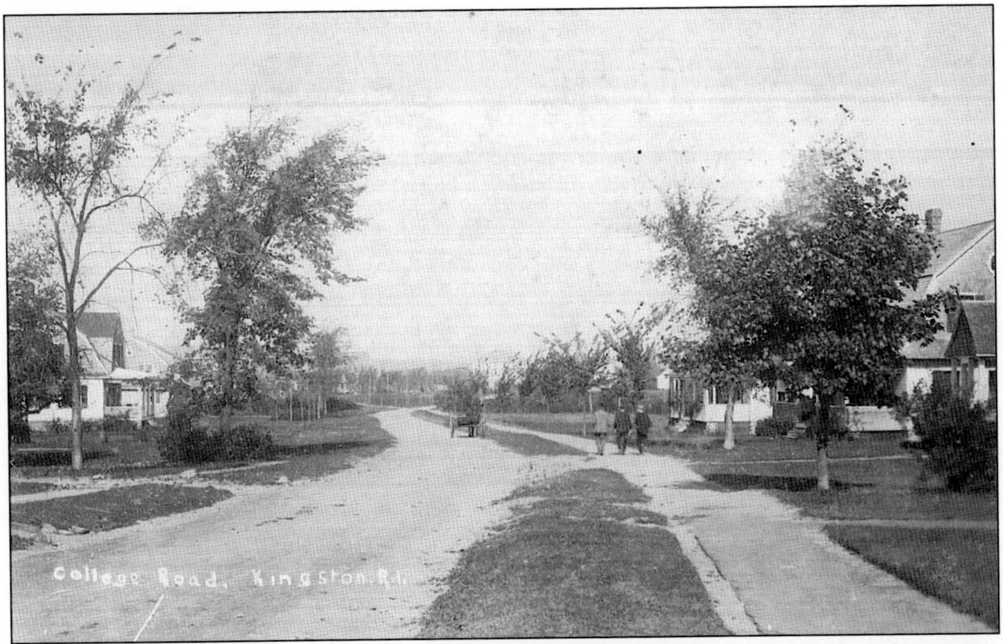

This tree-lined street was called the College Road or Upper Campus Road before the current name of Upper College Road was chosen. The street eventually became home to several faculty members. (Courtesy Pettaquamscutt Historical Society.)

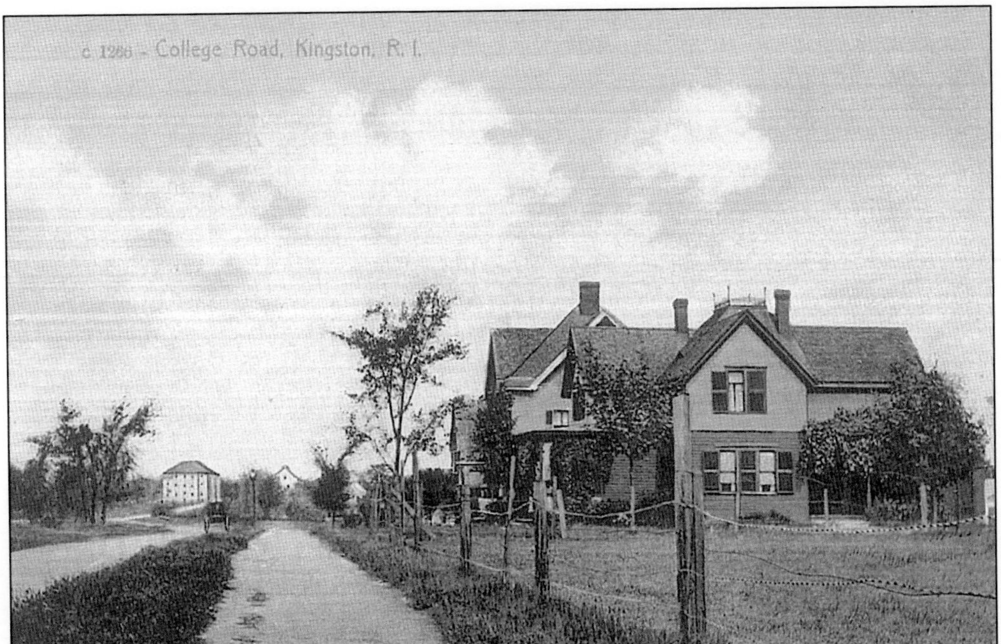

A campus building can be seen far in the distance in this 1903 postcard of Upper College Road. (Courtesy Elaine Pereira.)

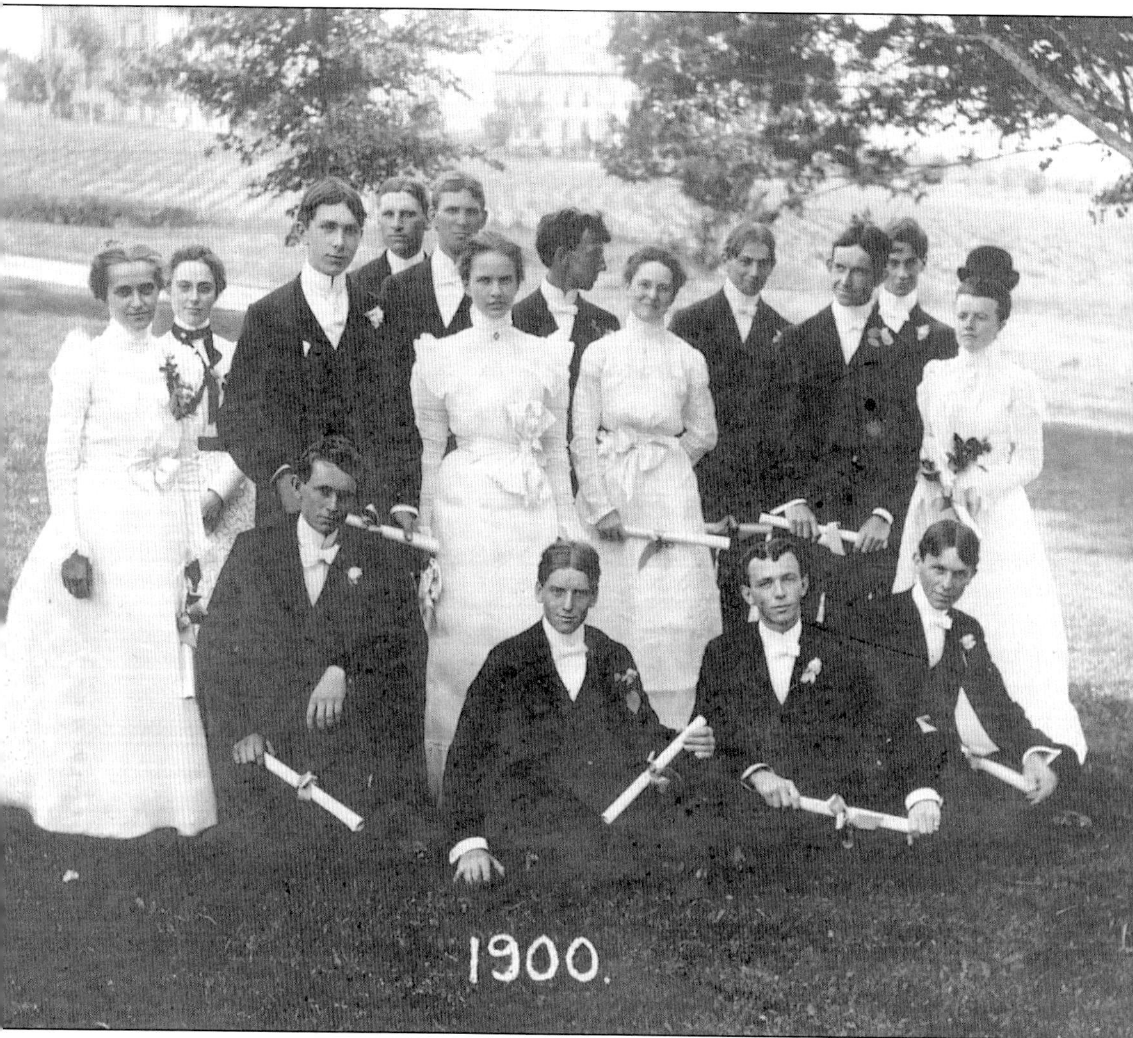

The class of 1900 was the seventh graduating class in the history of the Rhode Island College of Agricultural and Mechanic Arts. Commencement week began on Monday, June 18, with orations for the annual Lippitt Prizes and an evening faculty reception for community members at Lippitt Hall. On Tuesday, commencement was held at Lippitt Hall, with Governor William Gregory making his first official visit to the campus. Graduates read theses, and a luncheon was served after the ceremony. The *Narragansett Times* listed the following graduates with their hometowns: Maxon Brightman, Westerly; Charles Clarke Cross, Narragansett; John Raleigh Eldred, Kingston; Gertrude Sarah Fison, Peace Dale; Edith Goddard, Brockton, Massachusetts; Amos Langworthy Kenyon, Wood River Junction; Arthur Earle Munro, Quonochontaug; Ralph Nelson Soule, East Greenwich; Anthony Enoch Steere, Chepachet; Lenora Estelle Stillman, Kenyon; Bertha Douglas Tucker, Swansea Centre, Massachusetts; Charles Noyes Wheeler, Shannock; and Joseph Robert Wilson, Allenton. Receiving four-year certificates were Robert Joseph Sherman of Usquepaugh and Levi Eugene Wightman of South Scituate. Although there are 16 people in the photograph, the newspaper listed only 15 names. (Courtesy Pettaquamscutt Historical Society.)

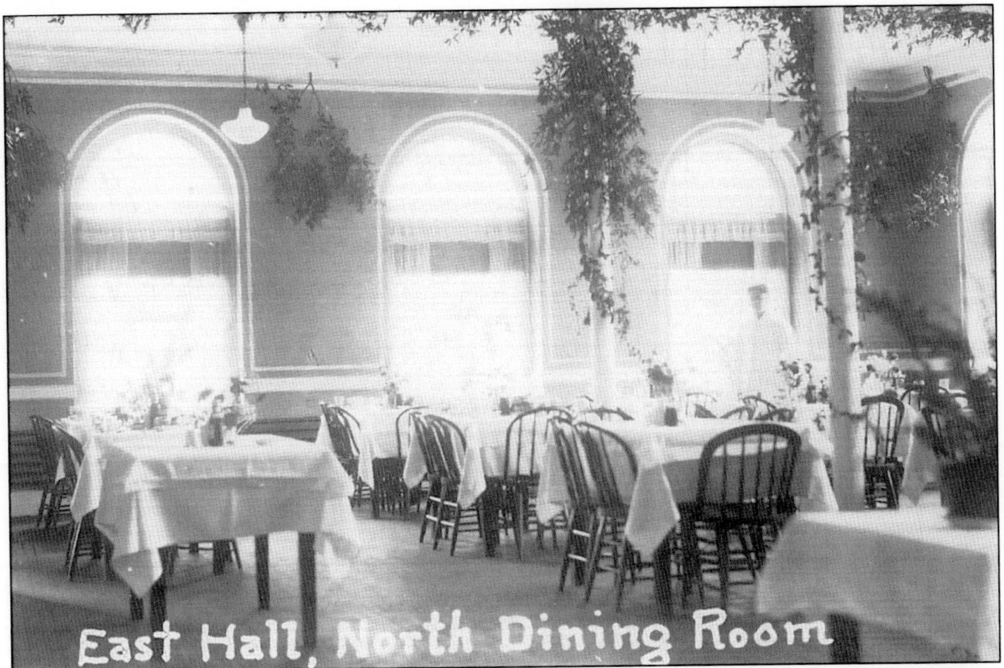

This is the dining room of East Hall. Located on the east side of the quadrangle, the three-story hall also contained a chapel, a kitchen, a social room, and 22 living suites. (Courtesy Diane Smith.)

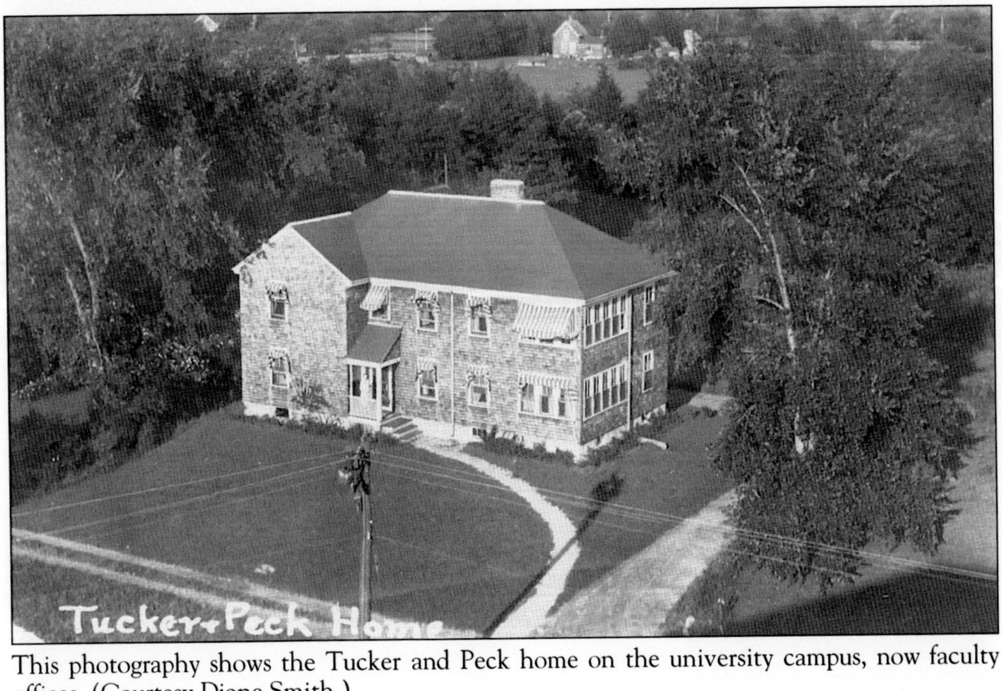

This photography shows the Tucker and Peck home on the university campus, now faculty offices. (Courtesy Diane Smith.)

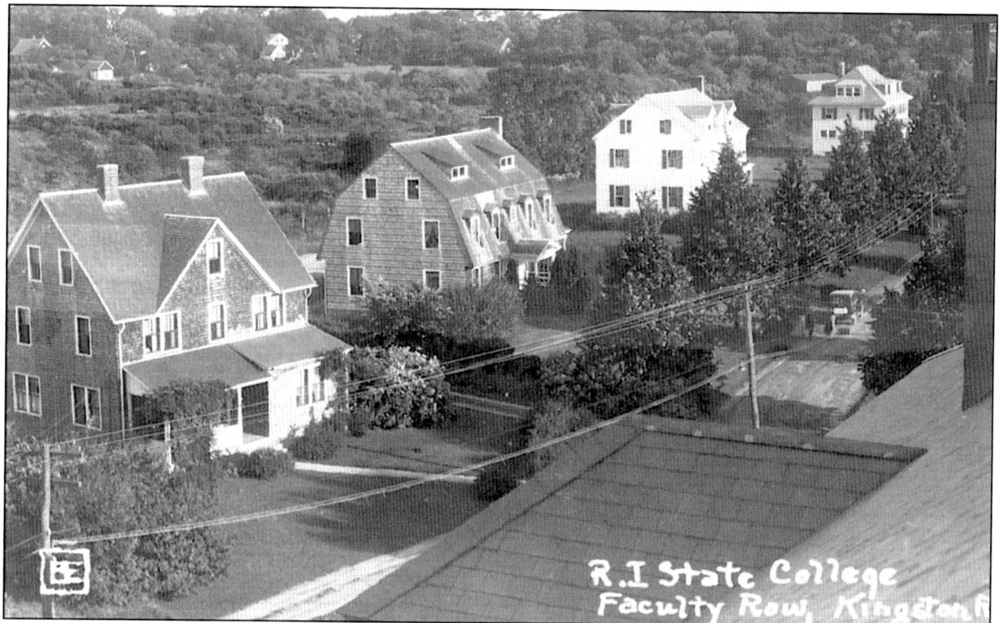

Faculty homes, some in the Dutch Colonial style, were built near campus as the college began to expand. (Courtesy Diane Smith.)

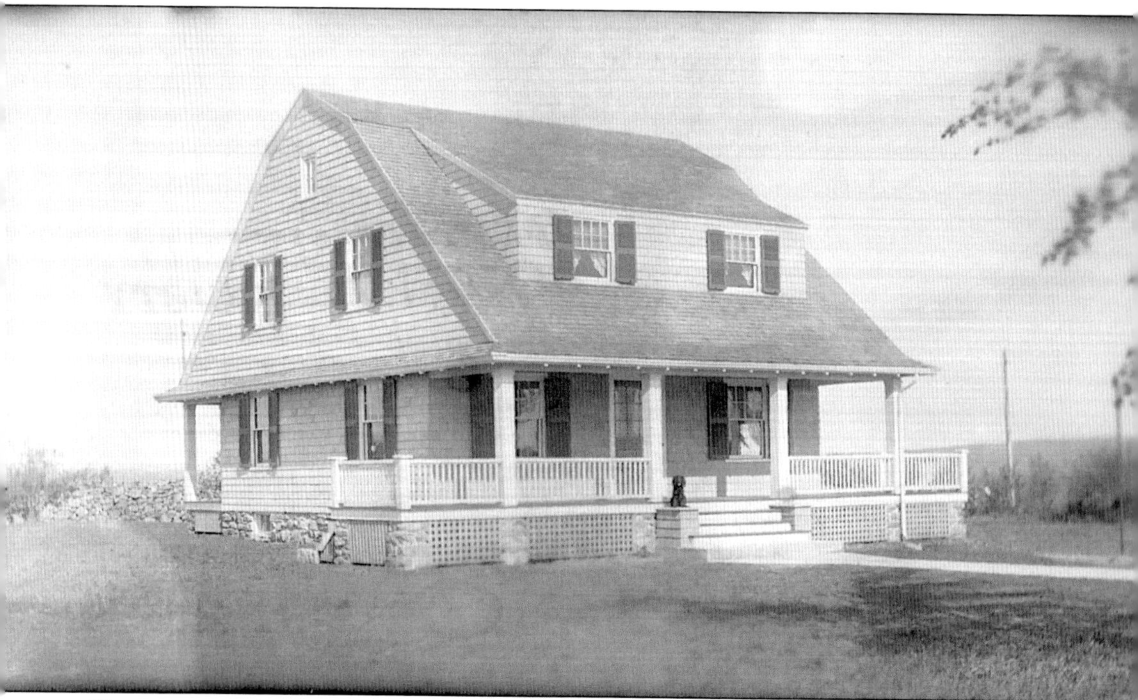

This appears to be the home of the late Francis H. Horn (1908–1998), president emeritus of the University of Rhode Island. Horn traveled widely, although he returned to live in Kingston in 1985 after serving as president of several institutions. (Courtesy Pettaquamscutt Historical Society.)

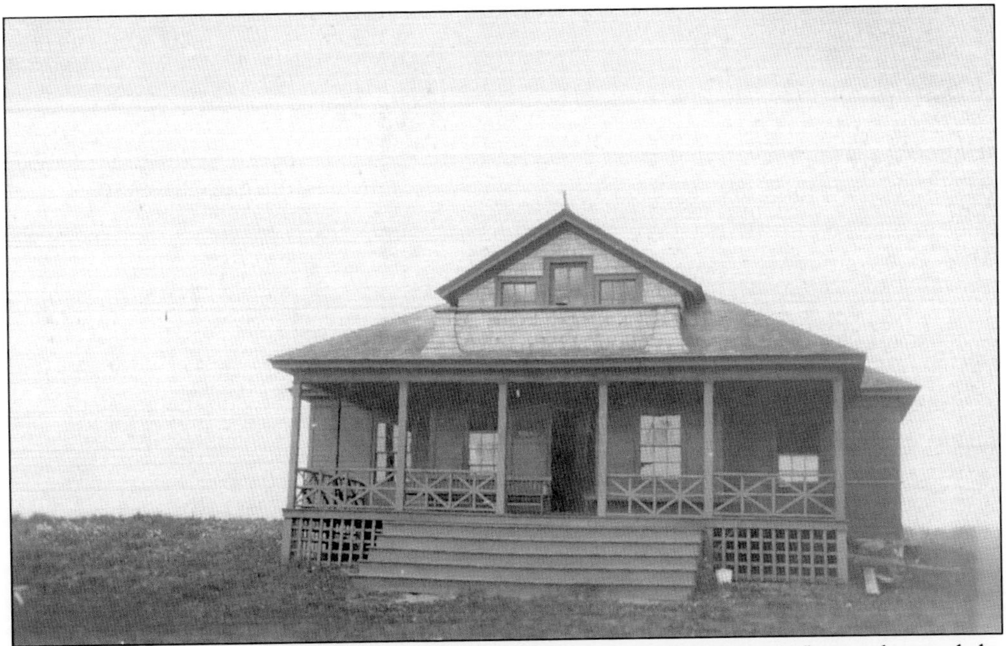

This is the athletic house at the state college. Athletics at the college were influenced strongly by two men, famed basketball coach Frank W. Keaney and coach and former Olympian Frederick D. Tootell. (Courtesy Pettaquamscutt Historical Society.)

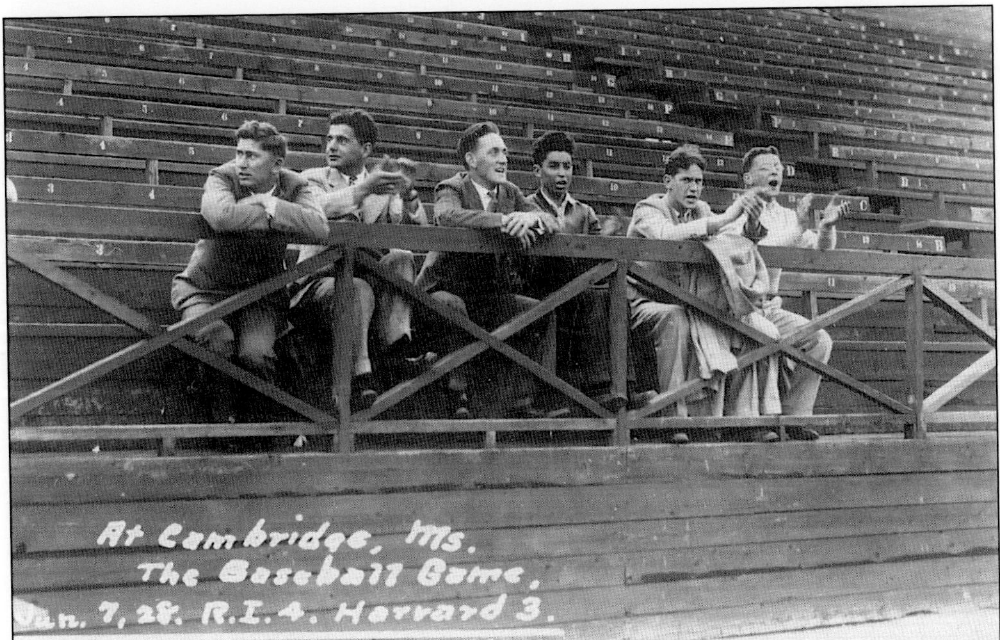

Few fans made the trip to Cambridge to watch the Rhode Island State College baseball team trounce Harvard, 4-3, in 1928. Despite the small cheering section, 1928 was "the best year of the decade" for the team, reported historian Herman F. Eschenbacher, who wrote that the players lost only to Colby College that year. (Courtesy Diane Smith.)

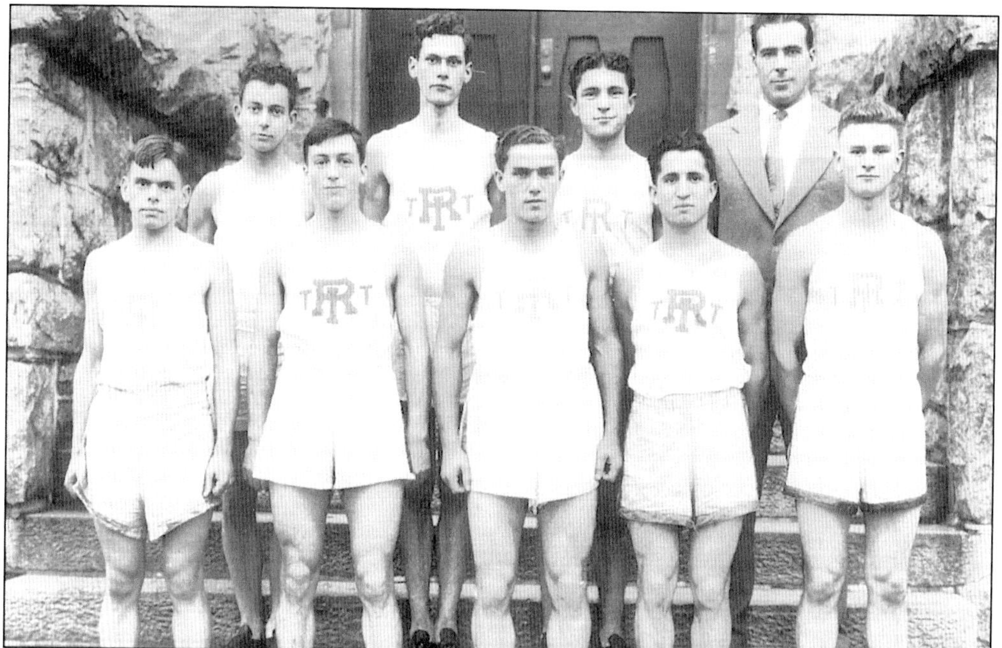

The track team at Rhode Island State College for 1927–28 ran for coach Frederick D. Tootell, a former Olympian who came to the college in 1925 and soon built a strong track program. Herman F. Eschenbacher, in his history of the college, reported that the team won 28 of its 33 meets between 1931 and 1939. (Courtesy Diane Smith.)

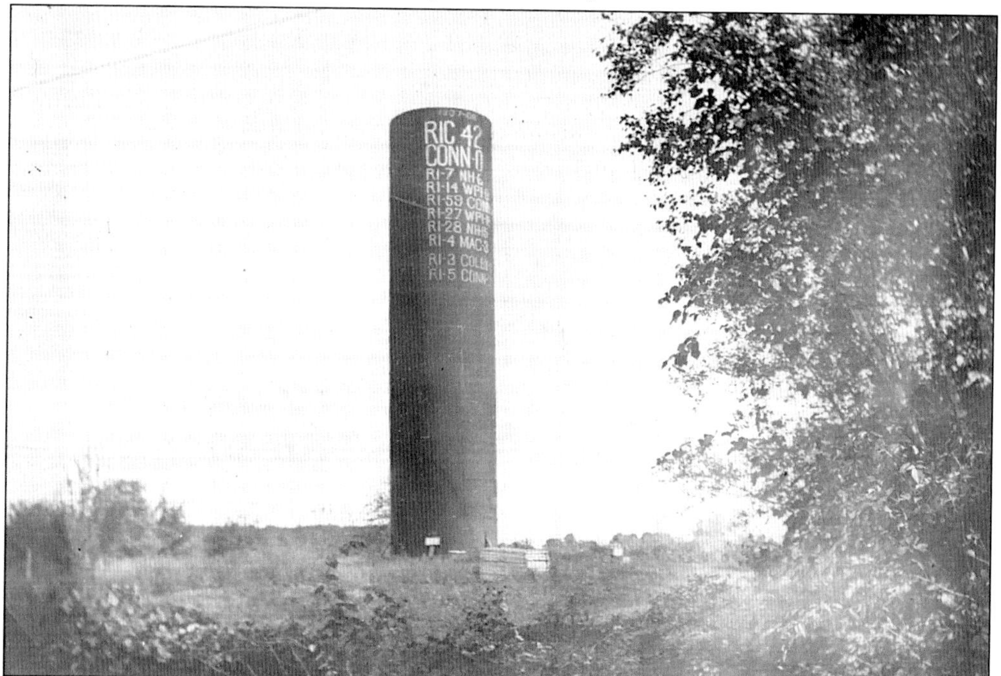

Rhode Island State College kept score on this tower, particularly noting a 42-0 victory over arch rival Connecticut. The sport being recorded is probably football. (Courtesy Pettaquamscutt Historical Society.)

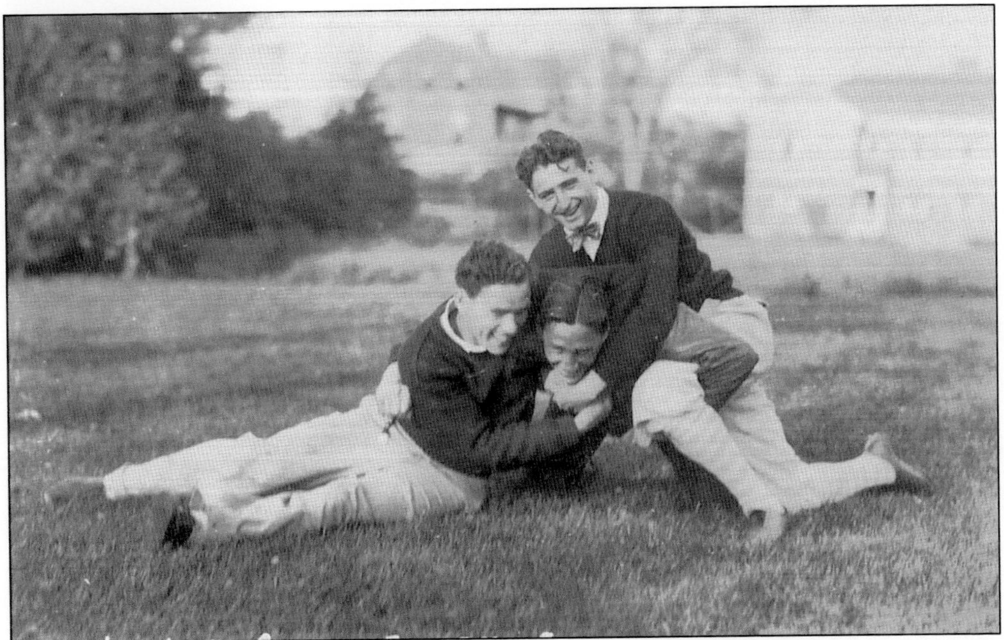

This moment of campus fun was captured in 1928. (Courtesy Diane Smith.)

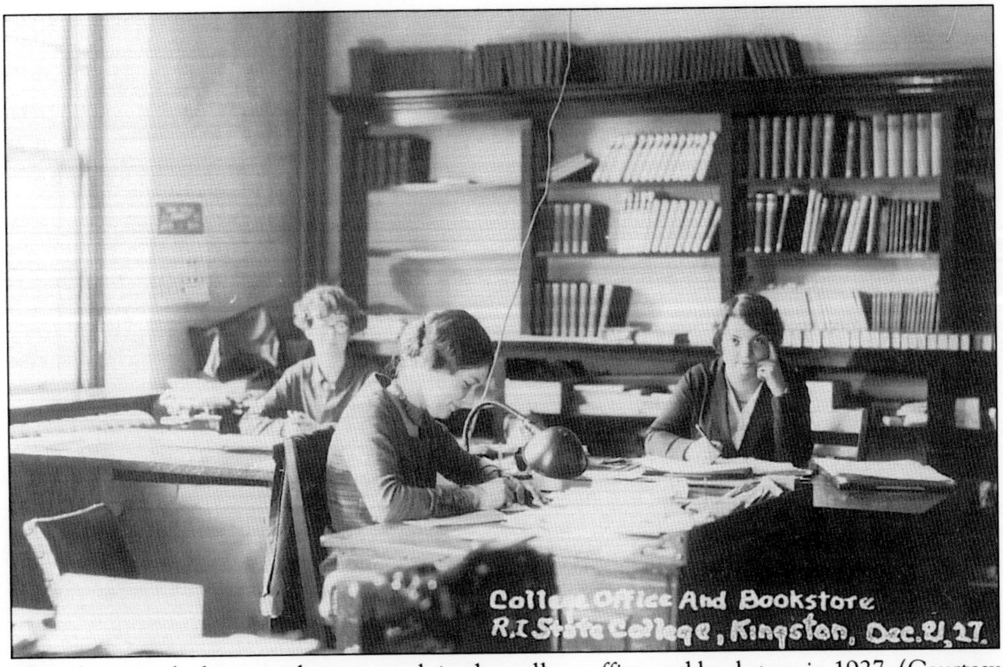

This photograph shows students at work in the college office and bookstore in 1927. (Courtesy Diane Smith.)

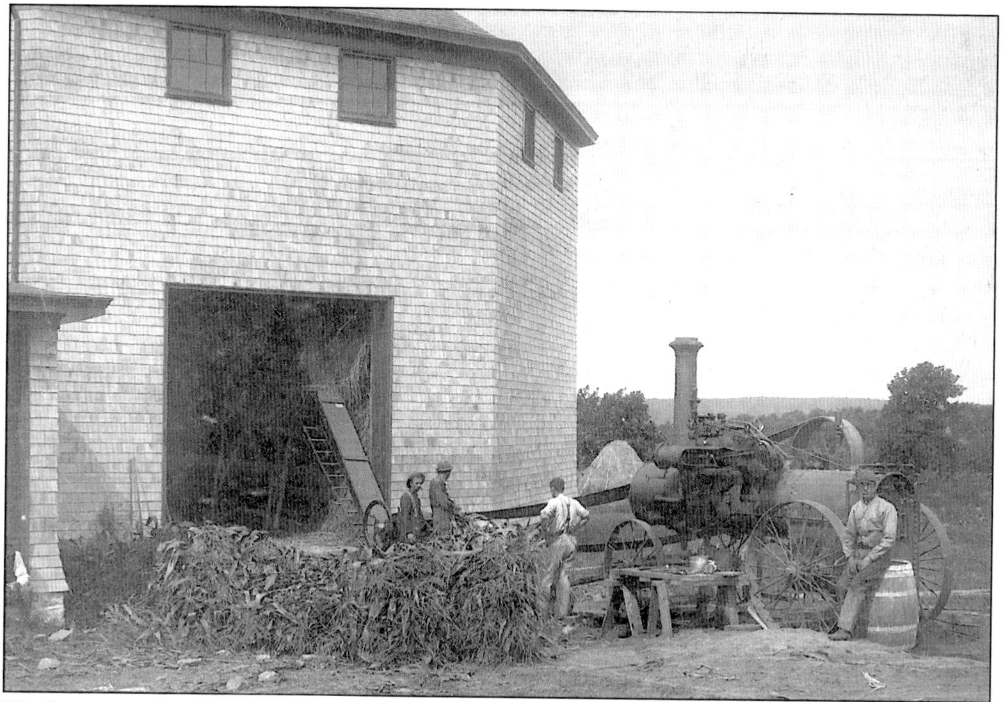

Workers put silage in the old campus dairy barn. Despite its roots as an agricultural school, Rhode Island State College and then the University of Rhode Island gradually moved away from keeping dairy cows, chickens, and other animals, concentrating instead on turf grass, oceanography, and aquaculture. (Courtesy Pettaquamscutt Historical Society.)

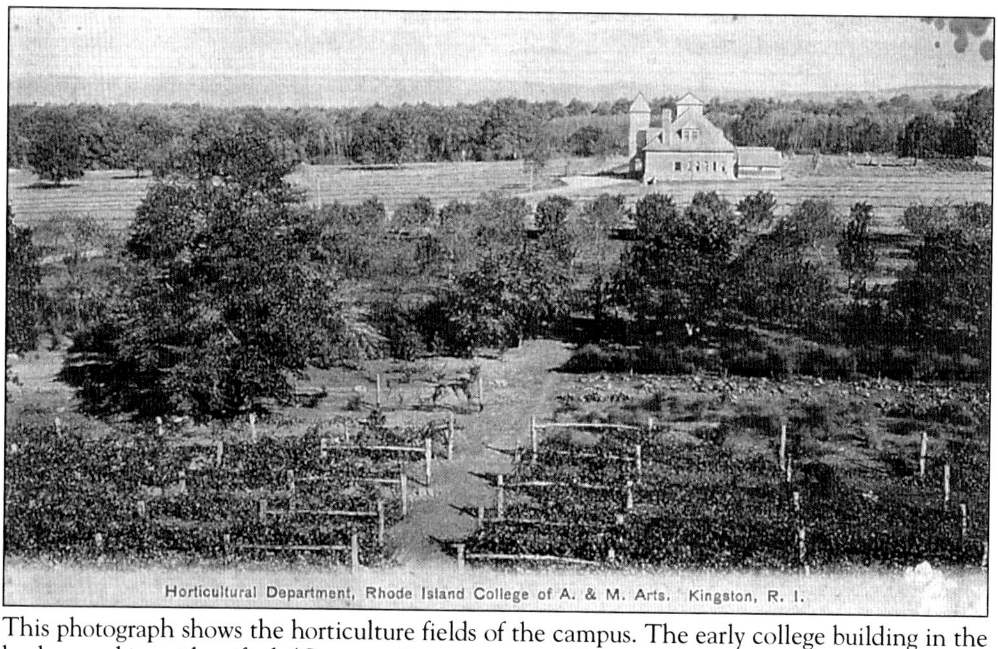

This photograph shows the horticulture fields of the campus. The early college building in the background is unidentified. (Courtesy Pettaquamscutt Historical Society.)

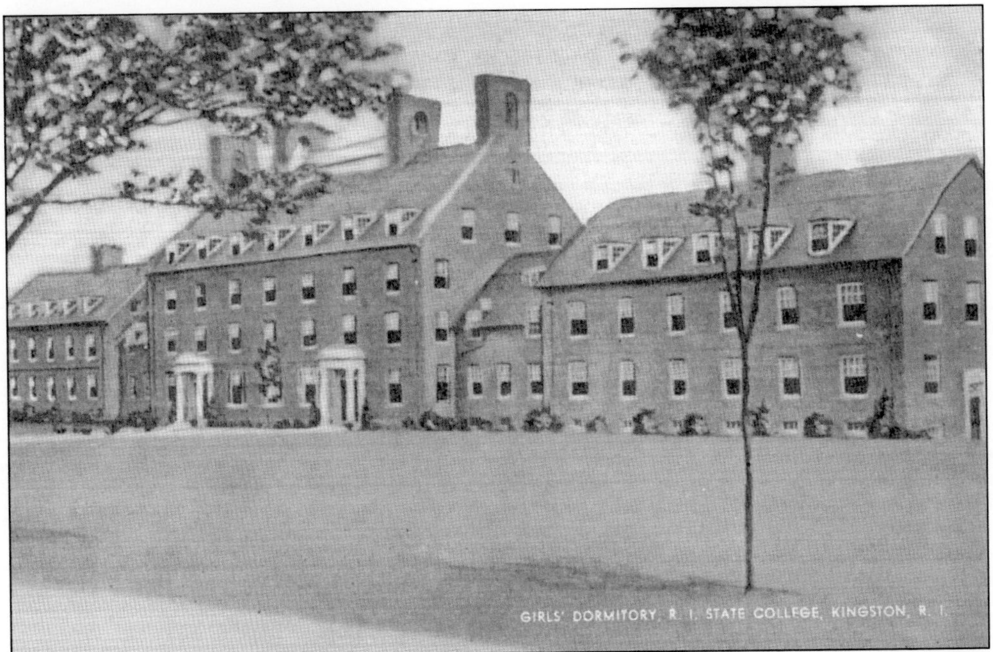

Eleanor Roosevelt Hall was built in 1938 as a women's dormitory. It was named for the first lady. The dormitory was built to accommodate 90 women. (Courtesy Diane Smith.)

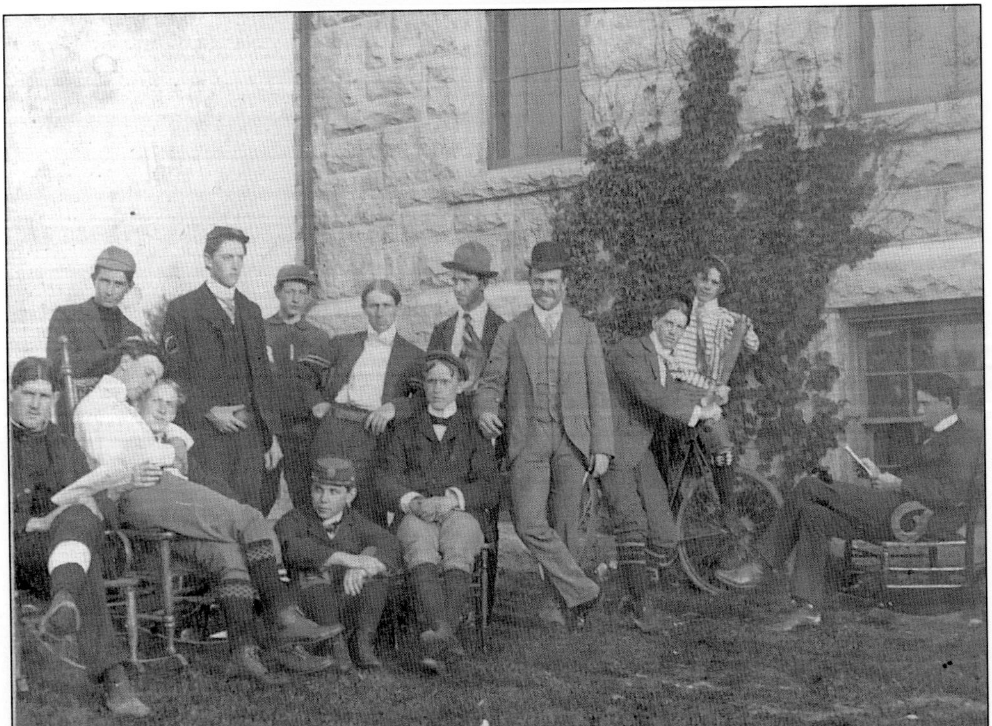

Students gather in front of Davis Hall. The ivy already had begun to grow up the side of the building's granite walls. (Courtesy Pettaquamscutt Historical Society.)

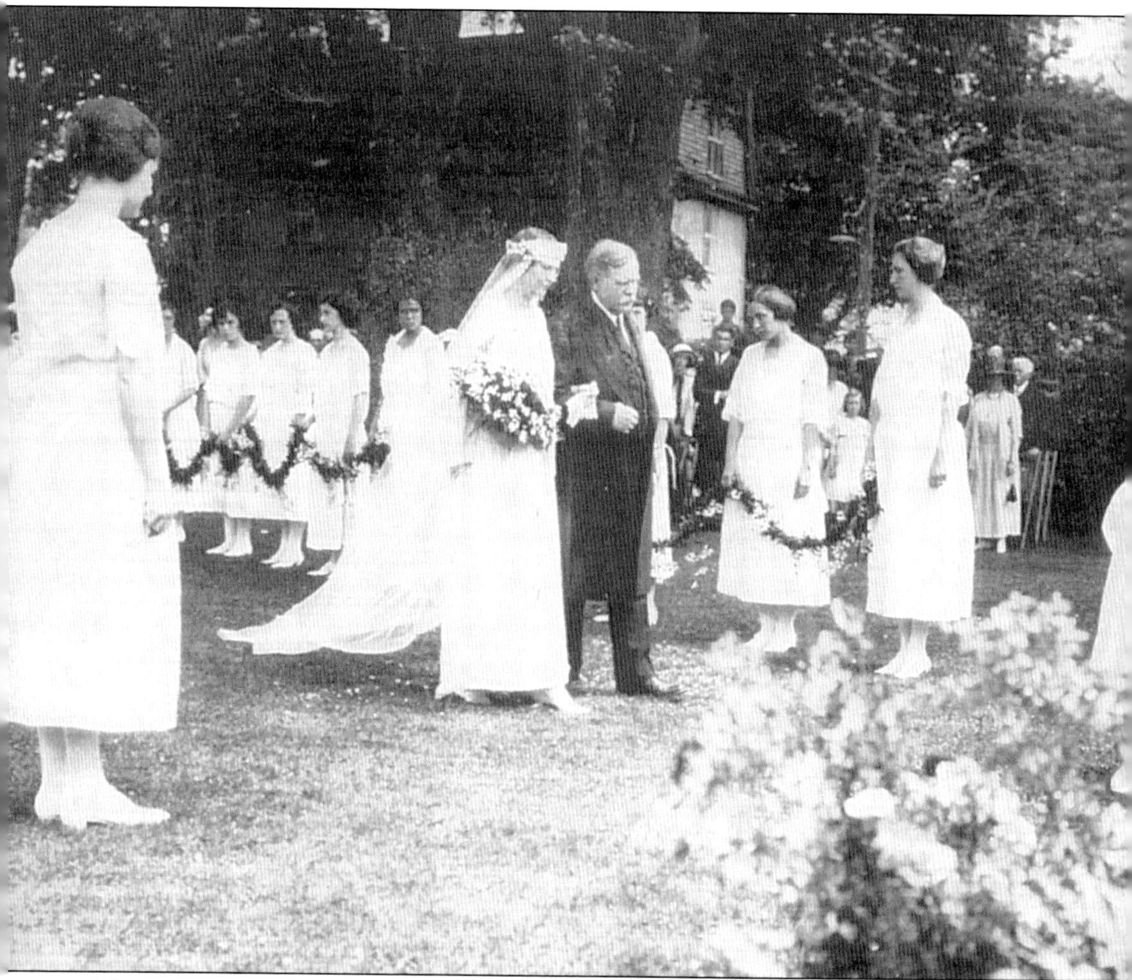

The campus was dressed to the nines in June 1923 for the wedding of Mildred Edwards, the daughter of college president Howard Edwards. The bride wore embroidered white crepe and was escorted to the altar by a "guard of honor composed of college girls from [her] national sorority, Sigma Kappa of the Rhode Island State College," the *Narragansett Times* reported. Miss Edwards, a 1920 graduate of the school, was wed to Hobart Wadsworth Spring of Braintree, Massachusetts, and was given away by her father. Among her attendants was Helena Kinney of Kingston. The *Times* reported that the lawn was decorated with evergreen, lilacs, and shrubbery under the direction of Professor Wilden of the college greenhouses. Among the bride's gifts was $200 in gold from the faculty. Sadly, the marriage was short-lived, as Mildred Edwards Spring died in childbirth in 1924. (Courtesy Betty Faella.)

Eight

West Kingston

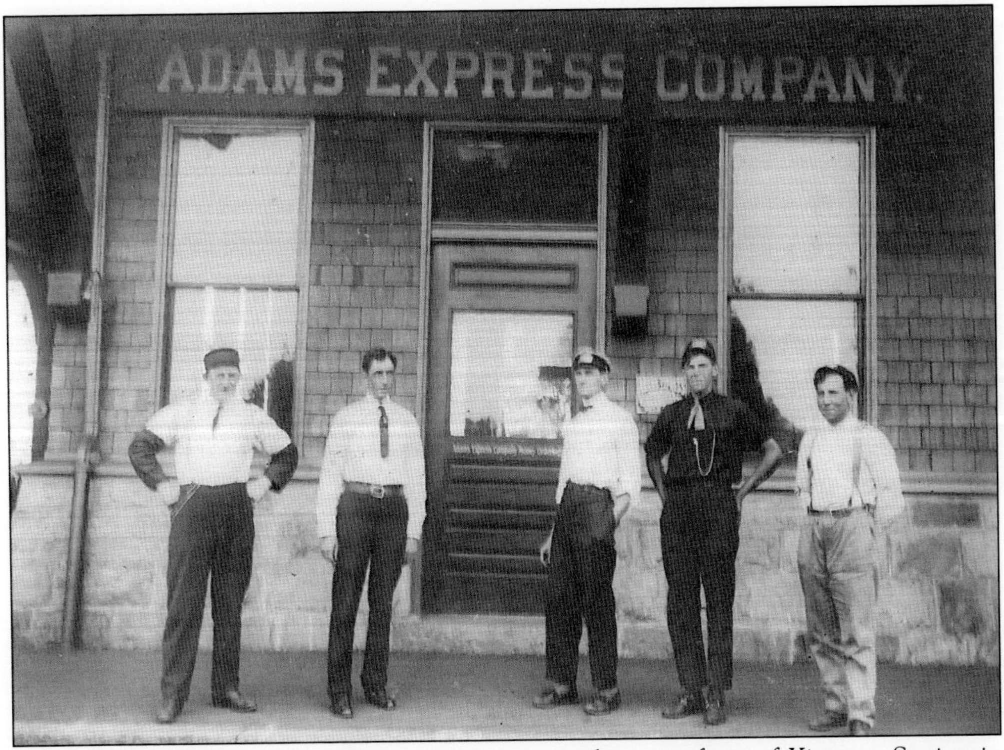

The employees of the Adams Express Company are shown in front of Kingston Station in West Kingston. The railroad passed west of the village in 1837. (Courtesy Pettaquamscutt Historical Society.)

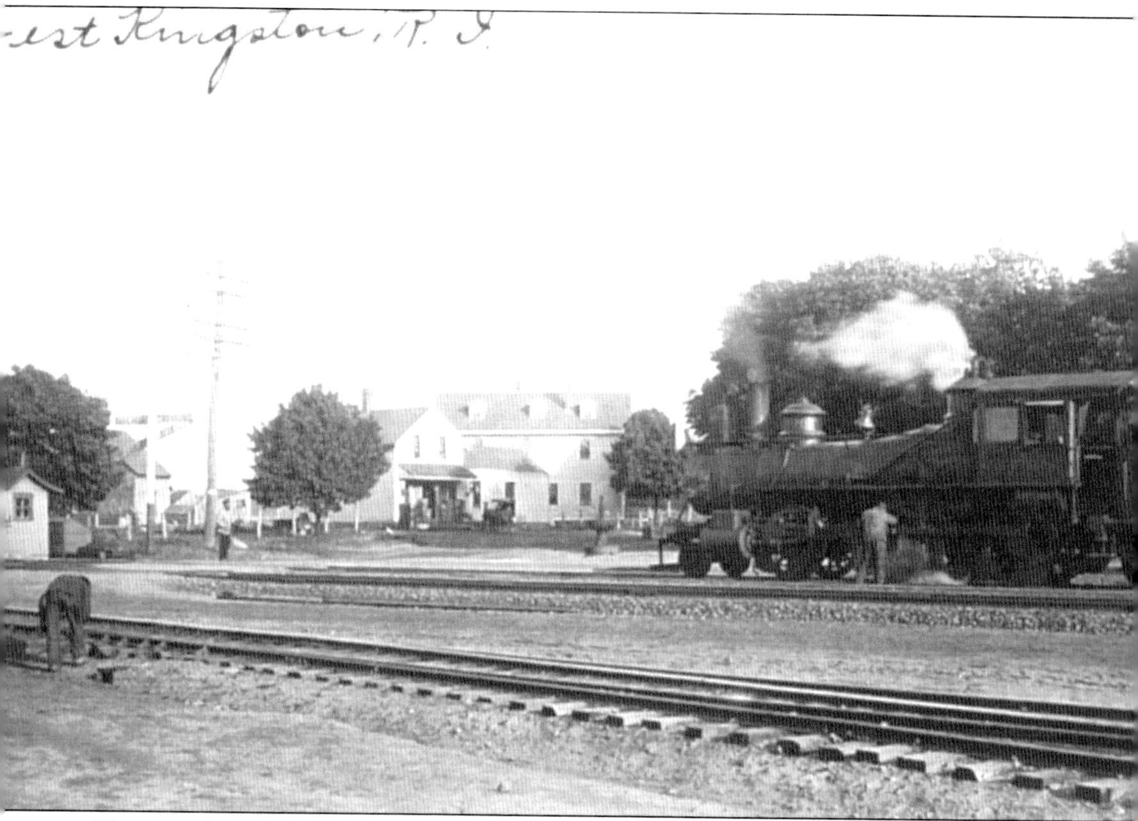

This rare photograph shows what is now the intersection of Kingstown Road (Route 138) and the railway lines before a bridge was built over the railroad tracks. A settlement of houses sprang up near Waites Corner Road as a result of the railroad's coming in 1837. In his history of Washington County, J.R. Cole reported that Benjamin Watson built a trading store nearby soon after the railroad was built. Cole also stated that John A. Woodmansie (probably Woodmansee) and O.C. Howard were still conducting "a lively business" in a nearby building in 1889. J.B. Watson and J. Henry Wells built a store where first the Sherman family and later the Tuckers conducted business. (Courtesy Elaine Pereira.)

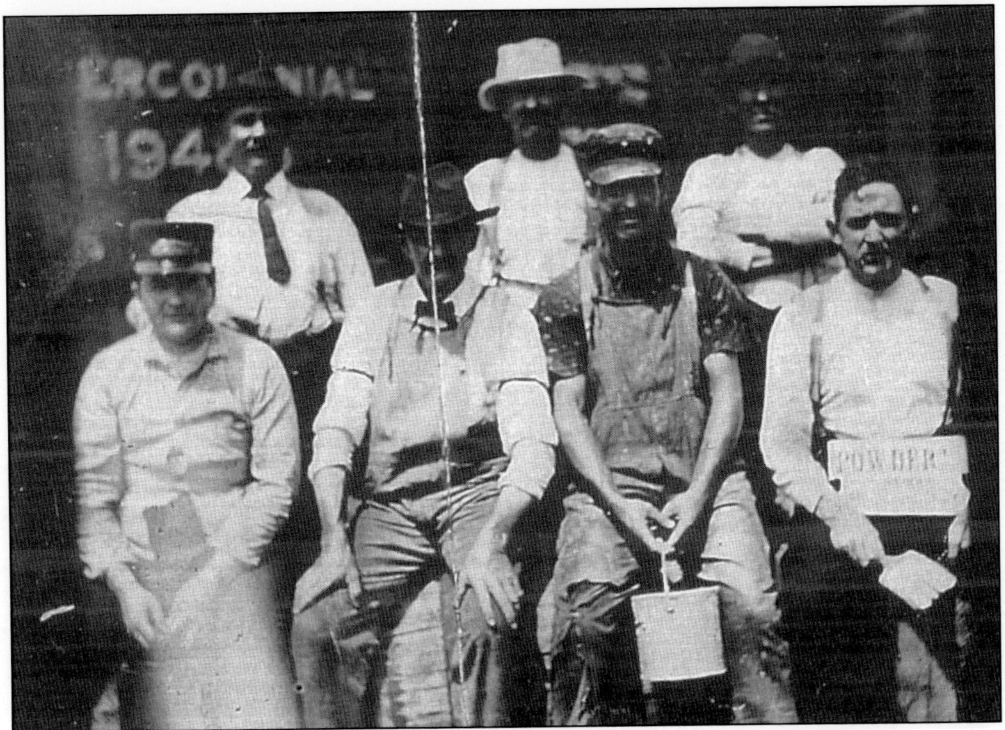

Charlie Stafford, the agent at West Kingston Station, is shown sitting on the left, with George L. Young, signalman, on the right. Both were from West Kingston. This photograph was taken at the railroad station in 1904. (Courtesy Pettaquamscutt Historical Society.)

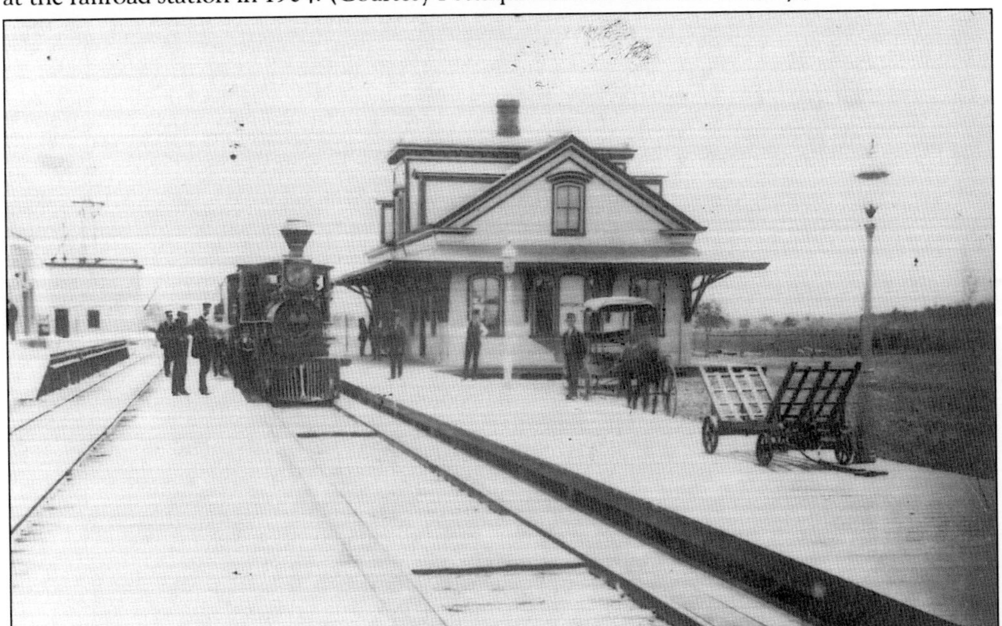

A train pulls into Kingston Station in West Kingston in this undated photograph. Note what appears to be a handcar on the right. (Courtesy Pettaquamscutt Historical Society.)

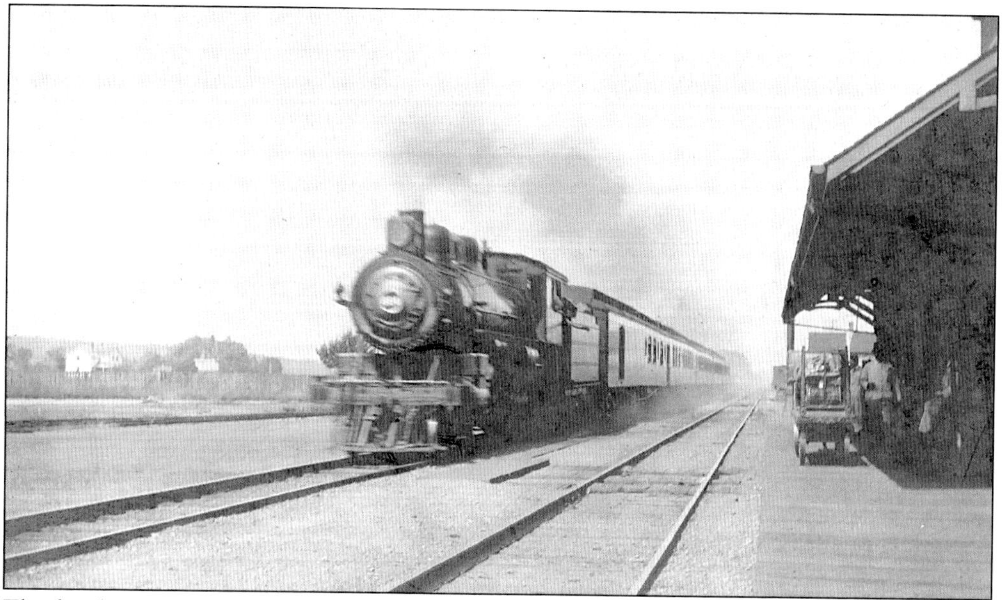

The five-hour train pulls in from Boston, in this photograph by George D. Crandall Sr. Today, with electrification, that same route takes one fifth the time. (Courtesy Pettaquamscutt Historical Society.)

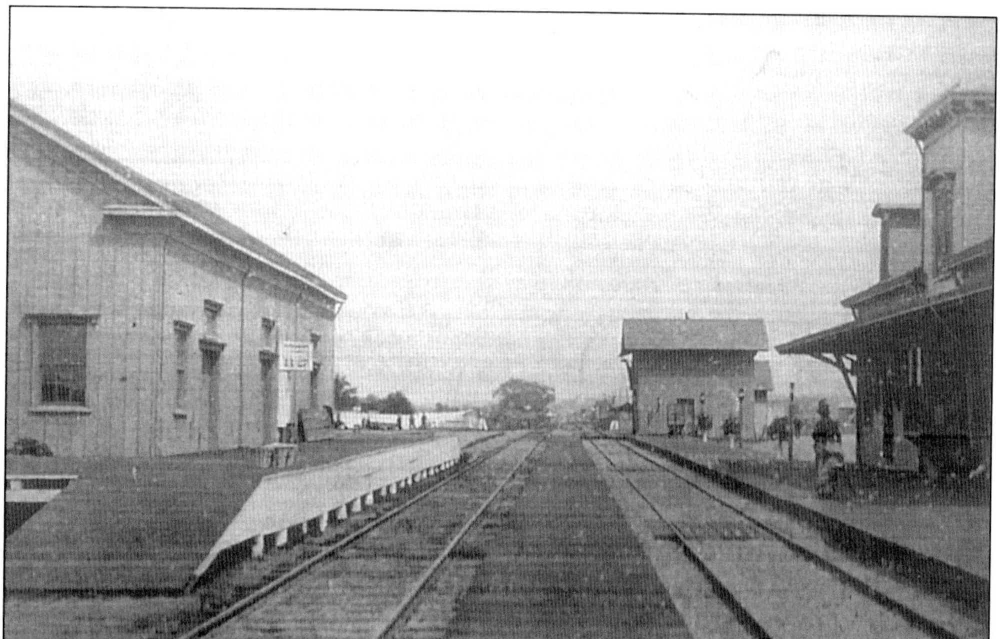

This view of the station shows some of its other buildings. The station was built in 1876 slightly south of the first station, which was built near Waites Corner Road. Kingstown Road did not exist when the railroad came through West Kingston in 1837. (Courtesy Pettaquamscutt Historical Society.)

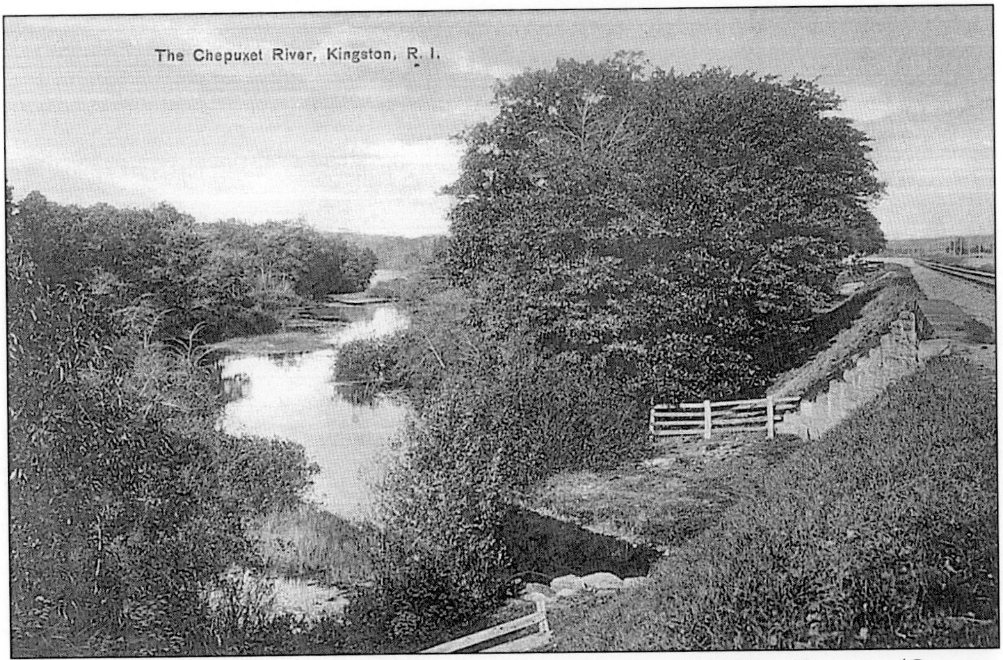

The Chipuxet River is shown where it flows near the railroad tracks in West Kingston. (Courtesy Elaine Pereira.)

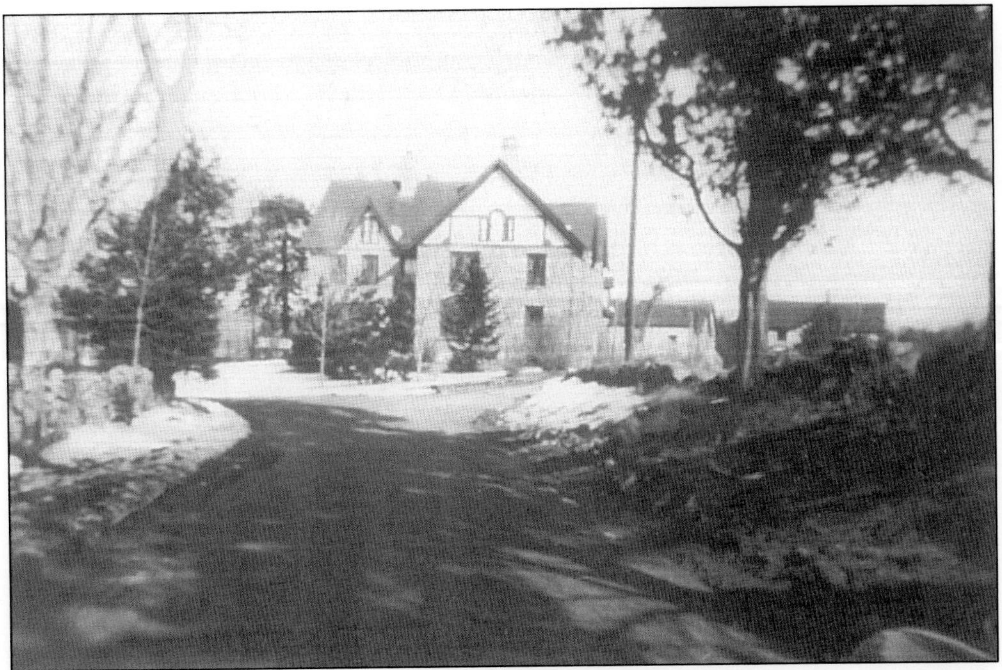

Built in 1889 on Liberty Lane, the Clark or Clarke homestead was home to John G. Clarke II, a State Supreme Court clerk from 1865 to 1883 and a member of the Rhode Island General Assembly. Originally a gambrel-roofed farm stood on the site. (Courtesy Everett J. Hopkins.)

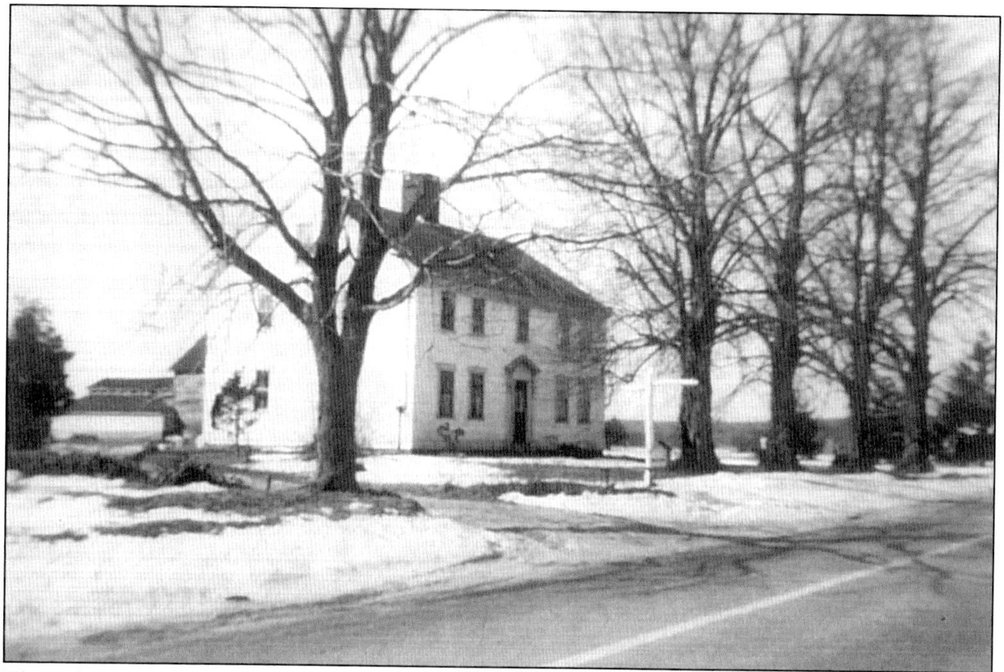

The Thomas Hopkins homestead on Usquepaugh Road (Route 138) was home to one of the original Providence Plantation owners. His descendants John and Isaac also lived here. (Courtesy Everett J. Hopkins.)

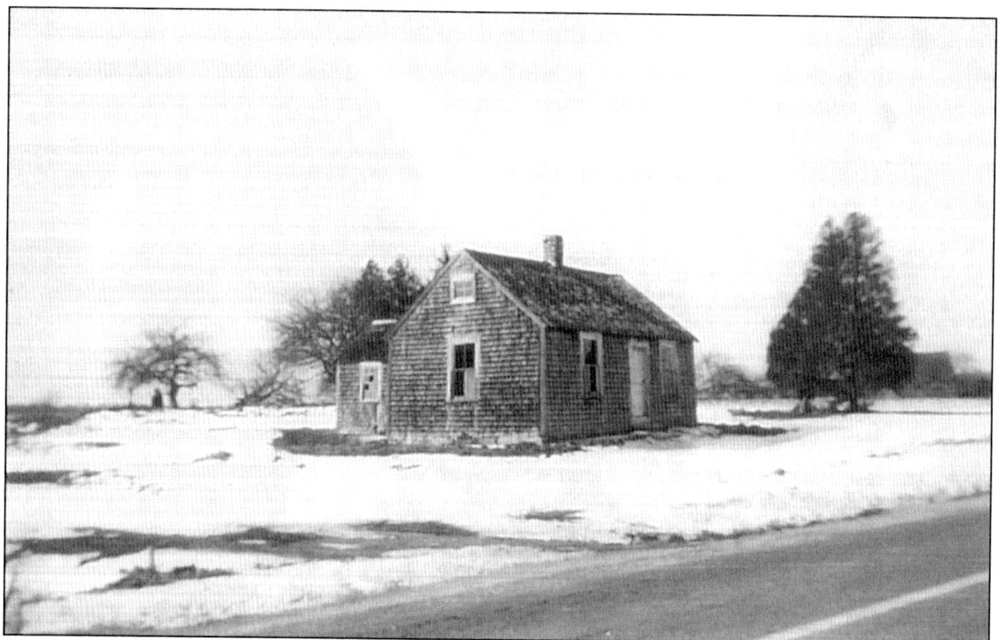

This house, the John J. Hopkins house in Usquepaugh, is no longer standing. It included a cemetery in back of the house where seven slaves are buried. (Courtesy Everett J. Hopkins.)

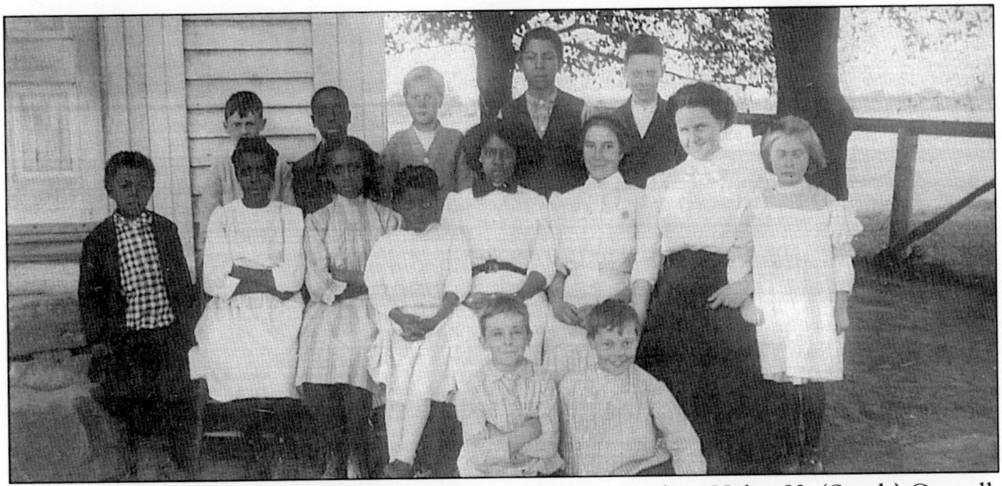

The 1912 class at Usquepaugh School gathers with their teacher, Helen H. (Smith) Cottrell. This was one of the last years of the school, which was located next to the cemetery at the Queen's River Baptist Church on Route 138. The school committee report of 1913 shows no record of the school, and after that date students were sent to school in West Kingston or the Beaver River section of Richmond. Mrs. Cottrell, who graduated from Hope Valley High School, received $400 to teach in 1911–12. Her students were, from left to right, as follows: (front row) Henry Dodge and Harold Holgate; (middle row) Charles Walmsley of Usquepaugh, Mary Elizabeth (Robinson) Walmsley of West Kingston, Bessie (Perry) Slaughter of Ashaway, Susie Robinson, Lillian Twyne, Pearl Davis, Mrs. Cottrell, and Jennie Davis; (back row) Earl Kenyon, Walter Robinson, Clinton Davis, Jerry Walmsley, and Russell Kenyon. (Courtesy Virginia Arnold.)

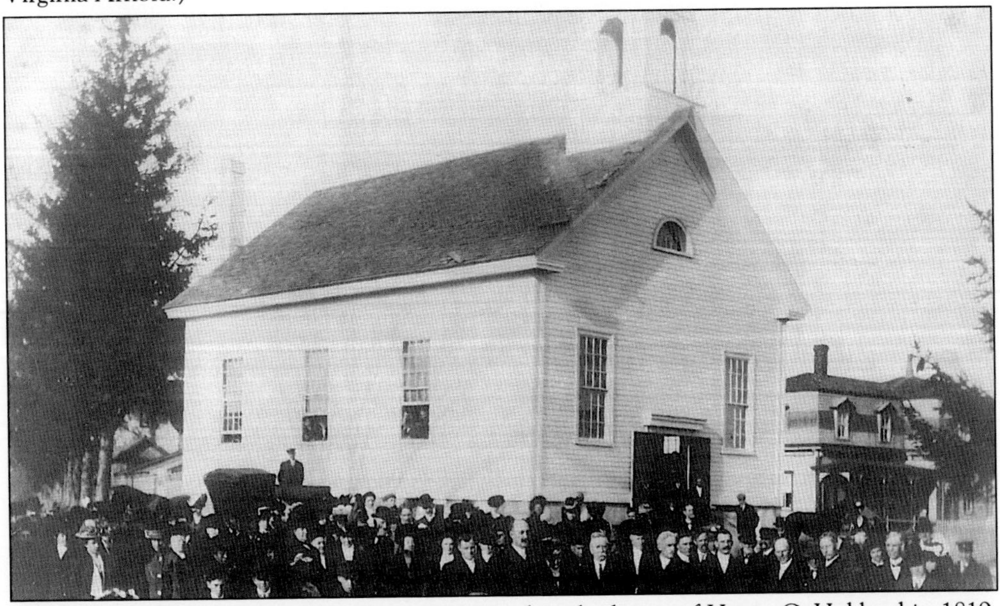

The Queen's River Baptist Church was organized in the home of Henry C. Hubbard in 1819, and its first church was built c. 1844. That structure was destroyed by lightning on August 5, 1908, and was rebuilt over the next nine years at a cost of nearly $3,000. The church celebrated its centennial a year early, in 1918, and that celebration may have been the occasion of this photograph. (Courtesy Virginia Arnold.)

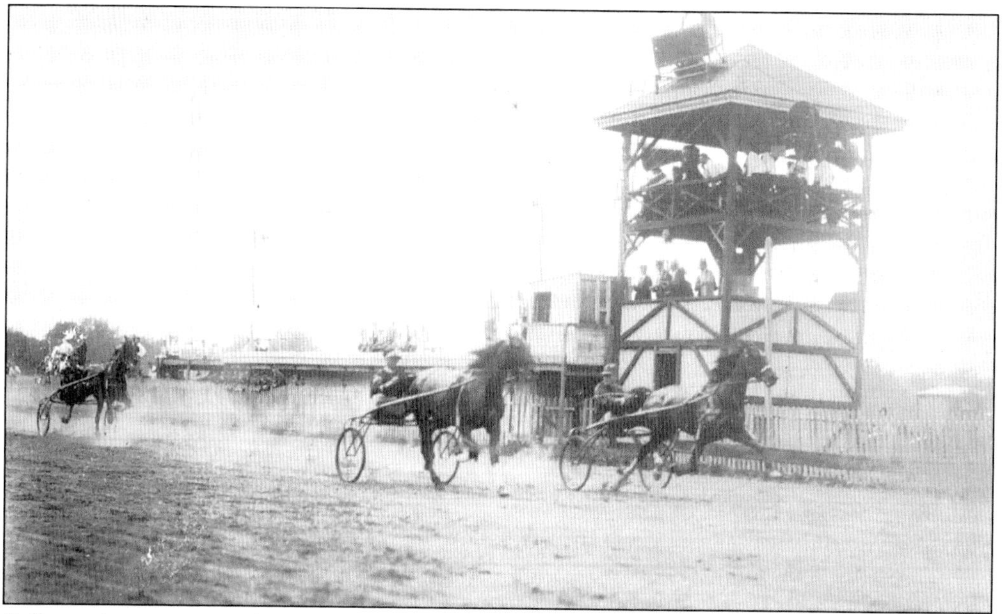

Sulky racing was a popular attraction at the Washington County Agricultural Fair, also called the Kingston Fair or the State Fair. Trainloads of people would pour into Kingston Station to attend the fair, held each September on Fairgrounds Road, near what is now American Power Conversion. (Courtesy Pettaquamscutt Historical Society.)

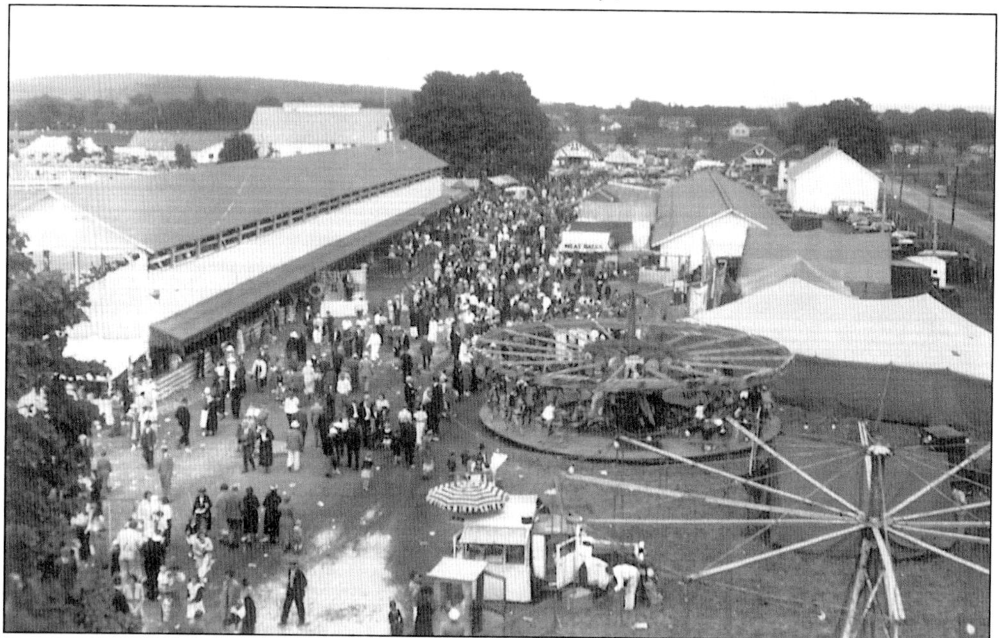

The Washington County Agricultural Fair was organized in 1874 by the Washington County Agricultural Society. The first fairs were held in Wakefield. Later, they were held at the Bradford farm, which was bought by the fair organizers. At the farm, located near the train station in West Kingston, a number of permanent structures were erected and used at other times of the year for various purposes, including temperance meetings. (Courtesy Pettaquamscutt Historical Society.)

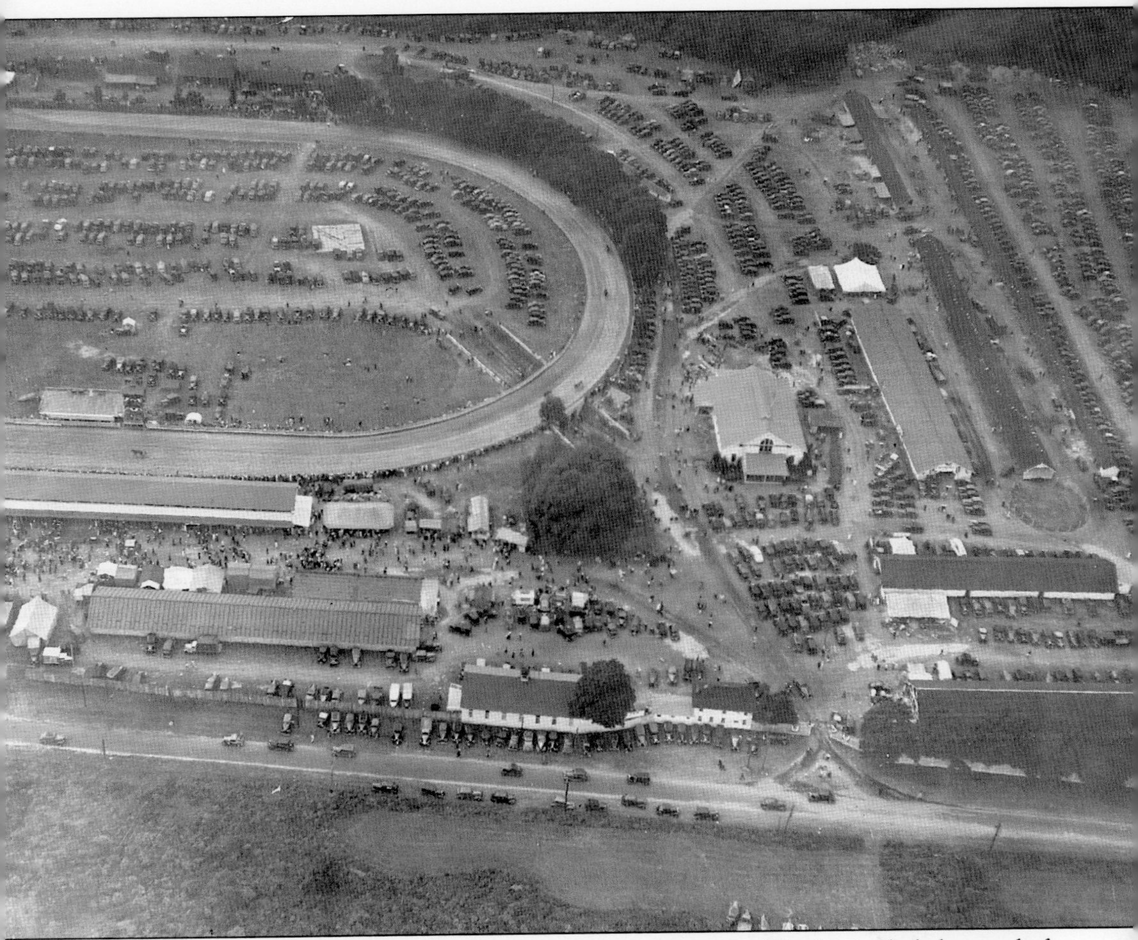

This photograph shows an aerial view of the fair in West Kingston. The fair included no end of unusual attractions. In 1912, Ruth Bancroft Law, "the only lady operator of a standard Wright biplane," made a successful flight over the racetrack. The *Narragansett Times* apparently was impressed, noting that she "did not lose her nerve." In 1913, besides the usual agricultural exhibits, the Immigration Bureau of Canada displayed grains from Canada, a popular exhibit. Also that year, Hazard Hall on the fairgrounds was transformed into a moving picture theater by Charles Webster of the Scenic at Narragansett Pier. In addition, a number of restaurants catered to every taste, and Maine's I Scream was sold on the grounds. (Courtesy Pettaquamscutt Historical Society.)

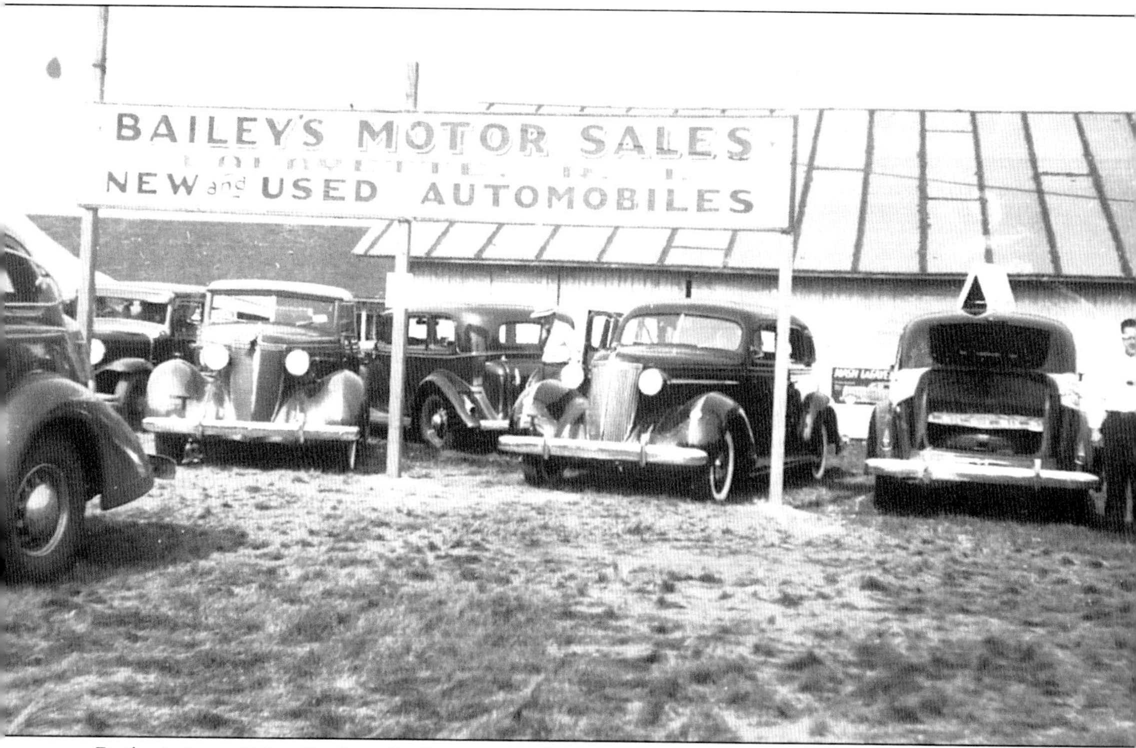

Bailey's Auto Sales displays the latest models in an exhibit at the fair. The long reign of the fair was dealt a sharp blow in 1924 when the grandstand and three buildings were destroyed by fire. On May 8, 1958, the Gilbane Building Company burned the last remains of the fairgrounds to make way for an industrial park. (Courtesy Pettaquamscutt Historical Society.)

Bibliography

"Annual Report of the School Committee of South Kingstown" for the years ending June 30, 1912, 1913, and 1916.

Biographic Cyclopedia of Representative Men of Rhode Island. Providence: National Biographical Publication Company, 1881.

Clawson, J. Earl. "Two Elisha Potters Gave State Service of Real Value." *Providence Journal*, undated 1936 clipping.

Cole, J.R. *History of Washington and Kent Counties, Rhode Island.* New York: W.W. Preston & Company, 1889.

Eschenbacher, Herman F. *The University of Rhode Island, A History of Land-Grant Education in Rhode Island.* New York: Appleton-Century-Crofts, 1967.

Hazard, Thomas Robinson. *The Jonny-Cake Papers of 'Shepherd Tom.'* Boston: D.B. Updike/The Merrymount Press, 1915.

"The Helen Mason Grose Collection at Kingston Free Library." Pamphlet.

Helme, Nathaniel. Unpublished diaries, 1886–89, 1898, and 1927.

Higbee, Holly. *Historic Kingston Rhode Island.* The Milkweed Art Press, 1971.

"Historic Kingston House Tour." Pamphlet of the Pettaquamscutt Historical Society.

"History of Kingston Congregational Church." Pamphlet.

Kaye, Alda Ganze. "Weaver Rose: A New Perspective." *Shuttle, Spindle & Dyepot*, issue 30, Vol. VIII, No. 2, spring 1977.

Leslie, James W. "The Key to URI's Beginnings." *Horizons*, a publication of The URI Alumni Association, February 1988.

MacKenzie, Louise. *Strolling through Kingston formerly known as Little Rest.* Westerly: Narragansett Graphics, 1986.

McBurney, Christian M. *Kingston: A Forgotten History.* Kingston: Pettaquamscutt Historical Society, 1975.

Metz, William D. *History of the Kingston Congregational Church.* Kingston: Kingston Congregational Church, 1996.

Narragansett Times, July 25, 1890; Aug. 22, 1890; Aug. 5, 1898; Oct. 28, 1898; June 22, 1900; April 15, 1910; Aug. 5, 1910; June 14, 1912; Sept. 13, 1912; Sept. 20, 1912; Oct. 18, 1912; Dec. 27, 1912; Sept. 12, 1913; June 8, 1923; Sept. 12, 1924; and Jan. 17, 1947, plus several undated clippings.

National Society of the Colonial Dames in the State of Rhode Island and Providence Plantations. *Old houses in the South County of Rhode Island*. Providence, 1932. Privately printed.

Rhode Island Historical Preservation Commission. "State of Rhode Island and Providence Plantations Preliminary Survey Report Town of South Kingstown." Providence: Rhode Island Historical Preservation Commission, 1984.

Providence Evening Bulletin, May 9, 1958.

Richmond Historical Society. *Driftways into the Past*. Ed. Lucy Tootell. Westerly: The Utter Company, 1977.

St. Amour, Lynda S. "The Kingston Free Library, Kingston, Rhode Island." Winter 1994. Unpublished manuscript.

Wells, the Reverend J. Hagadorn. "Kingston Annals, Reminiscences of Little Rest." 1897.

Stedman, Oliver H. A *Stroll Through Memory Lane*. Ed. Stella Burns. Vols. I and II. West Kingston: Kingston Press, 1999.

Taylor, Philip Kittredge. "Little Rest." *The New England Magazine*, Vol. XXVIII No. 2, April 1903.

Thresher, John C. "More Information about the Eldred Family." *The Reporter*, the quarterly journal of the Pettaquamscutt Historical Society, summer 1998.

Thresher, John C. "Education in Kingston, Part Two— Kingston Grammar School." *The Reporter*, the quarterly journal of the Pettaquamscutt Historical Society, spring 1998.

Woodward, Carl R. "A Profile in Dedication: Sarah Harris and the Fayerweather Family." *The New England Galaxy*, Vol. XV No. 1, summer 1973.

Woodward, Carl R. "Kingston's Cultural Heritage." *Rhode Island Yearbook*, 1970.